D1391417

OUR ROOTS GROW DEEPER
THAN WE KNOW

OUR ROOTS GROW DEEPER THAN WE KNOW

PENNSYLVANIA WRITERS
PENNSYLVANIA LIFE

LEE GUTKIND, *Editor*

University of Pittsburgh Press

Published by the University of Pittsburgh Press, Pittsburgh, Pa. 15260
Copyright © 1985, Lee Gutkind
All rights reserved
Feffer and Simons, Inc., London
Manufactured in the United States of America

Library of Congress Cataloging in Publication Data

Main entry under title:

Our roots grow deeper than we know.

    1. Pennsylvania—Social life and customs—Addresses,
essays, lectures. 2. Pennsylvania—Fiction.
3. American fiction—Pennsylvania. I. Gutkind, Lee.
F149.5.097 1985   974.8   85-40338
ISBN 0-8229-3523-6
ISBN 0-8229-5374-9 (pbk.)

*This family of prose is dedicated to the members of my family
—my grandfather, my parents, my brothers, my uncle Steve—
who have always been loving and supportive.*

Contents

ACKNOWLEDGMENTS

Anthologies are usually team efforts, and this more than most. My team included research assistants Monette Tiernan and Stephen Murabito; Kathleen McLaughlin, editorial assistant at the University of Pittsburgh Press, who copyedited the manuscript and doggedly sought out most of the permissions necessary to publish the book; Patricia Park, my best friend, who helped guide me. I thank them for their dedication, their painstaking work, their appreciation for detail.

I also want to thank Professor Mary Briscoe, Chairman, and Professor Robert Hinman, Director of the Graduate Program, Department of English, University of Pittsburgh; Frederick A. Hetzel, Director of the University of Pittsburgh Press; Philip Hallen, Chairman of the Pennsylvania Humanities Council and President of the Maurice Falk Medical Fund for their faith in this project and their continued support.

Grateful acknowledgment is made to the following publishers and individuals for permission to reprint the stories in this book:

"In the Valley of Death," by David McCullough. From *The Johnstown Flood*, copyright © 1968 by David G. McCullough. Reprinted by permission of Simon & Schuster, Inc.

"197903042100 (Sunday)," by David Bradley. From *The Chaneysville Incident* by David Bradley. Copyright © 1981 by David H. Bradley, Jr. Reprinted by permission of Harper & Row, Publishers, Inc.

"Teeth," by Lee Gutkind. From *The People of Penn's Woods West*. (University of Pittsburgh Press, 1984).

"Grids and Doglegs," by Clark Blaise. From *Tribal Justice*, by Clark Blaise (Doubleday, 1974). Copyright © 1974 by Clark Blaise. Reprinted by permission of Russell & Volkening, Inc. as agent for the author.

"Where Are Our M.I.A.'s?" by Robert Taylor, Jr. Originally published in *Kansas Quarterly*. Copyright © 1979 by *Kansas Quarterly*. Reprinted by permission of *Kansas Quarterly* and the author.

"Comfort Stations," by John Griesemer. Originally published in *West Branch* (No. 10, 1982). Reprinted by permission of *West Branch* and the author.

"The Student," by Myron Taube. Originally published in *The University Review* (University of Missouri at Kansas City, 1968). Reprinted by permission of the author.

"Elegy to the Carlton House Hotel," by Roy McHugh. Originally published in *The Pittsburgh Press* (20 September 1980). Reprinted by permission of *The Pittsburgh Press*.

"Shillington," by John Updike. Originally appeared under the title "The Dogwood Tree: A Boyhood," in *Five Boyhoods*, edited by Martin Levin (Doubleday, 1962). Copyright © 1962 by Martin Levin. Reprinted by permission of Martin Levin.

"Innocence Lost," by Mike Vargo. Originally published in *Pennsylvania Illustrated* (August 1979). Reprinted by permission of *Pennsylvania Illustrated*.

"Makeup," by Michael Clark. First appeared in *The Arizona Quarterly* (Autumn 1982). Copyright © 1983 by *The Arizona Quarterly*. Reprinted by permission of *The Arizona Quarterly* and the author.

"Gus Zernial and Me," by Jerry Spinelli. Originally published in *Philadelphia Magazine* (1982) and anthologized in *The Best Sports Stories of 1982*. Copyright © 1982 by Jerry Spinelli. Reprinted by permission of the author.

"Waiting for Her Train," by Audrey Lee. From *What We Must See: Young Black Storytellers*, edited by Orde Coombs (Dodd, Mead & Co., 1971). Copyright © 1971 by Audrey Lee. Reprinted by permission of the author.

"Why I Did It," by William D. Ehrhart. Copyright © 1980 by W. D. Ehrhart. First published in *The Virginia Quarterly Review* (Winter 1980); reprinted in *Vietnam-Perkasie*, by W. D. Ehrhart (McFarland & Co., 1983). Appears by permission of the author.

"You Taught Us Good," by Claude Koch. Originally published in *Four Quarters* (Spring 1981). Copyright © 1969 by *Four Quarters*. Reprinted by permission of *Four Quarters*.

"The Last Miracle Show," by Evan Pattak. Originally appeared in *Pittsburgh Magazine* (April 1976). Reprinted by permission of *Pittsburgh Magazine*.

"Distances," by W. S. Merwin. Originally appeared under the title "Tomatoes," in *Unframed Originals: Recollections*, copyright © 1982 by W. S. Merwin. Reprinted with the permission of Atheneum Publishers.

"Tommy," by John Wideman. From *Damballah* (Avon Books, New York, 1981). Copyright © 1981 by John Edgar Wideman. Reprinted by permission of the Andrew Wylie Agency as agent for the author.

PREFACE

LEE GUTKIND

"YOU COME ALL the way from Pennsylvania on that motorcycle?"

"From Pittsburgh," I said.

The old man, leaning on a parking meter, eyeing my bedroll, my bulging saddlebags, my Pennsylvania license plates, looked up at me.

"I been to Pittsburg," he said, nodding. "But I ain't never been to Pennsylvania."

That quick conversation took place in 1971 in Cedar Springs, Texas, about one hundred miles from another tiny Texas town called Pittsburg. But it could have also happened in California, Illinois, Kansas, New Hampshire, Kentucky, or God knows how many other areas across the United States where Pittsburgh, Pittsburg, or Pitsburg, as in Ohio, exists. It was, however, the first time I had ever seriously thought of myself as anything other than an American or a Pittsburgher. Pennsylvania, its laws, its elected and appointed officials, its very borders, seemed somehow superfluous. I understood the practical importance of Pennsylvania; but to me the state had always been a necessary evil, another form to calculate during tax time, another check to write each time I purchased a new car. The realization that I was much more intimately connected to the Commonwealth dawned on me slowly, over a period of years and only after a series of excursions across the United States.

My conversation with the old man occured during a time when I was researching a book about cross-country motorcycling and the subculture surrounding the two-wheeled machine. I did all I could to avoid the cities and freeways, following the many bits and pieces of backroad, east to west, south to north, ribbons of dust and asphalt

xiii

that connect the heart of the country. I met many people—families who watched television, drove pickup trucks, ate frozen dinners—who did not know the name of the vice-president of the United States, or that Pittsburgh was the steel capital of the world. More people recognized the Pirates and the Steelers; they were sports teams from somewhere in the East. But to the man, woman, and child, they all knew about Pennsylvania, about William Penn and Benjamin Franklin and Abraham Lincoln's Gettysburg Address. Through the rest of my time on the road, I began to identify myself as coming from Pennsylvania (I couldn't quite bring myself to use *Pennsylvanian*, however), and only when people would ask for more information ("What part of Pennsylvania?") would I volunteer, "Pittsburgh."

When I returned to Pittsburgh in 1972 to write my book, I continued to take excursions on my motorcycle, but for hours, or weekends at the most, rather than months at a time, and it was then that I began to discover the great diversity of our state. Fifty miles out of the city, evidence of city life would nearly disappear, and I would find myself in another country.

"There are towns in this state that seem caught in time warps," says novelist David Bradley, "people who know nothing, it seems, of progress. Old men and old women who seem to have been cloned from the original pioneers. They have passions and ignorance and honor and wisdom that seem to me almost mythical. You could call them stereotypes, but they are real in a way no sophisticated New Yorker could ever be, at least in my mind."

Not long after, I went back on the road with cross-country truckers and subsequently with baseball umpires, but whenever I returned to Pittsburgh I would periodically find myself on my motorcycle, beating a fast retreat into the depths of western Pennsylvania's backwoods: Penn's Woods West. During one of these excursions I suddenly realized that I had been chasing all over the country looking for stories to write and people to write about when all along the place in which I felt most comfortable was rich with material that inspired me.

The idea for this anthology stemmed from my growing interest in Pennsylvania, triggered by the designation of 1985 by the Pennsylvania Humanities Council as "The Year of the Pennsylvania Writer." There are many important writers missing from this collection, I should point out: John O'Hara, Edwin Peterson, Gladys Schmidt, to name a few who are no longer living; Joseph Wambaugh, James Michener, and John Barth, Pennsylvanians who have yet to write about their connections or their feelings for the state. These were my parameters as I began reading the hundreds of stories, excerpts, and essays located in the library or submitted to me: that the writers would still be living, that they would have roots or special connections to the state, and that their feelings for Pennsylvania would, in one way or another, be reflected in the fiction or nonfiction I selected.

I subsequently contacted each of the writers whose work I selected and asked how they felt about Pennsylvania and about being a writer and writing here. A few, such as John Updike or W. S. Merwin, have left Pennsylvania with their families years ago and have no intention of returning permanently. Others, such as novelist Karen Rile, would like to return but can't at this time because of personal commitments. Novelist John Wideman, though living in Wyoming, has written four books about life in the Homewood section of Pittsburgh, but requires the distance in order to see the place of his birth, and the people with whom he grew up, more clearly. Most of the writers, however, have had revelations similar to mine; they have traveled extensively but, for one reason or another, seem to have ended up back where they started.

Of all the personal statements I received from the writers collected here, I thought that William D. Ehrhart was most eloquent and most accurate: in fact, it is Ehrhart who has given title to this anthology. Ehrhart has also traveled widely, but now finds himself in Doylestown, just down the road from Perkasie in Bucks County, where he grew up.

"I get to see my parents often, which is nice," he says, "and I travel the same roads I used to pedal on my bicycle and drive in the family car back in those heady days after I'd first gotten my license. I have no idea how long I'll stay this time, but Anne and I are happy here, and we're in no particular hurry to leave. For me, it's—well—familiar, comfortable, like a well-worn easy chair or an old friend. And maybe there's a reason I keep coming back. My roots grow deeper than I know. I never really thought about it much. But I guess this is home."

OUR ROOTS GROW DEEPER
THAN WE KNOW

In the Valley of Death

David McCullough

"I had the best kind of time growing up in Pennsylvania, and I honestly can't say whether I enjoyed more the city (Pittsburgh) or the country in summer (near the little railroad town of New Florence). I saw my first professional theatrical production at the old Nixon (it was Harvey with Frank Fay). I went to my first concert at the Syria Mosque one Sunday afternoon when I was eight. (I have no memory of what was played, only of the excitement in the street when my older brother and I came out afterward, because news had come of the attack on Pearl Harbor.) I went to borrow my first book from the Carnegie Library, alone by bus to Oakland, and remember perfectly that it was A Tree Grows in Brooklyn.

"In the country, from the time school let out, my brothers and I were largely, wonderfully on our own nearly the whole summer long. We had a victory garden in those war years, and chores. We learned about bird dogs and tractors and helped bring in hay on the neighboring farms, but best were the days exploring in the mountains and the stories we heard from the old time people who were still about then.

"A writer has to draw on the past. So maybe the imprint of home ground and its associations mean more to a writer; I don't know. But I'm sure I knew all along, well before I had any clear aspirations to a writing life, that there was a particular power and importance to 'my' part of the world. It wasn't West, it wasn't East certainly, but it sure was someplace on the map. The imagination raced, in city or country. Everything, it seemed, had a story. And everybody worked, city or country, which is a lesson no writer can learn too soon.

"Pittsburgh has figured in all my books in one way or another, and I expect it will again many times, in the books I hope to write. As a historian, I think about Pennsylvania and Pittsburgh more and more, as a kind of prism through which the whole of American history might be seen, up to and including the momentous changes

3

taking place with the decline of the old industrial empires that seemed so majestic and impregnable for so long. As I said, everything has a story."

*   *   *

Twice the winner of the prestigious National Book Award, David McCullough is the host of the Public Broadcasting System's "Smithsonian World" series and the author of The Great Bridge (1972), the story of the building of the Brooklyn Bridge; The Path Between the Seas (1977), the history of the Panama Canal; Mornings on Horseback, the story of Theodore Roosevelt's struggle to manhood; and The Johnstown Flood (1968), from which this excerpt is taken.

IT WAS NEARLY morning when the strange quiet began. Until then there had been almost no letup from the hideous sounds from below. Few people had been able to sleep, and several of the war veterans were saying it was the worst night they had ever been through.

But in the last chill hour before light, the valley seemed to hang suspended in an unearthly stillness, almost as unnerving in its way as everything else that had happened. And it was then, for the first time, that people began to realize that all those harsh, incessant noises which had been such a part of their lives—mill whistles screeching, wagons clattering over cobblestones, coal trains rumbling past day and night—had stopped, absolutely, every one of them.

About five the first dim shapes began emerging from the darkness. But even by six very little stood out in detail. There were no shadows, no clear edges to anything. Some survivors, years later, would swear it had been a bright, warm morning, with a spotless blue sky, which, after the night they had been through, it may well have seemed. But the fact is that though the rain had at last stopped, the weather on that morning of June 1 was nearly as foul as it had been the morning before. The valley looked smothered in a smoky gray film. The hills appeared to be made of some kind of soft, gray-green stuff and were just barely distinguishable from a damp, low sky that was the color of pewter. Odd patches of the valley were completely lost in low-hanging ribbons of mist, and the over-all visibility was reduced to perhaps a mile at best.

Still the view that morning would be etched sharply in the memories of everyone who took it in. Along the Frankstown Road on Green Hill some three thousand people had gathered. On the rim of Prospect Hill and on the slopes above Kernville, Woodvale, and Cambria City the crowds were nearly as big. Chilled to the bone, hungry, many of them badly injured, hundreds without shoes or only partly clothed against the biting air, they huddled under dripping trees or stood along narrow footpaths ankle-deep in mud, straining their eyes to see and trying hard to understand.

Spread out below them was a vast sea of muck and rubble and filthy water. Nearly all of Johnstown had been destroyed. That it was even the same place was very difficult to comprehend.

There were still a few buildings standing where they had been. The Methodist Church and the B & O station, the schoolhouse on Adams Street, Alma Hall, and the Union Street School could be seen plain enough, right where they were meant to be. The Iron Company's red-brick offices were still standing, as was Wood, Morrell & Company next door. But everywhere else there seemed nothing but bewildering desolation. The only immediately familiar parts of the landscape were the two rivers churning toward the stone bridge, both still swollen and full of debris.

From Woodvale to the bridge ran an unbroken swath of destruction that was a quarter of a mile wide in places and a good two miles long. From Locust Street over to the Little Conemaugh was open space now, an empty tract of mud, rock, and scattered wreckage, where before saloons, stores, hotels, and houses had been as thick as it had been possible to build them. Washington Street was gone except for the B & O station. Along Main, where a cluster of buildings and gutted houses still stood like a small, ravaged island, the wreckage was piled as high as the roofs of the houses.

At the eastern end of town all that remained between Jackson and Clinton was a piece of St. John's Convent. At the corner of Jackson and Locust the blackened rafters of St. John's Church were still smoking, and where the Quinn house had stood, fifty feet away, there was now only a jumble of rubbish.

Across the Stony Creek, Kernville had been swept clean for blocks. Virtually everything was gone, as though that whole section had been hosed down to the raw earth. The entire western end of town, near the Point, was now a broad, flooded wasteland. Every bridge was gone except the stone bridge and against it now lay a good part of what had been Johnstown in a gigantic blazing heap.

Below the stone bridge the ironworks, though still standing, looked all askew, with stacks toppled over and one of the biggest buildings caved in at the end as though it had been tramped on by an immense heel. Cambria City had been ravaged past recognition. At least two-thirds of the houses had been wiped out, and down the entire length of its main street a tremendous pile of mud and rock had been dumped.

With the light the first small groups of people who had survived the night down in the drowned city could be seen making their way across the debris, most of them heading for Green Hill, where dry ground could be reached without having to cross a river. From Alma Hall and the Union Street School they came in steady little batches, moving up and down over the incredible flotsam. Then, at the same time from Frankstown Road and other near hills, men started moving down into town. And as they came closer, the dim sweep of destruction began to take on a different look. Slowly things came into ever sharper focus.

The Morrell house could be seen with a part of its side sheared off. Dr. Lowman's house stood alone on the park, the only big house still there, but its two-story front porch had been squashed and every window punched in. Colonel Linton's place on lower Main looked as though it had been blasted in two by dynamite, and the black span of an iron bridge was resting where the yard had been. Beyond, houses were dumped every which way, crushed, broken, split clean in half, or lying belly up in the mire, with their floor beams showing like the ribs of butchered animals.

Telephone poles, giant chunks of machinery, trees with all their bark shredded off, dead horses and pieces of dead horses, and countless human corpses were strewn everywhere. "Hands of the dead stuck out of the ruins. Dead everywhere you went, their arms stretched above their heads almost without exception—the last instinct of expiring humanity grasping at a straw," wrote George Gibbs, one of the reporters from the *Tribune*.

And now, too, all the litter of thousands of lives could be seen in sharp detail. Shattered tables and chairs, tools, toys, account books, broken dishes, chamber pots and bicycle wheels, nail kegs, bedquilts, millions of planks and shingles were thrown up in grotesque heaps ten, twenty, thirty feet high, or lay gently shifting back and forth in huge pools of water that covered much of the valley floor like a brown soup.

"It were vain to undertake to tell the world how or what we felt, when shoeless, hatless, and many of us almost naked, some bruised and broken, we stood there and looked upon that scene of death and desolation." David Beale wrote.

The flood and the night that had followed, for all their terror and destruction and suffering, had had a certain terrible majesty. Many people had thought it was Judgment Day, God's time of anger come at last, the Day of Reckoning. They thought that the whole world was being destroyed and not just Johnstown. It had been the "horrible tempest," with flood and fire "come as a destruction from the Almighty." It had been awful, but it had been God Awful.

This that lay before them now in the dismal cold was just ugly and sordid and heartbreaking; and already it was beginning to smell.

Rescue parties got to work bringing the marooned down from rooftops and went searching among the wreckage for signs of life. Men scrambled over piles of debris to get to the upstairs windows of buildings that looked as though they might fall in at any minute. They crawled across slippery, cockeyed roofs to squeeze through attic windows or groped their way down dripping back hallways where the mud was over their boot tops. It was treacherous work and slow going. Walls were still falling in and fires were breaking out.

At the stone bridge, gangs of men and boys, many of whom had been there through the night, were still working to free people trapped alive within the burning pile. Young Victor Heiser, who had succeeded in reaching solid ground after his night in a Kernville attic, had made his way down the west bank of the Stony Creek as far as the bridge, where, as he wrote later, "I joined the rescue squads, and we struggled for hours trying to release them from this funeral pyre, but our efforts were tragically hampered by the lack of axes and other tools. We could not save them all. It was horrible to watch helplessly while people, many of whom I actually knew, were being devoured in the holocaust."

Across the whole of the valley the dead were being found in increasing numbers. And as the morning passed, more and more people came down from the hillsides to look at the bodies, to search for missing husbands and children, or just to get their bearings, if possible. They slogged through the mud, asking after a six-year-old boy "about so high," or a wife or a father. They picked their way through mountains of rubbish, trying to find a recognizable landmark to tell them where their house or store had been, or even a suggestion of the street where they had lived. Or they stood silently staring about, a numb, blank look on their faces. Over and over, later, when the day had passed, people would talk about how expressionless everyone had looked and how there had been so few people crying.

There was some shouting back and forth among the men. People who had been separated during the night would suddenly find one another. "What strange meetings there were," wrote one man. "People who had hardly known each other before the flood embraced one another, while those who found relations rushed into each other's arms and cried for very gladness that they were alive. All ordinary rules of decorum and differences of religion, politics and position were forgotten."

Lone stragglers went poking about looking for only they knew what, many of them strangely clad in whatever odd bits of clothing they had been able to lay hands on. One man, hatless and with a woman's red shawl across his shoulders, came limping along in his stocking feet, using a piece of lath for a cane. He was looking for his wife, Mrs. Brinker, who, as he would soon discover, had survived the night inside the Methodist parsonage and who had long since given him up for dead.

People recovered some pathetic belonging or other and carried it carefully back to high ground or began building little personal piles of salvage. There was no order to what went on, no organization, and not much sense. Most people were unable even to look after themselves; they were stunned, confused, trying, as much as anything, to grasp what had happened and what was left of their lives. Where they went from there was something they were not yet ready to think about. Many of them struck off into the country, with no special destination. They just kept walking for hours, looking for food or a dry place to lie down for the night, or, very often, just trying to put as many miles as possible between themselves and the devastated city. They were afraid of the place and wanted no more part of it.

The problems to be faced immediately were enormous and critical. People were ravenously hungry, most everyone having gone twenty-four hours or more without anything to eat, and now there was virtually no food anywhere. The few provisions uncovered among the ruins were nearly all unfit for eating, and what little else people had was given to the injured and to the children. Moreover, there was no water that anyone felt was safe to drink. Thousands were homeless, hundreds were severely injured. Mrs. John Geis, for example, little Gertrude Quinn's grandmother, had had her scalp torn off from her forehead back to the nape of her neck. Hundreds of others were dazed by lack of sleep or in a state of shock. Dozens of people, as a result of exposure, were already in the early stages of pneumonia. There was almost no dry clothing to be had and no medicines.

People had no money, except what change they may have had in their pockets at the time the water struck, and even if they did, there were no stores left at which to buy anything. There was no gas or electric light. Fires were burning in a dozen different places, and no one knew when a gas main might explode. Every telegraph and telephone line to the outside world was down. Bridges were gone, roads impassable. The railroad had been destroyed. And with the dead lying about everywhere, plus hundreds of carcasses of drowned horses, cows, pigs, dogs, cats, birds, rats, the threat of a violent epidemic was very serious indeed.

But by noon things had begun to happen, if only in a small way. Rafts had been built to cross the rivers and to get over to those buildings still surrounded by water. People on the hillsides whose houses had escaped harm and farmers from miles out in the country began coming into town bringing food, water, and clothing. At the corner of Adams and Main milk was passed out in big tinfuls. Unclaimed children were looked after. A rope bridge had been strung across the Little Conemaugh near the depot, and, most important of all as it would turn out, up at the Haws Cement Works, on the hill at the western end of the stone bridge, several bedraggled-looking newspaper correspondents had established headquarters in a coal shed and were in the process of rigging their own wire down the river to Sang Hollow.

The men had reached Johnstown about seven in the morning, and like everyone else were cold, dirty, hollow-eyed from no sleep. There remains some question as to which of them arrived first, but William Connelly, who was the Associated Press correspondent in western Pennsylvania, Harry Orr, a telegraph operator for the A.P., and Claude

Wetmore, a free-lance reporter working for the New York *World*, are generally given the credit. Others kept straggling in from New Florence through the rest of the day. But until nightfall the major stories were still being filed out of the little railroad crossing on the other side of Laurel Hill.

New Florence, Pa. June 1 . . . Seven bodies have been found on the shore near this town, two being on a tree where the tide had carried them. The country people are coming into the news centers in large numbers, telling stories of disaster along the river banks in sequestered places. . . . The body of another woman has just been discovered in the river here. Only her foot was above the water. A rope was fastened about it and tied to a tree. . . . R. B. Rogers, Justice of the Peace at Nineveh, has wired the Coroner at Greensburg that 100 bodies have been found at that place, and he asks what to do with them.

That afternoon, at three, a meeting was called in Johnstown to decide what ought to be done there. Every able-bodied man who could be rounded up crowded into the Adams Street schoolhouse. The first step, it was quickly agreed, was to elect a "dictator." John Fulton was the obvious choice, but he was nowhere to be found, so it was assumed he was dead, which he was not. He had left town some days earlier and was at that moment, like hundreds of others, trying desperately to get to Johnstown.

The second choice was Arthur J. Moxham, a remarkable young Welshman who had moved to Johnstown a few years before to start a new business making steel rails for trolley-car lines. In the short time he had been there Moxham had about convinced everyone that he was the best newcomer to arrive in the valley since D. J. Morrell. His business had prospered rapidly, and it was earlier that spring that he had opened a sprawling new complex of mills up the Stony Creek beside the new town he had developed. He named the business the Johnson Steel Street Rail Company, after his lively young partner, Tom L. Johnson, who, in turn, had named the town Moxham. They paid their men regularly each week, in cash, and did not maintain a company store—all of which had had a marked impact on the town's economic well-being and a good deal to do with their own popularity.

Both men were energetic, able executives. Both were already wealthy, and both, interestingly enough, were devout followers of the great economic reformer of the time, Henry George, and were equally well known in Johnstown for their impassioned oratory on George's single-tax scheme.

Moxham was a fortunate choice. He took charge immediately and organized citizens' committees to look after the most pressing and obvious problems. Morgues were to be established under the direction of the Reverends Beale and Chapman. Charles Zimmerman and Tom Johnson were put in charge of removing dead animals and wreckage. (That anyone could have even considered cleaning up the mess at that point is extraordinary, but apparently the work began right away, against all odds, against all reason. Trying to bail the rivers dry with buckets would have seemed not much more futile.)

Dr. Lowman and Dr. Matthews were responsible for establishing temporary hospitals. Captain Hart was to organize a police force. There was a committee for supplies and one for finance, to which George Swank and Cyrus Elder were assigned.

Captain Hart deputized some seventy-five men, most of whom were employees of the Johnson Company sent down from Moxham. They cut tin stars from tomato cans found in the wreckage, threw a cordon around the First National and Dibert banks, and, according to a report made days later, recovered some $6,000 in cash from trunks, valises, and bureau drawers lying about.

As dusk gathered, the search for the living as well as the dead went on in earnest. There seemed to be no one who was not missing some member of his family. James Quinn had already found little Gertrude, but he was still looking for his son Vincent, his sister-in-law and her infant son, and Libby Hipp, the nursegirl, though he had little hope of finding any of them except his son. That Gertrude was alive seemed almost beyond belief.

He and his other daughters had been luckier than most and had spent the night in a house on Green Hill. At daybreak he had been outside washing his face in a basin when his sister, Barbara Foster, came running up shouting that she had found Gertrude. She had seen her on the porch of the Metz house, still speechless with fright, still unidentified, and almost unrecognizable with her blonde hair tangled and matted with mud, her dark eyes quick with terror. Quinn at first found it impossible to accept what he heard, but started off at a run, the lather still on his face, and the other little girls running behind.

"When he came near the house," Gertrude wrote later, "I saw him and recognized him at once. I fairly flew down the steps. Just as he put his foot on the first step, I landed on his knee and put both my arms around his neck while he embraced me."

Quinn gathered up the child. They both began crying. A small crowd had assembled by now, on the porch and on the street below, and the scene caused several people to break down for perhaps the first time. Then there was a lot of handshaking and Quinn set off with his children to find his son.

Victor Heiser had spent most of the day searching for his mother and father, hoping against hope that somehow they had come through it all alive and in one piece. His own survival seemed such a miracle to him that he could not help feeling there was a chance they might be somewhere in the oncoming darkness looking for him.

At the bridge late in the afternoon an old man and his daughter were rescued from a house wedged among the burning wreckage. The old man made quite a reputation for himself when, on being helped down into a rowboat, he asked his rescuers, "Which one of you gentlemen would be good enough to give me a chew of tobacco?" And on the hillside a few hundred yards away two young ladies who had been stripped naked by the flood were found cowering in the bushes, where they had been hiding through the long day, too ashamed to venture out before dark.

Cyrus Elder's wife and daughter were missing. Horace Rose did not learn until late in the afternoon that the two sons, Winter and Percy, from whom he had been separated during the flood were still alive, and that he was the only member of his large family who had even been injured.

His neighbor John Dibert had already been identified among the dead, as had Mrs. Fronheiser, whom Rose had last seen in her window next door. The bodies of Samuel Eldridge, one of the best-known policemen in town, and Elizabeth Bryan of Philadelphia, who had been on the *Day Express*, had also been found. But of the other dead found only a small number had as yet been identified for sure.

At the Adams Street schoolhouse and a saloon in Morrellville, where the first two emergency morgues had been opened, the bodies were piling up faster than they could be properly handled. They came in on planks, doors, anything that would serve as a stretcher, and with no wagons or horses as yet on hand, the work of carrying them through the mud and water was terribly difficult.

Each body was cleaned up as much as possible, and any valuables found were put aside for safekeeping. Those in charge tried hard to maintain order, but people kept pushing in and out to look, and the confusion was terrific.

"We had no record books," David Beale wrote, "not even paper, on which to make our records, and had to use with great economy that which we gathered amid the debris or happened to have in our pockets."

One way or other the bodies were numbered and identified, whenever that was possible. Many were in ghastly condition, stripped of their clothes, badly cut, limbs torn off, battered, bloated, some already turning black. Others looked as though they had suffered hardly at all and, except for their wet, filthy clothes, appeared very much at peace.

A Harrisburg newspaperman named J. J. MacLaurin, who had been near Johnstown at the time the flood struck, described a visit to the Adams Street School early Sunday afternoon, where he counted fifty-three bodies stretched on boards along the tops of the desks. "Next to the entrance lay, in her damp clothing, the waiter-girl who had served my last dinner at the Hulbert House, with another of the dining room girls by her side."

How many dead there were in all no one had any way of knowing, since there was, as yet, almost no communication between various parts of town. But wild estimates were everywhere by nightfall, and with more bodies being discovered wherever the wreckage had been pulled apart it was generally agreed that the final count would run far into the thousands. Some were saying it would be as much as ten thousand by the time the losses were added up from South Fork to Johnstown, and few people found that at all hard to believe. What may have happened on down the river at Nineveh or New Florence or Bolivar was anyone's guess.

Within another day the Pennsylvania station and the Presbyterian Church, a soap factory, a house in Kernville, the Millville School, and the Catholic Church in Cambria City would be converted into emergency morgues. But it would be a week before things got down to a system at these places, and not for months would there be a realistic count of the dead. Actually, there never would be an exact, final count, though it is certain that well over two thousand people were killed, and 2,209 is generally accepted as the official total.

Hundreds of people who were lost would never be found. One out of every three bodies that was found would never be identified beyond what was put down in the morgue records. With all the anguish and turmoil of the first few days, such entries were at best a line or two.

... 11. Unknown.
        A female. "FL.F." on envelope.
... 17. Unknown.
        A man about fifty years of age. Short hair, smooth face.
... 25. Unknown.
        Female. Light hair. About fifteen years.

Later, more care would be taken to be as explicit as possible.

... 181. Unknown.
         Female. Age forty-five. Height 5 feet 6 inches. Weight 100. White. Very long black hair, mixed with grey. White handkerchief with red border. Black striped waist. Black dress. Plain gold ring on third finger of left hand. Red flannel underwear. Black stockings. Five pennies in purse. Bunch of keys.
... 182. Unknown.
         Male. Age five years. Sandy hair. Checkered waist. Ribbed knee pants. Red undershirt. Black stockings darned in both heels.
... 204. Unknown.
         Male. Age fifty. Weight 160. Height 5 feet 9 inches. Sandy hair. Plain ring on third finger of left hand (with initials inside "C.R. 1869.") Pair blood stone cuff-buttons. Black alpaca coat. Navy blue vest and pants. Congress gaiters. Red stockings. Pocketbook. Knife and pencil. $13.30 in change. Open-faced silver watch. Heavy plaited chain and locket. Inside of locket a star with S.H., words trade-mark alone a star. Chain trinket with Washington head. Reverse the Lord's prayer. Odd Fellow's badge on pin.

In all, 663 bodies would be listed as unknown. A few were not identifiable because they had been decapitated. Close to a hundred had been burned beyond recognition, and some so badly that it was impossible even to tell what sex they had been. And many of the bodies found in late June or on into the summer and fall would be so decomposed as to be totally unrecognizable.

Part of the problem, too, was the fact that on the afternoon of May 31 Johnstown had had its usual share of strangers in town, nameless faces even when they had been alive, foreigners who had been living there only a short time, tramps, traveling men new to the territory, passengers on board any one of the several trains stalled along the line, countrypeople who had decided to stay over after Memorial Day. They made up a good part of the unknown dead, and doubtless many of them were among those who were never found at all.

Among the known dead were such very well-known figures as Dr. John Lee; Theodore Zimmerman, the lawyer; Squire Fisher, the Justice of the Peace, and his entire family; C. T. Schubert, editor of the German newspaper; and Ben Hoffman, the hackman, who, according to one account, "always got you to the depot in plenty of time" and whose voice was "as familiar as train whistle, iron works, or the clock bells." (Hoffman had gone upstairs to take a nap shortly before the flood struck and was found with his socks in his pockets.)

The Reverend Alonzo Diller, the new rector of St. Mark's Episcopal Church, was dead, along with his wife and child. George Wagoner, who was a dentist as well as a part-time preacher, and so one of the best-known men in town, was dead, as were his wife and three daughters. Emil Young, the jeweler, was dead; Sam Lenhart, the harness dealer, was dead; Henry Goldenberg, the clothier, Arthur Benshoff, the bookseller, Christian Kempel, the undertaker, were all dead. Mrs. Hirst, the librarian, lay crushed beneath a heap of bricks, slate, and books that stood where the public library had been.

Vincent Quinn was dead, as were Abbie Geis, her child, and Libby Hipp. Mrs. Cyrus Elder and her daughter Nan, Hettie Ogle and her daughter Minnie were dead, and their bodies would never be identified. George and Mathilde Heiser were dead.

Ninety-nine whole families had been wiped out. Three hundred and ninety-six children aged ten years or less had been killed. Ninety-eight children lost both parents. One hundred and twenty-four women were left widows; 198 men lost their wives.

One woman, Mrs. John Fenn, wife of the tinsmith on Locust Street, lost her husband and seven children. Christ Fitzharris, the saloonkeeper, his wife, father, and eight children were all drowned. Charles Murr and six of his children went down with his cigar store on Washington Street; only his wife and one child survived. In a house owned by John Ryan on Washington Street, twenty-one people drowned, including a man named Gottfried Hoffman, his wife and nine children.

At "Morgue A," the Adams Street schoolhouse, 301 bodies would be recorded in the logbooks. At the Presbyterian Church, which was "Morgue B," there would be ninety-two; at "Morgue C," in the Millville schoolhouse, the total would come to 551 by the time the last entry was made ("Unknown") on December 3. And along with the prominent merchants and doctors, the lawyers and preachers, there were hundreds of people with names like Allison, Burns, Evans, Shumaker, Llewellyn, and Hesselbein, Berkebile, Mayhew, McHugh, Miller, Lambreski, Rosensteel, Brown, Smith, and Jones. They made up most of the lists, and in the town directory that was to have been published that June they were entered as schoolteacher, porter, or drayman, clerk, miner, molder, barber, sawyer, dressmaker, or domestic. Dozens of them were listed as steelworker, or simply as laborer, and quite often as widow.

In that part of the valley through which the flood had passed, the population on the afternoon of the 31st had been approximately twenty-three thousand people, which means that the flood killed just about one person out of every ten. In Johnstown proper, it killed about one out of nine.

But there were no statistics for anyone to go on that Saturday night. It would be weeks before even a reasonably accurate estimate would be made on the death toll. The business of finding the dead just went very slowly. Young Vincent Quinn's body, for example, was not uncovered until June 7, buried beneath the wreckage in Jacob Zimmerman's yard. Victor Heiser's mother was found about the same time, her clothing still much intact, her body scarcely marked in any way; but the search for George Heiser went on for weeks after, and his body never was identified for certain. Toward the end of June a body was found which Victor was told was his father, but it was by then in such dreadful condition that he was not permitted to look at it.

In July there would be many days when ten to fifteen corpses would be uncovered. About thirty bodies would be found in August, including that of little Bessie Fronheiser; and so it would go on through the fall. In fact, for years to come bodies would keep turning up in and near the city. Two bodies would be found west of New Florence as late as 1906.

But by dark that Saturday only a small part of the dead had been accounted for, perhaps no more than three hundred or four hundred, and only a very few had been buried. Most of the living found shelter well back from the city, on Prospect Hill or Green Hill, or on up the Stony Creek, where against the dark mountains tiny windows glowed like strings of orange lanterns. Or they walked to little towns like Brownstown, which was set in a high valley above Cambria City. Victor Heiser spent the next several nights there, along with more than one thousand other refugees from the flood who were all housed, one way or other, by Brownstown's fifty-three resident families.

Houses, barns, stables, schools, churches, every remaining upright structure for miles around was put into service. Crude tents were fashioned from blankets and bedspreads. Lean-tos were built of planks and doors dragged from the wreckage.

One man later described smelling the odor of ham frying as he walked along the front street on Prospect Hill, and how he was invited into a small house "filled with a strangely composed company." There were two or three women who had been just recently rescued, and who were "pitiably pale, and with eyes ghastly at the flood horror." There was the hostess, who carried an infant on one hip, "a divine, a physician, a lawyer, two or three merchants," and several others. The dining room was too small to hold everyone, so they ate in shifts, waiting their turn out on the front porch. Below them, almost at their feet it seemed, lay the devastated valley.

The cold was nearly as cruel as it had been the night before. Pitch-blackness closed down over the mountainsides that crowded so close; but across the valley floor bonfires blazed, torches moved among the dark ruins, and the rivers and big pools of dead water were lighted by the fire that raged on at the stone bridge.

And with the deep night, for nearly everyone, came dreadful fear. There was the rational and quite justifiable fear of typhoid fever and of famine. It was entirely possible that a worse catastrophe than the flood itself could sweep the valley in a matter of days if help did not get through.

There were also rumors of thieves prowling through the night and of gangs of toughs who had come into the valley looking for trouble. Great quantities of whiskey were supposedly being found among the ruins, and drunken brawls were breaking out. People were warned to be on the lookout, that there would be looting and rape before the night was over; and men who had not slept since Thursday night took turns standing guard through the night, watching over their families or what little they may have had left of any earthly value.

Perhaps worst of all, however, was the wholly irrational fear of the very night itself and the nameless horrors it concealed. The valley was full of unburied dead; they were down there among the cold, vile remains of the city, waiting in the dark, and no one could get that idea out of his head for very long. If there were such a thing as ghosts, the night was full of them.

But despite it all, the hunger, the grief, the despair and fear, people gradually did what they had to; they slept. They put everything else out of their minds, for the moment, because they had to; and they slept.

197903042100 (SUNDAY)

DAVID BRADLEY

"There are towns in this state that seem caught in time warps, people who know nothing, it seems, of progress. Old men and women who seem to have been cloned from the original pioneers. They have passions and ignorance and honor and wisdom that seem to me almost mythical. You could call them stereotypes, but they are real in a way no sophisticated New Yorker could ever be, at least in my mind.

"I suppose it's a shame for some people that Pennsylvania isn't really sexy, you know? Like Virginia, or Texas, or California. We don't have an image, unless you're thinking about the Pittsburgh Steelers. What we do have is everything in human doses. Which means, I guess, the heavy hitting poets go for the Greek Islands or Timbuktu, and the visual artists go looking for pyramids. For a novelist, though, the rivers here are wide enough, the mountains high enough, and the people deep enough to give you stuff to write about for years."

*   *   *

The Chaneysville Incident, the novel for which David Bradley won the prestigious PEN/Faulkner Award in 1981, is the story of a quest that takes a young black historian, John Washington, back through the secrets of his heritage. In this excerpt, Old Jack Crawley, his father's closest friend, who is ill and dying, continues relating a tale that has become a mystery to Washington — one that he has pledged to unravel.

Bradley, who lives in Philadelphia and teaches writing at Temple University, but was born and raised in Bedford County, has invoked in his work the richness of his past and the distinctiveness of his home state; the places of the book, Chaneysville and Southampton, are real and can be located on any reasonably detailed Pennsylvania map. This was where Bradley was born and where he grew up. How much of this particular excerpt is true, only Bradley knows but, as he says: "I remember going to college and getting William Faulkner dropped on me like a ton of bituminous. Great imagination, my professors said. Made up his own county, put all these weird, wonderful characters in it. Wonder where he got them from; sheer genius. Well, maybe so. But I knew those kinds of people, those kinds of places. I grew up watching them. Grew up smelling fresh hay and manure. So I didn't need to be a genius; all I had to do was look and listen and smell and taste – and remember."

"I KNOWED THE South County. I had reason to know it. If there was anyplace in this whole part a the country a colored man would want to steer clear of, the South County was it. All them folks down there had come up from Maryland an' Virginia, an' some of 'em didn't know the Civil War was over, or, leastways, didn't know which side won. Anyways, I was thinkin' maybe I oughta get maself together an' go on down there with Josh. An' I was thinkin', too, that maybe I ought to let Mose in on what was goin' on, 'cause sure God if there was gonna be any kinda trouble, we was gonna need Mose. But on the other hand, I more or less give Josh ma word that I wasn't gonna say nothin' to nobody, least of all Mose. So I polished an' I pondered. Wasn't payin' too much attention to what them fellas was sayin'; most times it didn't amount to a hill a beans anyways, an' when it did, I usually knowed it 'fore they did. But 'long 'bout one o'clock, one a the fools that worked in some damn office or other, shufflin' papers in between takin' bribes, come over an' set his butt up there an' tells me to shine, but 'fore I can get started good he leans over an' gives me that fishy-eyeball look white folks toss at you when they're tryin' to act dangerous. I can't recall his name now; I do recollect that he bought his shoes outa the Montgomery Ward catalog, an' his heels was always run over, an' I recall he was so damn stupid they caught him takin' bribes. Now I think on it, he mighta been so damn dumb he wasn't takin' bribes, so the rest a them crooks had to make it look like he was, jest to get shut a him. Anyways, he leans over an' he says to me, 'Jack,' he says, 'I want you to know you're a good fella. You're a credit to your race.' Well, I thanked him kindly an' kept on shinin';

when they start with that it's best to jest ignore 'em; they don't mean no harm. But he wasn't through. 'Jack,' he says, 'I want you to know some folks come to me today, astin' 'bout you. Seems they heard some colored boy was nosin' 'round with a young lady down in Southampton.' *That* made me stop polishin'. But I managed to play dumb. 'Southampton?' I says. 'Why, I wouldn't be seein' no gal down there. Ain't a colored family —' 'I said a young *lady*, Jack,' he says. 'Well, like I was sayin' . . . Oh,' I says. Like I jest caught on. 'Well, you ain't got to worry none, Jack,' he says. 'I told them folks that you was too much a credit to your race to be actin' that way towards a young lady. Now ain't that the truth?' Well, I was about ready to fall offa ma stool, but leastways I could keep ma head down an' shine, so I says, 'Yes, sir, that surely is the truth.' He says, 'Well, I'm glad to hear it. On accounta these folks was mighty upset. Bad enough, boy even thinkin' 'bout interferin' with a young lady, but the way they tell it, he's bein' perty slick, goin' down there to Southampton an' actin' like he was workin' for the young lady's father, an' then hangin' 'round down there, tryin' to talk that young lady into doin' unspeakable things. You wouldn't know any niggers that slick, would you, Jack?' Well, there was enough trouble brewin' 'thout me startin' a pot, but I wasn't about to take that crap from nobody. So I put the polish down an' I stood up an' I looked him right in the eye an' I said, 'Mister, I don't *know* no niggers.' Well, he faded clean to pale white, jest like a catfish's belly. That's when white folks scare me; when they gets that fish-belly white color. Unpredictable as a copperhead, an' could be the bite's poison too; I couldn't say. But he got up an' he didn't say a damn thing. He jest looked at me, 'sif to say, If I had me a book, your name would sure God be in it, an' then he went away.

"Well, in a way it was good that it happened like it done, on accounta it settled ma mind on jest about everything. So as soon as I could get outa there I set out lookin' for Mose.

"Now, Mose wasn't the easiest fella to find, 'specially that time a year. What he'd be was holed up somewheres cleanin' his equipment so he'd be ready when they harvested the corn, or he'd be trampin' over half the County lookin' for God knows what. He done that all the time. I don't know why; he already knowed the County bettern God knowed Creation. Anyways, you couldn't find him if he was holed up; places where he kept his worms an' his kettles an' whatnot was the closest-kept secret this side a Eleanor Roosevelt's underwear. You couldn't track him if he was explorin'; wasn't a man alive could track Mose 'thout a bloodhound, an' maybe not then. But what we done a long time 'fore all this was to set up a couple signs; I had ma signs an' Mose had his an' Josh had his. So the first thing I done was to head for a old hollow tree about two mile northwest, out towards Wolfsburg, an' when I got there I felt around inside it for a while an' come up with an acorn. Which meant that he wasn't holed up—in which case he wouldn'ta left nothin' an' ma butt woulda been busted— an' that he had headed south from there. Which may not sound like a whole lotta help, but if you know where a man started an' which direction he headed in, you oughta be able to find him 'thout too much trouble. So I found me a creek, an' I followed that upstream— which was what Mose woulda done jest in case somebody decided to track him with some dogs—lookin' for high ground, an' when I found some I headed south again, right up over Kintons Knob.

"I was halfways to Manns Choice when I heard him comin'. He was singin'. He always done that. May sound strange for a man to take all that trouble hidin' his trail from dogs that ain't even there an' then go around makin' noise like that, but Mose claimed that it didn't make no difference, on accounta what he sung was spirituals an' couldn't nobody but colored folks hear 'em, an' even they couldn't hear 'em too far. Well, he musta been right, 'cause I could hear him comin'—an' well, more like I could feel him, on accounta his voice was so—low—an' it wasn't moren five seconds later that I seen him. I tell you, it was always a sight to see Mose movin' through the woods. You'd see him in town, or even up to Hawley's, an' you'd start to think maybe he wasn't so much, nothin' moren any other man. But you see him in the woods, movin' along over dry leaves without makin' a sound, movin' in big long strides that done to distance what a flame does to wax, you'd jest about want to head for town an' streetlights an' side- walks 'cause you'd know you never had no more business in the woods than a catfish in a foot race.

"I stopped an' he come up to me. Says, 'Hey, Jack, what you doin' out here with your pants wet?' I still hadn't dried off from wadin' in that damn creek. 'I been pissin' in 'em,' I says, 'an' you gonna be pissin' in yours when you hear what I got to say. Siddown.' An' he done it, an' I told it all to him. Well, not all of it. I didn't tell him about the

sunset-starin' an' whatnot, on accounta he wouldn'ta understood it;
Mose wasn't never crazy enough over a woman to do anything like
that. He had a hard enough time understandin' it as it was.

"'Damnation,' he says when I'd done finished tellin' him. Says, 'I
can't see why a man'd want to go an' get messed up with a white woman
for.' 'Hell,' I says. 'You can't see what a man'd want to get messed up
with any kinda woman for. But this here ain't no time to be gettin'
into that. This here's the time to be catchin' up to Josh.' Well, he seen
the sense a that, even if he didn't see the sense a nothin' else, an' we
set out.

"Well, it was 'bout four o'clock when we got back; Mose coulda
made it faster, I imagine, but I held him back a bit. So we was too
late. When we come up the Hill—we come up the back way, a course—
we could jest about smell the fact that old Josh'd already lit out; you
could hear his dogs a yippin' an' yappin' like they only done when
they'd got fed recent an' knowed they wasn't gonna get left out to run
nothin'. But we stopped by Josh's place anyways, jest to make sure.
Well, he was gone, all right, an' it didn't look like he'd done changed
his mind about what he was gonna do—you could see where he'd took
a bath an' shaved, an' his overhauls was hung up on a nail, so he musta
been wearin' that suit didn't nobody believe he owned. Mose looked
the place over for a minute or two an' then he looks at me. 'I ain't
never seen this fool this neat,' he says. 'Me neither,' I says. 'This place
don't smell a nothin' 'sides pine tar soap,' he says. 'Surely don't,' I
says. 'He ain't had a woman in here, 'cause you can't smell that,' he
says. 'Surely can't,' I says. He shook his head. 'You mean to tell me
some little old pasty woman can do all that to a man?' 'Mose,' I says,
'I think what's important here is that she's a woman. Now, we know
white men ain't worth dog dung, but it strikes me that any kinda
woman is a mighty powerful thing to fool with.' Mose shook his head
again an' went outside. I knowed where he was goin', so I jest waited.
He come back in about a minute. 'Sonofabitch,' he says. 'The sonofabitch limed his sonofabitchin' outhouse!' You could tell he was struck
with it. 'Hell,' he says, 'maybe he is fool enough to go down there
an' ast a white man can he marry his daughter.' 'Well, damn,' I says,
'I tole you that. Tole you he was fixin' to get his butt busted.' Mose
looks at me real sharp. '*His* butt? *Your* butt. Every black butt this
side a Pittsburgh. You think they gonna let it go at his butt? Why,

the first damn thing them white folks is gonna get to thinkin' is if one nigger can quit sneakin' in the back winda an' start knockin' at the front door, we all gonna be linin' up on the porch. What you think they gonna do?'

"Well, Mose may not a been the smartest fella when it come to men an' women, but he sure knowed a good bit about politics. I tell you, I had never even thought that far, but I seen he was dead right. I heard 'bout the riots they had right down in Philadelphia an' out there to St. Louis maybe two, three years before this all went on. Way I heard it, that St. Louis thing started on accounta some little boy went swimmin' in the white folks' water, an' they throwed rocks at him till he drowned, an' if they done that to a little boy that went swimmin' in the wrong swimmin' hole, I hated to think what they was gonna do to a full-growed man that started tryin' to marry somebody's white daughter. So I thought about that for a half a second, an' then I says, 'Well, we best not be settin' 'round here talkin' about outhouses, then. We best find that fool an' pound some sense into his head.' Mose nods. 'Yeah,' he says, 'only we gonna have a damn hard time, seein' as the way I judge it he's got about a half-hour lead, an' he's gonna be on horse-back.' I thought hard, an' then I says, 'Would be, 'ceptin' he's gonna be ridin' slow, on accounta the road'll be dusty an' he won't wanna mess up his suit. An' we can borrow a horse from Hawley. An' you know every shortcut for thirty miles, so we shouldn't have no problem.' 'Well,' says Mose, 'we do got one. We don't know where he's goin'.'

"Which was true. So there we was; half an hour behind already, an' we didn't even know where the finish line was. All I could do was stand there. 'Come on,' Mose says, an' he starts out the door. 'Come on where?' I says. 'Well, hell, Jack,' he says, 'we know he's headed south. We'll head that way an' maybe we'll get an idea.'

"So we lit out. Went chargin' down to Hawley's, but he wasn't there, so we jest told his missus we was borrowin' the horse. Turned out he took the horse with him. So we hotfooted it down the west side a the Hill, headin' for the swingin' bridge into town—that was standin' then—so's we could hit the Springs Road, but then, jest like Mose said, an idea hit me. Well, all it was was me recallin' what that white fella had said 'bout Southampton Township; but I guess you could call it an idea. Anyways, I jest says, 'We go east,' an' Mose didn't even bother to say what the hell or give me a funny look; he jest swing off an' we went hightailin' it down towards the Narrows. I tried to get up enough breath to tell him what was happenin', but he waved me off. I was grateful for it too, on accounta travelin' with Mose on foot was somethin' that took all the breath you could spare, leastways till you caught your second wind. So I didn't try to explain nothin' else, I jest kept movin', an' pretty soon it come to me what we was doin': we was trailin'. Not trackin', now; trailin'. Anybody that's spent jest a little bit a time in the woods knows there's a world a difference. Maybe you got a pack a dogs, an' they'll all take after a bear, an' every one of 'em will head off one way, followin' the scent. Trackin'. But there'll be one old hound—mostly it's an old hound, though I seen a couple pups that could do it—an' he'll circle around an' whine an' sniff an' whine some more, an' then he'll take off in some damnfool direction that don't make no sense. He won't act like he's got a scent, on accounta he don't; he'll jest act like he knowed right where he was goin', an' jest what he was doin'. An' if you're out for the exercise, you follow the pack, but if you want bear meat, you follow that hound, on accounta what he done is put hisself right into that old bear's head. Started thinkin' jest like him. Knows where that bear is goin' an' what he's gonna do, jest as soon as the bear knows.

"Now Mose, he wasn't no fool. He knowed I'd knowed Josh a sight longern him, an' he knowed we was still a sight closer, an' he figured I knowed, jest *knowed*, what the man'd do. An' I started to tell him he was wrong, but then I says to maself, Jack, maybe you do know. So I forgot about where I was goin'; I jest let the spirit move me, so to speak, an' old Mose come whippin' along beside me, never sayin' a word, never astin' a question. We was trailin'.

"An' we was movin' too, I mean to tell you. We covered some ground in the next hour or so. 'Bout a mile, mile an' a half down, we cut off from the river an' headed south on that road, runs down that side a the mountain, down towards Charlesville, an' we went on down there lickety-split. Might not a been too hard on Mose, but it was a pace that shoulda been gettin' to me. Only it wasn't, on accounta I had that knowin' feelin'. I seen old hound dogs that'll go like that all night, long as they got a scent. An' I had it, so we kept on. Musta covered seven, eight mile in that hour, all told. But then the feelin' left me. Jest like that, an' soon as it did, the strength went outa me too, an' I stopped dead.

"Or anyways, I tried to. Mose wouldn't let me. We dropped back to walk, but he made me keep movin'. He knowed jest what had happened, too. 'Lost it?' he says. I was too outa breath to do nothin' but nod. An' then, 'thout knowin' why, I looked up in the sky, an' I seen the sun.

"I stopped dead in ma tracks. I says, 'Mose, if you was to want to get up on top a mountain to watch the sun go down, which one would you pick?' Well, I think that shook his faith, a little bit anyways, on accounta he says, 'Jest what the hell would I be wantin' to watch the sun go down for?' Well, I didn't want to tell him. I didn't know *how* to tell him. So I says, 'Look, you're on your way to see this fella about marryin' his daughter, an' you figure seein' as he's white an' you're colored it might be the last damn sunset you're ever gonna see, so you want to get a good long look, an' the fella you got to see is down in Southampton Township.' Mose shook his head. 'Well,' he says, 'if I had me a horse, an' I was comin' down this way—' I stopped him there, on accounta the fella that said he seen Josh said he seen him on the Springs Road. 'Naw,' I says, 'you're comin' down—' 'The Springs Road,' Mose says. An' I knowed I didn't have to say no more. 'Yeah,' Mose says, an' he was starin' up at the sky, which was a mite dangerous on accounta we was pacin' along perty good again. 'I come down the Springs Road. Reason I'm on the Springs Road is so won't nobody know where I'm headed—' 'An' on accounta you couldn't borrow no horse from Hawley an' the onliest other place for a colored man to get one is to pay Les down to the Springs for one a them ridin'-stable nags.' 'Uh huh,' Mose says. 'So it takes me a while to get down there an' pay Les his dime an' ride out—' 'Saddle up an' ride out, on accounta Les ain't gonna be saddlin' up no horse for no damn dime.' 'Uh huh, an' I ride on down the valley as fast as I can go—' 'No, not that fast, on accounta it's dusty an' I'm wearin' ma suit.' 'Uh huh, an' I get to Patience an' cut off an' head up over the mountain, then I come down through Rainsburg an' head up over the mountain again, an' jest about sundown. . . .' An' he looked at me an' I looked at him, 'cause now we knowed where Josh was gonna be. He was either gonna be goin' so slow he'd be on Evitts Mountain, west of Rainsburg, or he was gonna be pushin' to get to the top a Tussey Mountain, east a Rainsburg, an' all we had to do was get up on that east mountain 'fore the sun was clean down, an' either we'd catch him or we'd be ahead of him. So we lit out.

"Now, I don't recall too much more 'bout that part of it, mainly on accounta the fact that Mose wasn't 'xactly human when it come to coverin' ground in a hurry. I seen him run moren one dog into the ground, an' there was stories that he'd outdistanced a pair of fellas that was after him on horseback. You may not believe it, but I sure as hell do, on accounta that night was like the Goddamn trottin' races at the county fair, so far as I'm concerned. I won't say the trees went flyin' by, but there sure wasn't no time to be carvin' your name into the bark. An' I know we passed up moren one farmer's wagon. Don't know how many; couldn't count an' move at the same time. But it was a lot. An' jest 'bout the time the sun started touchin' the tree-tops, we seen some smudges a smoke an' 'fore we knowed it we was in Rainsburg. Wasn't much of a town—still ain't. Couple houses, a general store, an' a couple churches. Well, for a small town there was a goodly amount of commotion goin' on; bunch a farmers at the store, settin', but we didn't have no time to stop an' pass the time a day. We jest hightailed it to the south end a town, an' we cut up over the ridge an' we had to slow down, but we made the best time we could, an' even Mose was puffin' a shade when we hit the top. Me, I was damn near dead. An' I damn near died for real when we got there, 'cause the sun was gone, an' so was Josh. There was enough light for us to find the place where Josh'd tied the horse.

"We headed off again; there was a chance we might catch him 'fore he got to the fork in the road at the bottom of the mountain. We mighta too, if it hadn't been so damn dark an' that road hadn't been so damn windy. Time we got to the bottom I felt like I jest come through a prizefight with three dozen pine trees. So we sat at the bottom an' caught our breath; wasn't nothin' more to do till the moon come up.

"Soon as we caught our breath Mose says, 'I don't like this. I don't like all them farmers back there, an' I don't like all them wagons on the road.' Well, I told him I didn't like it neither, but I had worse things to worry about. 'Like what?' he says. 'Well, for one thing,' I says, 'you an' me figured out somethin' that ain't gonna make us too damn comfortable is likely to happen if we don't catch up to Josh.' 'Yeah,' says Mose. 'Now, jest what do you think that might be?' Well, I hadn't really thought 'bout 'xactly what it might be, an' I said so. 'Well,' Mose says, 'jest 'xactly what you think is gonna make us any more uncomfortable than a bunch a redneck farmers with shotguns in their hands an' likker in their guts, 'cept maybe a bunch a redneck farmers with shotguns an' full a whiskey that's got wind of a colored boy tryin' to marry up with a white girl?'

"Well, then it hit me. An' I was jest about to start gettin' religion real quick when two things happened, right at the same time. First thing was, the moon come pokin' over Warrior Ridge; a big, full orangey moon, looked like it was swole up like a blood blister. Second was, we heard harness jinglin' an' hoofbeats comin' from up the mountain, on the road we jest come down. Lots a harness. Lots a hoofbeats. An' voices, the way drunk men sound when they think they're bein' sneaky. I looked at Mose, an' I swear to Jesus, it was the onliest time up till then I ever seen that man scared. Wasn't scared when that damnfool Langford Beegle hired us to kill a bear for him an' didn't bother to tell us he'd winged the sonofabitch already, so when we got there the bear come chargin' out of a thicket maddern Joseph after Mary said she was interfered with by an angel. Wasn't scared when the sheriff took his money an' then tried to kill us an' take the whiskey. But he was scared that night, let me tell you. Me, I wasn't scared, I was pure terrified. An' I looked at him an' he looked at me, an' the same damn thought come to us both at the same damn time: headin' for trouble like we knowed we was, an' hadn't neither one of us thought to bring a gun. All we had was Mose's huntin' knife.

"Course, even if we hada had a gun, we wasn't gonna do nothin' right then, 'cept what we did, which was slink off into the woods aside of the road, an' set there, waitin' for 'em to come past, hopin' to God they wouldn't see us, or smell the fear comin' offa us, which was a damn sight more likely. 'Jesus, Mose,' I says, 'I hope they ain't got dogs.' 'Dogs?' Mose says. 'What the hell would they want dogs for?' 'Why, to try . . .' an' I stopped. 'Cause I seen somethin'. They wasn't gonna need no dogs, 'cause they knowed where Josh was goin' even if we didn't. All we had to do was follow 'em. 'Mose,' I says, 'Mose all we got to do—' 'Is follow 'em. Yeah, I know that. But since you're so smart, what the hell we gonna do after we follow 'em?' Well, I didn't have the answer to that one, an' it didn't matter anyways, on accounta they was damn near on top a us by then.

"They come by us, ridin' slow. I wanted to be 'bout six miles away, downwind, but where we was 'bout four feet from the edge a the road, sucked up right to a birch log. We couldn't half breathe. What we could do was watch, an' what we seen was 'bout thirty old white farmers with faces that looked like somebody shoulda made shoes outa 'em. They was likkered—they was *well* likkered—you could smell it. But you couldn't see it in their faces. Those faces was set. An' they set in their saddles, them that had saddles to set in, straightern hell. Every one of 'em had a shotgun or a rifle. An' I could moren see 'em. I could smell 'em—smell the whiskey an' the horses an' the sweat an' all that, but mostly I could smell the angry. Maybe you don't think angry has a smell, but it does. Smells just like hot iron, only its jest a shade softern that, jest a touch more fleshy. In a funny way, it's like a woman's smell. A woman, first thing, when she's fresh an' young, she smells sweet an' tangy. You can let her be for a while, couple years, maybe, an' she's still got that sweetness, maybe a little more salt to her, but that don't hurt. But you let her set for too long 'thout touchin' her an' it all turns sour. Not lemon sour; rotten sour, like the way milk tastes if you take it atop a maple syrup. An' that's what happens to the angry smell. An' that's what'd happened down there, 'cause the angry I was smellin' was an old-smellin' angry, an' I knowed soon as I smelled it somebody was gonna die that night.

"We waited till they passed, then we straightened up a shade. I looked at Mose, an' Mose looked at me, an' I knowed he'd been snif-fin' the angry same as I done. But there wasn't nothin' to do 'cept light out after 'em, so I stood. Or I tried to; jest 'bout the time I got to ma knees, Mose hauls me back down. I wasn't fool enough to say nothin'; I jest looked around till I seen what he seen. An' presently I did. They had a rear guard; one fella on horseback, with canvas tied 'round his horseshoes so's they wouldn't make no noise. He had hisself a shotgun, jest like the rest. But that wasn't all. He was all dressed up, wearin' a hood, made outa some kinda white cloth, came to a point at the top an' hung clean down to his chest, an' a kinda sheet over the rest of him that hung down to his knees. He rode by slow an' quiet. An' we watched him till he was near outa sight, then we crawled out onto the road an' set off after him.

"We didn't have to worry 'bout him seein' us. Fool runs around in a white sheet on a moonlit night is gonna stay in sight to you a damn sight longer than you're gonna stay in sight to him. What we had to worry 'bout was stayin' outa earshot. So we couldn't talk. An' that was a problem, on accounta I wanted to tell Moses somethin'. Which was that I knowed who that last fella was. Could tell him by his boots. Pair I shined damn near every day for years. Belonged to Parker Adams. Parker, he'd been round the courthouse longern the man on the monument. You wanted somethin' done, you went to see Parker, an' Parker knowed who to talk to, an' he'd talk to 'em, an' he'd tell you yes or no, an' how much it was gonna cost. Parker took the money, an' I guess if any of it had ever come out, it woulda been Parker that went to jail, only none of it never did. Thing was, Parker wasn't no freelance. He done what he done on accounta it worked both ways, an' come election time he was right out there twistin' arms for the party. I wouldn't say they owned him, but wasn't no question a whose side he was on, an' who he took orders from. Which jest let you know 'xactly how far the whole thing had gone. 'Cause havin' Parker Adams there, dressed up in a sheet, was 'bout the same thing as havin' a speech by the mayor, an' the Presbyterian preacher handy to lead the prayer. Whatever they was gonna do to Josh, it wasn't gonna be no lynchin'. It was gonna be damn near as official as the Fourth of July.

"So we followed quiet. We knowed how to do that, an' you can bet we never done it no better. 'Bout two miles from the forks, or maybe it's closer to three, we come up to Chaneysville, which ain't much of a town, but there was likely to be somebody to see us, an' maybe call out or somethin', an' tip off Parker. Thing was, we couldn't take a chance on goin' around, on accounta the road splits off three different ways that I know of, an' maybe a couple more. So I was worryin', but it turned out that town was shut down tightern I don't know what. All the porches was empty an' all the curtains was drawn, an' there wasn't no lights showin' behind 'em. Wasn't nobody in that town takin' a chance on seein' something they wasn't wanted to see. Which was fine, since it meant they wasn't gonna be seein' us.

"Parker took the left-hand fork, or maybe it was the middle one, I don't recall too good, but anyways we followed him down the road an' past a few farmhouses, an' up over a couple hills, an' we was gettin' a little tired on accounta we couldn't hardly breathe right for fear a makin' noise, but we stuck to him. Had to. An' finely he stopped.

"I don't know how close he come to spottin' us. He jest stopped dead an' whirled that horse around an' looked over his backtrail, an' wasn't time for us to take cover; wasn't time for us to do nothin' 'cept freeze an' hope to God that whatever was behind us was dark enough to keep us hid. I swear I don't know how it was he didn't see us. But he didn't, 'cause after a long minute he turned off on a lane, an' that was that.

"I wanted to set there for a second an' shake, but we didn't have no time. Mose lit off through the woods fastern a scalded hound dog, an' I knowed he musta knowed a shortcut, so I jest tucked in close to Mose's butt an' kept ma head down, an' we went tearin' through them woods for maybe a quarter mile, an' then we come out into some old loggin' road, wasn't much moren a track but it was a hell of a lot clearer than the woods, an' we started runnin'. I don't know how we managed it—ma feet was 'bout ready to pack up any second, but I'll tell you, I knowed how bad things was gonna get an' a set of blistered-up toes was hardly gonna be the worst of it. So we run, an' about ten minutes later that track widened up a bit, an' Mose quit runnin' an' took to the woods again an' circled us around, an' we busted up onto some open fields, a pasture, a couple cornfields, an' then we slipped into a little ring a woods, an' come up back of a farmhouse.

"'Zis it?' I says. 'Better be,' Mose says. 'We beat 'em?' I says. 'How the hell do I know?' says Mose. Well, I didn't see nobody. The house was jest a big old two-story white farmhouse, with white curtains in the windows with yellow lamplight comin' through, an' a old glider swing on the porch. There was a front yard an' a back yard an' a barn an' a outhouse an' what looked like mighta been a separate stable. There was a faint odor a hog, but the pens musta been a good ways off 'cause I couldn't see no hogs or hear 'em grunt. What it all come down to was a perty picture of a country farmhouse, an' not a livin' soul in it.

"Mose waved his hand an' we backed outa there a ways. 'What we back out for?' I says. 'We busted our guts gettin' down here 'fore them peckerwoods, an' we ain't 'xactly got time to spare.' 'Yeah,' Mose says. 'We ain't got a lotta things. We ain't got no guns an' we ain't got no horse an' we ain't got the love a nobody this side a hell, so we sure God better have ourselves a plan.' Well, that's the way Mose was. 'Mose,' I says, 'this here ain't the kinda thing you want to go make a prayer meetin' outa. All we got to do is nip up to the back door there an' knock an' get in an' get Josh out, an' hightail it 'fore them bastards get here.' Mose shook his head. 'Jack, you ain't thought it—' 'Mose,' I says, 'I ain't got to think nothin' through, an' if I do, I'll do it when

I has to. Now, I know you ain't really got that much love for Josh, or nobody else for that matter, but he's like a brother to me, so you all jest set on your butt here an' plan, an' when I bring him back you tell us both about it.'

"Now, maybe I wasn't as careful as Mose, but I wasn't no hot-headed fool. I took a good look around 'fore I done nothin', an' I waited two seconds while the moon went behind a cloud, but once it did I didn't waste no time with sneakin' an' crawlin'. I busted right outa cover an' hightailed it across the back yard, prayin' whatever dog them folks had wouldn't start in to barkin'. I come up to the back door an' opened her up an' went in. Wasn't no time to be polite—if them farmers rode up I sure God didn't want to be outside.

"Soon as I come in I could see 'em settin' there, 'round the table. Josh was there, an' an old rawboned-lookin' fella had to be the father, an' two big dumb-lookin' country boys had to be the brothers. Wasn't no woman in sight.

"I hadn't made a whole lotta noise, an' I guess I come in so fast they didn't have no time to do nothin' about what I did make, so I took 'em all by surprise. I says, ''xcuse me, gentlemen, I hate to bust up the meetin', but I got some business to discuss with Mr. White here,' an' I jest reached right over an' grabbed old Josh by the shoulder an' tried to jest haul him away. An' when I pulled him he come all right, but the chair came with him. On accounta he was tied to it. Whole thing fell on the floor an' there he was, layin' on his side, lookin' up at me with his eyes widern the sky. I looked at him for a second, an' then I looked up an' I seen three pistols pointed at me, an' jest like I told Mose, I thought it through when I had to. An' then I put ma hands up, real slow.

"The old man looks at me an' he grins real wide, an' I could see where his teeth was goin' green. 'Why, boys,' he says, 'I guess we went to whole lotta trouble for nothin'. We wouldn'ta had to work on this one so hard if we'da knowed these fools was jest gonna come droppin' by.' The two boys laughed real good at that one. Real deep belly laughs; went 'Wheeyoo, wheeyoo.' 'That's enough now,' the old man says, an' the two of 'em shut up 'sif they was switched. He waves the gun at me, an' he nods toward the chair. 'Siddown, boy.' I sat. 'Merle,' he says, 'Merle, you come 'round behind me now an' go over there an' tie him up.' One a them fools come around, an' I damn near seen ma chance, 'cause he started to cut in 'tween us, but at the last minute he recollected what the old man told him ten seconds back an' went behind. He come around an' rummaged around in a cupboard for a while, with his behind stickin' up in the air, lookin' like a mountain covered over with denim. After a while he backs outa the cupboard. 'Pa,' he says, 'we done used up all the rope on that un there,' an' he gives a nod at Josh, who was still layin' there on the floor. The other lunk hadn't said nothin' up till then, but he chimes in on that, an' he says, 'That's right, Pa, we used her all up on this un here,' an' jest in case Pa didn't know which un where he was talkin' about, he fetched poor Josh a kick in the kidneys. I was lookin' right at him when it landed, an' it wasn't no love tap, neither, but Josh didn't show it. His eyes was blank, an' he hardly even winced. Well, up till then I hadn't really been thinkin'. But lookin' at Josh, seein' him hardly even wince when that dumb ox kicked him, well, I did start thinkin' 'bout how in hell we was gonna get outa there. An' the first thing I seen was we wasn't gonna get outa there. I had maybe an outside chance, 'cause I wasn't tied yet, an' with three of 'em there they was gonna have to be mighty careful how they fired them pistols, an' if Josh coulda maybe kicked one in the shins or somethin' to give me half a second's start, well, maybe I coulda made it. An' if I coulda got clear, maybe me an' Mose together could do somethin'. But none a that looked likely, on accounta Josh wasn't gonna be kickin' nobody to give nobody else half a second's nothin'. It didn't take much figurin' to know what had happened. His mind was ruint. On accounta he figgered out—too late, jest like I figgered out too late—that that girl had been settin' him up all along. Maybe he even figgered out that there was folks comin' to lynch him. An' if he figgered that far, he was surely gonna have figgered that when he swung she was gonna be right there, watchin' an' grinnin' an' fixin' to go gushy in her bloomers when he started jerkin' around. Anyways, I knowed I couldn't 'xpect no help from Josh. Meanwhile, Pa was tellin' the second one to take it easy, he didn't want Josh to die 'fore they was ready. 'Wayne,' he says, 'you go on out to the spring porch an' see if there ain't none a that there chain left hangin'.' 'Hey, Pa,' the first one says, 'there's a whole heap more rope out in the barn.' 'I know that, Merle,' the old man says, 'but I don't want nobody outside jest now.' Well, it turned out there was some chain, an' the two of 'em,

Merle an' Wayne, they chained me to the chair, an' the old man never once took his eyes off me, so I didn't have a chance to do nothin'. When they was done, Wayne says, 'Pa, we finished on this un here,' he slaps me upside the head jest so's there wasn't no mistake. 'You want I should set that un there on his feet?' 'You do that, Wayne,' the old man says, 'but stay outa ma line a fire.' 'This un here?' he says, an' he went to give me another crack. Onliest thing I could move was ma head, but I twisted around an' took the slap flush on the mouth, an' I got a mouthful a finger an' bit as hard as I could an' twisted ma head as sharp as I could, an' I heard the bone go snap jest 'fore Wayne started bellerin'. Sounded awful. An' it was an awful sight, let me tell you, a two-hundred-an'-fifty-pound farm boy starin' down at his pinkie finger that was pointin' south when the rest a his fingers was pointin' east, cryin' like a baby. The old man jest shook his head. 'Yeah, Wayne,' he says, 'that un there.'

"Well, I can't say what they mighta done to me—I suspect as how that wasn't ma smartest move—but they never got the chance, on accounta there come a knock on the front door. The old man told Merle to set Josh an' me aloose from the chairs, which he done, an' they herded us both down the hallway towards the parlor. Josh jest walked along, calm as you please, lookin' dead. I suspect it wouldn'ta mattered if they hadn'ta tied his hands. It was harder for me; them chains was the heaviest damn things you can imagine. They wasn't even tied to me, jest wrapped around, an' it woulda been easiern hell to whip 'em off if it hadn'ta been for the fact that ma arms was inside next to ma chest. There wasn't nothin' I could do, so I jest clanked along.

"Jest 'fore we got to the door I heard a sound. Funny sound. Like a dog makes when you hit it all the time. I stopped an' I turned around an' looked, an' then I seen her. The girl. She was standin' up to the top a the steps, lookin' down at us. She was a little bit of the thing, with long dark hair an' skin the color a snow an' these big black eyes; I could see 'em starin' at us. She was dressed all in white, in a dress that went clear to the floor, an' the wall behind her was white, an' there wasn't no light up there to speak of, so all you could see was the hair an' the eyes an' the size of her. But you could hear her voice; that was the sound.

"Well, the old man looked up at her an' he says, 'Clydette, I told you to get outa sight an' stay outa sight.' But she didn't pay him no attention. She says 'Joshua? Joshua?' I looked at Josh, but it was like he didn't hear her. I didn't blame him for not turning his head, I wouldn'ta turned my head for her no more neither, but it was like he didn't even hear her. But the old man heard her, an' went flyin' up them steps and fetched her a good clean slap an' knocked her sprawlin'. Then he come back, an' him an' Wayne an' Merle hauled us out inta the yard.

"They was waitin' out in the yard, all them farmers an' Parker Adams in his sheet, laid out in a half circle. They was all carryin' torches, an' the whole yard was lit up brightern day. Soon as they seen Josh, the whole bunch of 'em left out a roar like a mangled shebear, an' for the first time it come to me jest how bad it was. I had perty much figured out I was gonna die, but I'd been too close to that too many times to let it spook me. But hearin' that roar, I got to thinkin' 'bout what they might do to me 'forehand, things that, well, once they happen to a man, he'd jest as soon die, an' if you come along an' save his life afterwards, it ain't no kindness.

"Well, Parker waited till they quieted down, an' then he waved his hand an' some a them farmers come up on the porch an' laid hold a Josh. Then Merle gives me a shove an' I come out in the torchlight. I seen old Parker give a start, 'cause I knowed he recognized me. 'What the hell you got there, Mr. McElfish?' he says. Only he made his voice all high an' whispery, an' it come to me that didn't nobody else there know 'xactly who he was. 'Don't rightly know,' the old man says. 'He come bustin' into the party so's me an' the boys give him these chains for a door prize. Figger he must be hooked up with that un there. But I don't see it matters none; a nigger's a nigger, an' if you gonna have a lynchin', two's as good as one.' 'Maybe,' says Parker, 'but these two runs with a third one, an' if they're both here, third one can't be far off. You, Jack,' he says, 'where's Moses at?' I give ma voice a good shake, on accounta I seen a chance an' I wanted Parker to think I was scaredern I was, an' I says, 'He was right here, but he went to get the sheriff, an' when they get here you gonna be in some kinda trouble, an' if I was you I'd turn tail an' head back to Maryland fast as I could.' I wanted old Parker to get it in his head that I didn't know who he was. Only it damn near backfired. 'Mr. McElfish,' Parker says in that high whispery voice, 'you told this man where I was from?' 'No sir,' says the old man. 'He musta been listenin' for a while 'fore he come

bustin' in.' So I was safe; Parker musta let on to 'em he was from Maryland, which made all kindsa sense. "Sides,' the old man says, 'we gonna
kill him anyways, so it don't make no diff—' 'Listen here, McElfish,'
Parker says. 'You bear in mind who's runnin' this lynchin'. Now, maybe
we'll kill 'em both, an' maybe we'll let this one watch so he can go
back an' tell the rest. I ain't decided.' Well, jest about then Wayne perks
up a little, an' he says, 'If we only gonna lynch that un there, kin we
mess this un here up a little 'fore we leave him go?' Parker looks at
him. 'McElfish,' he says, 'you shut this lump of pork fat up 'fore I decide to lynch him too.' 'Shup, Wayne,' the old man says, an' Wayne
shut up.

"They put us up in front of a bunch of 'em an' they made us march.
Josh coulda run, maybe, but he looked deadern a two-day-old catfish,
an' I wasn't gonna get too far wearin' eighty pounds a chain. So we
jest walked along, me keepin' ma eyes peeled for a sign a Mose. I figgered he had to be doin' somethin', an' I knowed it wasn't goin' for
no sheriff. But he didn't show hisself, an' nothin' happened. So all I
could do was march.

"Well, they took us back down the lane to the main road, an' they
marched us south for maybe a mile or so. It musta been a sight: two
colored men walkin' along with ropes around their necks like they
was dogs an' thirty men with guns on horseback an' wagons, an' what
all. I got to thinkin' it musta looked jest like somebody goin' huntin'.
We was the dogs an' they was the hunters, an' the onliest thing we
needed was a coon, only we was the coons, an' they sure as damnit
was gonna tree us, or one of us anyways, an' that got all mixed up
in ma head, an' I started to laugh, real soft like, an' the chains started
to clinkin' a little when ma chest moved, not much, jest a little *clink,
clink, clink,* an' that was funny too, an' I started laughin' a little more,
an' I marched right along while we turned off the main road an' went
up over a hill, chucklin' an' clinkin', an' I mighta turned right into
the jolliest bastard in hell if it wasn't for the fact that when we got
to the other side a that hill there was a clearin' an' 'leven more fellas
in sheets an' a big oak tree an' underneath of it a pile a wood, an' it
come to me that when I said lynch I thought about hangin', but didn't
everybody think that way, some thought about burnin'. An' I stopped
chucklin'. I'm shamed to say it, but when them chains stopped clinkin'
I heard a funny sound, like hoofbeats far off. An' Wayne, he sings

out, 'Looky, Pa, looky, that un there wet hisself.' An' I looked down an' I seen he was right. But I couldn't feel it. Even when I seen it, I couldn't feel it.

"But nobody was payin' no attention. The 'leven sheets come trottin' up an' the farmers come up closer with the torches, an' they looked us over. Didn't say nothin'; didn't nobody say nothin'. It was so quiet all you could hear was a horse snort now an' again. They jest set there lookin'. After a minute Parker come up an' nods to the other sheets, an' they nodded to him, an' one of 'em says, 'Where'd *he* come from?' Said it in that same high whispery voice, so's wouldn't nobody know him. But I knowed him. I knowed 'em all. Knowed 'em by their boots. I'd shined every damn pair, that very day. Parker tole 'em how I'd come into the party, an' then he tole 'em how Mose was goin' to get the sheriff, an' they all chuckled a little, an' I knowed why: if he *hadda* gone to get the sheriff, you coulda bet dollars to double eagles there was least two deputies that wasn't gonna be handy. But after they was done chucklin' they stirred a little like they was uneasy. An' I seen why, right away: they wasn't sure they could kill me. If Josh was to disappear wouldn't nobody much know, or care. Me, I was another matter. Folks would miss me. An' somebody was maybe gonna look for me. An' the only way they was gonna be able to make folks stop lookin' was by tellin' 'em the truth, or somethin' like it, an' that wasn't gonna go down too easy. On accounta folks is funny; they'll get off their porches an' pull the shades an' keep their eyes screwed shut, but sometimes if you tell 'em what it is they ain't seein', they take notice.

"Well, Parker an' the rest a them sheets trotted aside to try an' figger out what to do. Me, I was feelin' mighty guilty, on accounta Josh was gonna die, an' I was feelin' good knowin' that I maybe wasn't. An' that's the way it was lookin', 'cause when the conference was over they hauled me over to the edge of the clearin' an' chained me to a tree an' they set Wayne to keep an eye on me, an' then they dismounted an' set about lynchin' Josh.

"It's funny how you see things. Why, a day before all that, if you was to a tole me I could set there an' watch the Klan lynch ma best friend an' not feel a thing, I woulda laughed in your face. But the truth is I can get more riled about it layin' here than I was then. It was jest like watchin' somebody butcher a hog. First they pulled his

clothes off him—coat, vest, tie, shirt, pants, long johns, everything—
an' they tossed the free end of a rope over the limb a that oak tree
an' looped the noose end 'round below his armpits, an' they hoisted
him up. Then Parker commenced to make some kinda speech. I couldn't
hear what he was sayin' but I knowed what he was gettin' at, on accounta he kept pointin' to Josh's privates an' every time he done it
them farmers would grumble. An' then he pulled out a knife an' held
it right upside Josh's parts, an' they left out a roar. But Josh didn't.
He jest hung there. An' that started gettin' to 'em; I guess it don't
make no sense to lynch a man that don't pay you no mind. So Parker
said somethin', an' one of them farmers went to his horse an' come
back with a whip. I guess they figured to get old Josh's attention.

"They sure as hell had Wayne's. He could barely keep his eyes off
'em while they was uncoilin' that whip an' gettin' people moved around
to give the sheet that had it enough room to swing. He started closer
an' closer so's he could get a good look at what was goin' on. Matter
a fact, one a the sheets seen how far from me Wayne was gettin' to
be, an' he come over to take care a that. That was what I figgered,
anyways. Only when that sheet came up to Wayne, he walked right
on by him. Or looked to. Then he stopped an' turned, an' went back
t'other way. An' I couldn't figger what *that* was all about, until all the
sudden Wayne goes 'Wheeyoo,' real soft like, an' falls on his face. The
sheet kept right on walkin'. It was too dark for me to see the boots,
but it wasn't too dark for me to count, an' when he got back to the
middle a the clearin' there was thirteen sheets there.

"I didn't waste no time.

"They hadn't bothered to chain me good, jest wrapped 'bout eighty
pounds a chain round me an' a tree. So I wriggled around as much
as I dared, made a little noise, but there wasn't nobody near enough
to hear 'sides Wayne, an' I was perty certain Wayne wasn't listenin'.
I twisted an' turned, an' I bruised maself on that chain, but I was gettin' a little play when they started in to whippin' Josh.

"The first crack made me jerk ma head up. Now, you gotta understand, that there wasn't no ridin' crop. It was a bullwhip. If it'd been
me I woulda screamed when the first one caught me, but Josh didn't
make a sound. The sheet that was whippin' him started windin' up
for another go; they was set on gettin' sound outa Josh. Only you don't
bullwhip a man too long—it ain't sound that comes out; it's his guts

to come out. I had to do somethin' fast. All I could think about was Wayne's pistol. I wanted that pistol so bad I could taste it. An' I started twistin' harder, an' pert soon I could see ma way out. I needed to give three good jerks, that was all. Trouble was, I was gonna have to make noise, lotsa noise. But if they heard that there chain clinkin', that was gonna be the end of everything. So I had to time it. I jest hoped Josh could take three more cracks.

"The second one come. Whip went slappin' through the air an' I twisted them chains. They give a little. Not enough. Josh, he didn't give at all. He jest swung there, his face jest as blank as a whitewashed board.

"The third one come. I got so close to bein' aloose I coulda cried. Close, but close ain't there. Josh still wasn't sayin' nothin'. I could see blood startin' to drip on the wood underneath him, but he didn't make a sound, he jest swung back an' forth like a scarecrow in the wind.

"The fourth one come. I got it that time, an' I left them chains fall easy as I could, an' I dropped an' scooted across the ground to where good old Wayne was layin' in the dust. It took a minute to work his pistol out from under him, but 'fore they was ready to give Josh another crack I was lined up. I waited. Sights was lined up perfect. That sheet wound up an' let the whip go, an' jest about the time it was halfways to Josh I squeezed that trigger jest as gentle as I could. I was aimin' for the chest but the slug dropped moren I'd figgered an' took the bastard in the hip. Blowed him halfways into the woods. Well, they stood there for a second, like they didn't know what the hell happened. I lined up on Parker. Coulda taken a closer shot, but I couldn't be sure about 'xactly who the others was, you see. Well, I was hurried an' the shot went high, but that second shot sure attracted some attention. One a them sheets looks over an' shouts, 'The nigger's loose,' an' one a the other sheets shouts, 'You all get him, I'll watch this sonofabitch.' An' then they come.

"Those bastards was stupid. Farmers can't do nothin' in the woods at night, an' them sheets was even worse—they was all the time gettin' their hems caught. I backed away real fast, an' soon as I was in the woods I left off the other three shots in the pistol to slow 'em down, an' then I lit out. I coulda got shed of 'em in two or three minutes, but I pulled 'em along for a good ten, lettin' 'em catch sight a me—they couldn't read sign worth a damn—takin' 'em uphill all the damn time so they'd wind theyselves good. After about a mile an' a half a dodgin' tree trunks an' playin' peekaboo, I cut back downhill an' left 'em play tag with theyselves.

"By the time I got back to the clearin', Mose had got his knife outa Wayne an' had Josh cut down from the tree an' tied onto a horse. Josh wasn't blank-lookin' no more. I guess that whip had cut loose a lotta things. He jest set there, cryin' like I ain't never seen a man cry. I don't know if it was the pain or the fear or the way that girl done him, but he wasn't good for nothin'. Soon as I was on horseback — Mose had picked out three good ones, an' run off the other horses — we rode out.

"We rode as hard as we could, but we couldn't make no time on accounta we couldn't keep Josh in the saddle. He wouldn't hold on. He wouldn't do nothin', 'cept cry. I wasn't too happy with him, but Mose was downright disgusted, an' he commenced to cussin' Josh three ways from Sunday. 'Damnit,' Mose says, 'we go through hell an' high water to rescue his pasty hind end an' all he wants to do is cry. Goddamn you, you mutilated sonofabitch, if you don't quit that cryin' an' start to ridin' I'm gonna lynch you ma own self.' 'Mose,' I says, 'go easy on him.' 'Easy, hell,' Mose says. 'You think them bastards are gonna go easy on us when they catch up? Which they gonna be doin' perty quick if we don't start ridin' hard. We got maybe ten minutes start in a two-hour ride outa this damn place, an' God knows what kinda fancy steppin' when we get back to someplace we can hide, an' we can't do none a that with a Goddamn dead man to cart around.' He reins in right there an' he says, 'Now, Josh, you listen to me. I know you been through a lot, but I swear 'fore God if you don't straighten yourself up an' start ridin' I'm gonna leave you here an' leave the bastards lynch you. I ain't entirely sure you ain't got it comin'.'

"Well, he was right in a way, an' he was wrong in a way, but 'fore I could say nothin' Josh looks up an' says, 'Leave me. I don't give a damn.' Mose jest stared at him. Then he says, 'All right. I got a life, an' I aim to keep it. Come on, Jack.'

"I says, 'Now wait a minute. Let me talk to him. Looka here, Josh,' I says, 'I know how you feel. I swear I do. But you dyin' ain't the way to do things. Why, what you oughta do is go back there an' take that bitch out in the woods an' beat her till there's no tomorrow. Kill her if you want to, I'll help you. But lettin' em kill you, that don't make no sense. That's what they wanted to begin with.'

"Mose looks at me an' he looks at Josh. ''Zat it? 'Zat *all?*' 'What you mean, 'zat all?' I says. 'The man was in love with that girl. He worked honest labor all damn summer jest to stay close to her. He give up other women to stay clean for her. He was fixin' to marry her. He trusted her. He was ready to pass for white, for *white,* so's he could be with her. Then she turns around an' tries to get him kilt, an' then you come along an' say 'zat all? Yea, that's all. Damn near all there is, anywhere. But what the hell would you know about that? You don't love nobody. You don't trust nobody. You don't give up nothin' for nobody. Well, maybe he was wrong, an' maybe he shoulda knowed better, an' maybe I think he's a damn fool too, but I tell you, I can't be real certain that if I was in his shoes I'd be too wild about stayin' alive maself. Now you ride on if you want. I'm gonna stay here an' talk to him, an' if I have to leave him, I swear, I'm gonna kill me a white girl.'

"Well, Mose, he looks at me, an' he shakes his head, an' he says, 'Jack, I swear, you as simple-minded as this here fool. Where you think I got this here sheet?' I couldn't think a nothin' to say, on accounta I didn't know where he got that sheet. So he told us. Told us how he'd gone on in that house, lookin' for a sheet, an' found that girl all beat an' bloodied, an' how she claimed she didn't have nothin' to do with it, that they musta been watchin' her an' Josh all along, an' waitin' for the right time, an' when they was ready they wanted her to tell 'em when he was comin' down to see her, an' she seen they didn't have nothin' good in mind, so they beat her an' made her tell, an' then they beat her again when they caught her tryin' to make some kinda signal to warn Josh off, an' how she begged him to save Josh somehow, an' give him the sheet, an' told him where they was takin' us.

"Well, I'll tell you, sometimes I useta get a little hot with Mose, on accounta the way he could lie easiern most folks breathe, but I was glad he could make stuff up that quick right then—or maybe he didn't have to make it up, maybe that was the guff she give him when he went in there to steal that sheet, to keep him from killin' her right then. I don't know. All I know is, Josh was whipped enough to believe it, an' he started ridin' better.

"Mose knowed a trail that ran along the top a Polish Mountain, an' we followed it almost to Evert. I was all for comin' on into town, but Mose kept sayin' he wasn't satisfied as to what was happenin'. I says to him, 'We know what's happenin', on accounta we jest finished puttin' a stop to it,' but Mose wouldn't listen. We finally holed up way up near dumb-butted town Mose called Oppenheimer. I hadn't never heard of it. It was a Godforsaken place to hole up, too; dry as dust, not a stream for miles. But Mose knowed a spring, an' he knowed a cave, an' it turned out he had some food cached up there, an' bandages an' some horse liniment, an' we cleaned Josh's back up an' bandaged him, an' then we ate an' then we had some whiskey, an' by the time the sun come up we was feelin' pretty good, most ways. 'Cept I could see that Josh wasn't comin' around the way he shoulda. He didn't say mucha anything. I knowed what it was, too; he finely seen through the lyin' Mose'd been doin' about that girl. I tried to tell Mose that, but he wouldn't listen. He jest wanted to go on an' on about politics, an' what them sheets was hopin' to accomplish by lynchin' Josh. I swear, Mose could make things about ten times as confusin' as they needed to be. An' I told him that. Said, 'Hell, Mose, we know what they was tryin' to accomplish.' 'Yeah,' Mose says, 'but why?'

"'Why?' I says. 'Hell, why ain't even a question. They done it on accounta white folks ain't noted for feelin' kindly towards colored folks, that's why. They're doin' the same damn thing all over the country all the damn time,' Well, Mose says, 'I know that, Jack. But there's more to why than jest that. There's "Why here?" an' there's "Why now?" an' there's—' 'Yeah,' I says, 'I know you know all the letters in the whatchemacallit, but I don't give a damn.' Well, he says, 'Jack, don'tcha see, we gotta figger out them whys so we can figger out who done it an' then begin to do somethin' about 'em. We can't jest go in there an' start beatin' on everybody white.' Well, I said, I didn't see why we couldn't, it sounded like they wasn't too particular about which nigger they started in on, but anyways, I already knowed who they was. An' I told 'em how I knowed, an' I told him who they was. An' Mose got real thoughtful.

"Well, we holed up that day an' the next, which was Sunday. Josh got so's he could move around pretty good, but his mind jest wasn't there. He still wasn't talkin'. Jest set there, sippin' whiskey, sayin' nothin'. By Sunday night, I was beginnin' to think we was gonna have to shoot him, like you do a horse with a busted leg—he was that bad. Finely

Mose sets down with him an' he says, 'Lookahere, Josh,' he says, 'we had about enough a this moonin' around. If you worryin' about that girl—' 'Hell with her,' Josh says, an' I begun to think that maybe that there whippin' was a good thing some ways; it got some sense in his head anyways. 'All right,' Mose says, 'hell with her. I ain't got no time to be huntin' down women anyways; we got twelve men to lay for.' Well, there he was, lyin' again, but I didn't mind it this time, neither, on accounta I seen that he was tryin' to get Josh's juices flowin'. Course there wasn't no way we was gonna ambush them twelve without causin' a whole lot a stir, but maybe we coulda done one or two, which mighta been enough to get Josh back whatever it was he left down there in the South County. So I says, 'That's right, Josh, we got twelve sheets that needs to be taken to the scrub board an' hung out to dry. An' if that ain't enough, we can go get that farmer an' the one fool son he's got left—' Well, to tell you the truth, I was beginnin' to warm to the idea. But Josh cut me off right there. 'Leave it be,' he says. That was all he said. But he said it in a voice that was lowern a mole's belly an' deadern Thursday night. An' that took the starch right outa me. An' I left it be.

"I left it be the next day when I come on in an' took to shinin' shoes. I shined every pair a shoes in the courthouse. An' I shined every pair a boots that was down there in Southampton—'cept one. Story was a tree fell an' busted up that one's hip. They told me that. Othern that, didn't nobody say nothin'. I didn't neither. I left it be.

"Next day Josh come on into town an' went down to Hawkin's an' bought hisself some Mail Pouch an' walked around town half the day, chewin' tobacco an' spittin' juice on the sidewalk, jest like Mose told him to do. Didn't nobody say nothin' to him; they was leavin' it be.

"An' the next day Mose come down, leadin' two horses an' ridin' the third, an' he hitched 'em to the post in front a the courthouse. Half the Town seen him doin' it but didn't nobody say nothin', an' an hour later them horses was gone, an' didn't nobody say nothin' 'bout that, neither. They left it be.

"That's the way it was. They left it all be. Course, Josh, he wasn't never the same. I don't think he ever did say moren three words at a time to anybody again. He'd walk aroun' town silent as the grave. He'd go into Hawkin's an' half the time he'd say what he wanted, an'

the rest a the time he'd jest point. I guess he was so mad he didn't
want to start talkin', 'fraid it would all come out. He left it be, too.

"But somebody didn't leave it be, on accounta every month or so
something bad would happen to one a them sheets. One went blind
from drinkin' leaded shine. One fell in a ditch an' broke his leg an'
caught pneumonia an' died. 'Nother one's wife left him. On like that.
Jest bad news. Not too much at any one time, but steady; somethin'
got every one of 'em. An' inside a 'bout three years wasn't none of
'em around here no more. Some moved on. 'Bout half was dead. Somebody didn't leave it be. . . ."

STREETCARS

ANNIE DILLARD

After winning the 1974 Pulitzer Prize (general nonfiction) for her first prose book,
Pilgrim at Tinker Creek, *a personal narrative set in southern Virginia, twenty-
nine-year-old Annie Dillard was deluged with opportunity: Vogue offered model-
ing assignments; broadcasting companies solicited her to do specials; one national
network wanted to showcase her talents in a regular half-hour show. There were
tempting propositions from the Hollywood movie moguls. "One time they offered
just huge sums of money to write a screenplay that was only supposed to be forty
pages long," says Dillard. "I could hear a little voice inside me going, 'Do it–do
it, honey!'"*

*She did not do it, however, preferring instead to continue, as always, to dedi-
cate time and effort to her writing. Over the next decade she produced four more
books, all highly acclaimed works of nonfiction:* Holy the Firm, Living by Fiction, Teaching a Stone to Talk *and most recently,* Encounters With Chinese
Writers.

*Although ten years younger than David McCullough, both writers were born
and raised on the same street in the Point Breeze section of Pittsburgh. McCullough's books often touch upon Pennsylvania, but only recently has Dillard returned
to her roots. Her current work-in-progress,* An American Childhood, *for which
she received a Guggenheim Foundation grant, focuses on Pittsburgh in the 1950s.
"Streetcars" is the first excerpt from that work to be published.*

S TREETCARS RAN ON Penn Avenue. Streetcars were orange, clangy, beloved things—loud, jerky, and old. They were powerless beasts compelled to travel stupidly with their wheels stuck in the tracks below them. Each streetcar had one central headlight which looked fixedly down its tracks and nowhere else. The single light advertised to drivers at night that something was coming that couldn't move over. When a streetcar's tracks and wires rounded a corner, the witless streetcar had to follow. Its heavy orange body bulged out and blocked two lanes; any car trapped beside it had to cringe stopped against the curb until it passed.

Sometimes a car parked at the curb blocked a streetcar's route. Then the great beast sounded its mournful bell: it emitted a long-suffering, monotonous bong . . . bong . . . bong . . . and men and women on the sidewalk shook their heads sympathetically at the motorman inside, the motorman more inferred than seen through the windshield's bright reflections.

You rode your bike across Penn Avenue with the light: a lane of asphalt, a sunken streetcar track just the width of a thin bike wheel, a few feet of brown cobblestones, another streetcar track, more cobblestones or some cement, more tracks, and another strip of asphalt. It was your whole body that knew those sidewalks and blocks of street. Your bones ached with them; you tasted their hot dust in your bleeding lip; their gravel worked into your palms and knees and stayed, blue under the new pale skin that grew over it.

The old cobblestones were pale humpy ovals like loaves. When you rode your bike over them, you vibrated all over. A particularly long humpy cobblestone could knock you down in a twinkling if it caught your bike's front wheel. So could the streetcar's tracks, and they often did; your handlebars twisted in your hands and threw you like a wrestler. So you had to pay attention, alas, and could not simply coast along over cobblestones, blissfully vibrating all over. Now the city was replacing all the cobblestones, block by block. The cobblestones had come from Pittsburgh's riverbeds. In the nineteenth century, children had earned pennies by dragging them up from the water and selling them to paving contractors. They had been a great and late improvement on mud.

Streetcars traveled with their lone trolley sticks pushed up by springs into overhead wires. A trolley stick carried a trolley wheel; the trolley wheel rolled along the track of hot electric wire overhead as the four wheels rolled along the cold grooved track below. At night, and whenever it rained, the streetcars' trolleys sparked. They shot a radiant fistful of sparks at every crossing of wires. Sometimes a streetcar accidentally "threw the trolley." Bumping over a switch or rounding a bend, the trolley lost the wire and the spring-loaded pole flew up and banged its bare side crazily against the hot wire. Big yellow sparks came crackling into the sky and fell glowing toward the roofs of cars. The motorman had to brake the streetcar, go around to its rear, and haul the wayward, sparking trolley stick down with a rope. This happened so often that there was a coil of rope for that purpose at the streetcar's stern, neat and cleated as a halyard on a mast.

So the big orange streetcars clanged and spat along; they stopped and started, tethered to their wires overhead and trapped in their grooves below. Every day at a hundred intersections they locked horns with cars that blocked their paths — cars driven by oblivious, semiconscious people, people who had just moved to town, teenagers learning to drive, the dread Ohio drivers, people sunk in rapturous conversation. Bong bong, bleated the stricken streetcar, bong, and its passengers tried to lean around to see what was holding it up, and its berserker motorman gestured helplessly, furiously, at the dumb dreaming car — a shrug, a wave, a fist:

> *I'm a streetcar!*
> *What can I do?*
> *What can I do*
> *but wait for you jerks*
> *to figure out that I'm a streetcar!*

TEETH

LEE GUTKIND

After roaming the country for nearly three years on my motorcycle to write my first book, Bike Fever, *and then traveling another year with a crew of National League baseball umpires for my second book,* The Best Seat In Baseball, But You Have To Stand!, *I began to focus my attention on familiar and friendly ground.*

My novel, God's Helicopter, *about three adolescent boys in the late fifties, is set in the Squirrel Hill-Greenfield section of Pittsburgh, where I grew up. My documentary film,* A Place Just Right, *focuses on four backwoods families in north-western Pennsylvania.*

I was inspired and excited by the wonderful people I met while making the film — trappers, rattlesnake hunters, modern-day mountain men and women — so much so that I dedicated the next few years to a collection of essays and profiles, The People of Penn's Woods West, *from which "Teeth" has been taken.*

AFTER BREAKFAST, her husband looked up from across the table and announced that he was taking her into town to have all her teeth pulled out. It took a while for the meaning of his words to penetrate. Even when he said he was getting her a new set of teeth, she stared at him blankly. The memory of that morning nearly six months ago, pained her even now.

"My teeth ain't perfect, but they never give me or my husband no

49

trouble," she said, rolling her eyes and shaking her head back and forth slowly. "And suddenly, there he wanted to go and pull them all out. I've never been so surprised in all my life."

She was sitting on a stoop in front of the tarpaper-covered cabin in which she and her husband lived, petting their old coon dog, curled in a grimy heap at her feet, and watching the tractor trailer trucks whoosh by. Each time a truck went up the road, she would wave and smile. The truckers would invariably wave back, as they roared by, bellowing smoke.

She told me that her loneliness was sometimes awful. It wasn't the mountains—she had lived here all her life and wasn't interested in anywhere else—but the fact that no one was around to talk to. The gloomy shadow that fell across her face blatantly telegraphed her desperation. Each time I visited, she went on and on, could hardly stop herself from talking.

She was a river of fat. Her body bulged and rippled in every direction, and her eyes, tucked into her pasty skin, looked like raisins pressed into cookie dough. Her hair was dirty gray, tangled and wooly, but you could tell her face had once been pretty. When she showed me her picture as an infant, I remarked that she looked like the Ivory Snow baby. Blushing, she covered her mouth and turned away. That was how we had first got on the subject of her teeth.

One day in town her husband was approached by the new dentist, a handsome young man in a white shirt and a blue and red striped tie, who explained that his house needed a new roof. Would he be interested in installing it in return for money or services?

Her husband was a short, wiry old man of seventy-two, who resembled a chicken hawk, with a hooked nose and arms that bowed out like furled wings. He hunched forward when he walked, as if he were about to take off flying. He told the dentist he would think on it for a while.

That evening, after supper, he stooped down and peered into her mouth, testing each of her teeth with his thumb and forefinger to see how well they were rooted. "Smile," he told her. "Laugh." She followed his instructions to the letter, as was her habit. Over the next few days, he watched her every chance he got. It was early autumn when he finally went back into town to make the deal. She never knew anything about it.

The woman explained that she and her husband had very little use for cash, bartering for almost everything they needed. They traded vegetables, cultivated on their tiny patch of land, for fruit—corn for peaches, tomatoes for apples, pickles for pears, beets for pretty blue-fire plums. He chopped wood in return for mason jars. Periodically, he repaired a car for a guy who owned a dry goods store in town in exchange for clothes for the both of them. By bartering instead of buying and selling, they hardly paid Uncle Sam a penny's worth of taxes.

Last summer, he raised a barn for some city folks, recently retired near here, in return for an old engine from a '64 Buick and a side of beef. The engine went into a pickup truck they had gotten for one hundred fifty dozen eggs. Paid out over a period of three months, the eggs came from their chicken coops out back. The pickup was then swapped to the owner of a local filling station for credit for two hundred gallons of gas, plus an assortment of parts and tools. Meanwhile, she boiled up the beef on the old black cast-iron stove that had belonged to his grandfather, and canned and stored most of it in the cold-cellar cave under the house. She cut the remainder of the beef in strips and hung them like wet socks above the stove, smoking and shriveling them down to jerky. From the spring to the fall, her husband went fishing each evening after dinner. When he collected a big batch of trout, she stewed them in the pressure cooker until the whole fish, bones and all, was white and meaty like tuna. This was what they would eat next winter and the winters thereafter. Their cave was stocked with years of stuff.

Her husband never talked about his work and what was owed to him in the way of goods and services, and she never asked. Despite her significant contribution, the actual swapping wasn't her business. Years ago, her daddy had told her in no uncertain terms exactly what she needed to know to get herself through life. He was a man much like her husband, didn't owe anyone and never wasted anything. No words were said in conversation, unless there was some specific point to be made. Otherwise, silence was golden.

One night, however, her father came outside and squeezed down on the stoop beside her. They lived in an old house along the side of the road, about the same size as the one in which she and her husband lived now. But her father only rented it for fifty dollars a month.

Neither her father nor his father before him had ever owned a piece
of property straight out.

At the time, she didn't know that the old man was dying from cancer.
Her mother had also died from cancer, and she had had to quit school
in the sixth grade to take care of the rest of the kids and keep house.
Recently, her two older brothers had joined the army, while the younger
kids were sent to foster homes. Now, she and her father were home
alone. She was fifteen at the time.

They sat side by side as the night grew colder. The moon shimmered in the glittering dish of sky, but the air felt like rain. Suddenly
he cleared his throat. The sound of his voice made her feel uncomfortable, similar to how she felt trying on a new pair of boots.

"What else is there in life?" He said this as if in summation after
a long conversation which she had somehow missed. Then, he paused.
She would never forget his face as they sat there. His hard, sharp features seemed to disintegrate in the darkness. The glitter reflecting from
the moonlight faded from the blue of his eyes.

"You work to eat, you eat to live, you live to work." He sighed.
"That's all there are to it."

The next morning, the man who was soon to become her husband
made himself known. Miraculously, all of the details had been worked
out between the man and her father in advance, without her having
the slightest idea of what was happening. The following afternoon,
the man came and took her away. Two weeks later, her father died.

She cleared her throat and motioned toward the house with her fat,
flesh-soaked arm. "We came right here to these two acres and moved
into an old shed out back. It ain't there no more. Tore it down to salvage the wood for this place. First we made sure we had good water,
then we started building. From start to finish it took two years to get
all set up. The winters were awful, but the summers weren't too bad."

All this happened some thirty years ago. Her husband had been
married once before. His first wife died or left him, she wasn't sure,
and his children, who she never met, were all grown up and living
somewhere in another part of the state. Once in a great while, there
was a letter, which he would read carefully, his lips moving, then stuff
into his pocket, shaking his head and muttering. He would go on,
muttering and cursing, shaking his head, for days at a time, without
so much as an explanation.

Her own brothers and sisters all lived near here, but hardly ever stopped by or invited her to visit. Like most everyone else, they were more than a little afraid of her somber, silent husband.

Once again, she paused to wave at a trucker, barreling up the narrow two-lane highway. Their shack had been built unusually close to the asphalt. Even from up in the sleeping loft inside, you could hear the cinders and feel the wind when the trucks rumbled by. She said she was so shocked and angry when she found out about the deal her husband had made with the new dentist that she started screaming and yelling. "I had never acted that way before, but I just couldn't help myself. All of a sudden, I went crazy. My husband didn't know what to do."

He had turned away, glaring in silence out the window. It was still early. The sun was just beginning its ascent up the hill toward them. His eyes narrowed. Time passed as he stared down the road. His brows, thick and hairy, cast a shadow, like umbrellas over his eyelids. When the sunlight reached up as far as their house, he got up and finished dressing. He bit off a plug of tobacco, stuffed it under his cheek, put on his old grimy baseball cap, climbed into his pickup, and turned her over. When he saw his wife come out onto the porch, he threw the truck into reverse, backed up, and leaned out the window. He wanted to have his say one more time. "We shook hands on a new set of teeth. It's owed to me."

She turned and walked back into the house without a word. He peeled out onto the asphalt, his tires spitting gravel.

In no time, her best clothes were out of the drawer and piled on the bed. She found an old suitcase, cleaned it inside and out carefully, before laying in her clothes. The last time she had been on any sort of trip was when her husband had come to take her from her daddy. They didn't have a suitcase then. All her possessions, including her mother's big black roasting pan, fit easily into a medium-sized cardboard box. Her father carried the box down to the road and they waited together until the man who was to become her husband arrived. The whole thing—packing, waiting, and driving away—all took about ten minutes. It went by in a blur, one moment stacked up on top of another.

Thinking back, she realized that her life had ended right about then. She had been isolated with this man who hardly talked to her and whom she hardly knew, a man who had refused to discuss his past for over thirty years. At least with her father there was evidence of some roots and another life somewhere behind the one he had been living. But this man's world was bleak, both behind and beyond. He offered little more than a nod or a grunt for sustenance each day. Her father's words, uttered with such sadness and resignation on that damp, dark night so many centuries ago, came back to her now. *You work to eat, you eat to live, you live to work. That's all there are to it.*

All right. She had lived her life in accordance with her father's wishes, had never asked for anything from anyone, never shirked her responsibilities or wasted a breath. She had always done whatever her husband had told her to do—and more. But giving up a part of her own body simply for the sake of a business deal was too much. It was going too far. A person has a God-given right to own certain things, especially when they were born with it.

The last thing she did before leaving was to go out to the pump house and peer into the mirror. The image she saw glaring back at her was awful. She was too old, too fat, and too dirty. But, if anything, her face had held up best of all. There was still a spark, a hint of the beauty that might have been.

Her daddy, who never had more than a dollar in his pocket at any one time, had always bragged that the Good Lord had made him rich by blessing him with a daughter with a million-dollar smile. Even now, she could hear the distant echo of his praise. She wasn't going to let that damn bastard she married squash the memory by pulling out her teeth.

She looked up at me. The shroud that had fallen over her face as she told her story momentarily lifted. "Used to be my husband would leave me alone from early morning until supper. But now, things is different. He's liable to ride by anytime, just to check and see if I'm still here. Sometimes I hide out behind the chicken coops and wait for him. When the house looks empty, he'll stop to see where I am. He always pretends he's come back for tools or materials, but I know I got him worried. It serves him right."

She dug her fingers into her scalp, shook her head vehemently, scratching simultaneously before continuing. "I left the house that morning, hitchhiked into town, and bought a ticket for Davenport, Iowa. Davenport was the only city in the state I could think of. My daddy traveled all over the country when he was younger. He told me you could drive for half a day in any one direction in Iowa and not see anything else but a green carpet of corn, just bending and stretching in the distance."

She pushed her big blubbery legs out into the grass, right near where the old coon dog was lying. Once in a while, the dog would thrash around and thump its tail against the ground. A couple of times, it pushed itself up and crawled over on top of us. The woman had on brown doubleknit slacks worn through at the knees. Her blouse was white with alternating pink and blue pastel stripes, although the colors were graying from repeated washings. This was the outfit she wore as she climbed aboard the bus and headed toward Davenport. Her clothes looked a lot better back then, she said.

It took nearly three hours to get to Pittsburgh, where they stopped and idled in the depot for about forty-five minutes. She did not get off the bus. They stopped twice on the highway in Ohio and once more in Indiana, but she remained in her seat, guarding her suitcase.

"I tell you, I've never done so much thinking in my entire life as I did on that bus, looking through the window, reading the neon signs and watching the headlights from the cars. Most of the people around me were sleeping, and none of them were too friendly. Not that I tried to do much talking. To tell the truth, I was scared half to death."

She wasn't actually thinking, she explained, as much as she was dreaming—with her eyes open. Her window was like an imaginary TV screen, and she could see the images of her past reflected before her. She saw her father carrying the cardboard box down to the side of the road. As the cancer took its toll, he had shriveled up like an old root. Then she saw the man who was to be her husband pull up. He put the cardboard box into the bed of the truck, opened up the passenger door, and helped her inside.

"I remember looking right into his face as he done this, the first time I had ever looked him full in the face. And then, as I sat in the darkness on that bus, I pictured how he had looked earlier that morning when he leaned across the table and told me he was going to take away my teeth. And you know what? He was the same. Those thirty years we had spent together had bloated me like a balloon and wrecked up my face but, except for a little more gray in his whiskers, that bastard ain't changed one bit."

She paused, shook her head, chuckled, then shook her head again and again. It wasn't easy to suddenly accept the reality of what had happened. The shiny sadness of her life reflected in her eyes.

I looked away, down behind the tarpaper shack toward the outhouse across the field. It had a three-hole bench. There were four or five old cars dumped into a gully behind the outhouse and an abandoned windowless schoolbus, teetering on the edge.

"I never made it to Davenport," she said, after a while. "But I got all the way to Chicago. You ever been to the bus station in Chicago? More people there than I ever seen, all in one place. Half of them don't speak English, and none of them was white. The moment I got off that bus, seeing all them coloreds and hearing all that foreign commotion, I was completely confused. I was hungry, but didn't want to spend any money. I also wanted to clean up a little, but with all them people, I was afraid to make a decision."

After a while, she found herself a bench back in the corner, out of the way, and sat down to try to think things out. She still had her ticket to Davenport, Iowa, but didn't particularly want to go there any more. She didn't want to go anywhere, as a matter of fact. She wasn't willing to move one inch from where she was. She must have dozed off, for the next thing she remembered was feeling a hand on her shoulder, shaking her gently. Someone was saying her name. No one would know her name in Chicago, so maybe she really was back home, about to emerge from a terrible dream.

But when she finally opened her eyes, an elderly man with horn-rimmed glasses and a tiny, pinched nose introduced himself as a representative of the Traveler's Aid Society, whatever that was. The man's voice was soft and reassuring. As he talked, he picked up her bag, wrapped his arm around her ample shoulders, helped her up, and led her across the bus station.

When her husband had discovered her missing, the man explained, he had contacted their minister, who somehow traced her to Pittsburgh, and subsequently to Chicago. There was also a Traveler's Aid representative waiting at the Davenport bus station, just in case she had made it that far.

They were moving at a brisk pace, passing the ticket counters and neatly wending their way through the milling crowd. She felt like a piece of livestock. "Where are you taking me?"

"There's a bus to Pittsburgh leaving in about ten minutes. Your husband already wired the money." He smiled and continued to talk to her in his quiet and reassuring manner, as they pushed through a big set of swinging doors and headed on down a broad cement runway toward a long line of idling buses. Drivers in neatly pressed gray uniforms stood by the doors of their respective vehicles puffing cigarettes and punching tickets, as she and the man hurried by.

"But I already have a ticket to Davenport, Iowa."

"You can cash it in when you get back home . . ." He paused, all the while continuing to lead her down along the row of buses. "Of course, I can't force you to do anything you don't want to do." He shrugged and smiled apologetically. "I can't even help you make up your mind."

By this time, they were approaching the bus to Pittsburgh. She felt his hand on her back, urging her gently toward the bus. He handed a ticket and her suitcase to the driver.

Meanwhile, she hesitated, momentarily resisting the pressure on her back. She tried desperately to think things out, but her mind was blank, as was her future.

With nothing better to do, she walked up the steps, dropped into a seat by the window, and closed her eyes. She did not allow herself to open her eyes until hours later, when the bus pulled into Pittsburgh. She was so confused and embarrassed, she had completely forgotten to say good-bye to the man with the horn-rimmed glasses who had helped her.

Now she looked up at me, smiling and winking. "My husband came to meet me." The thought evidently amused her, for she shook her head back and forth, chuckling. "On the way home, we talked things over, got everything out in the open for the very first time. I told him how lonely I was, how it wasn't fair the way he constantly mistreated me. I said that I should be consulted in his decisions about how we spend our money. I told him that I didn't have enough clothes, that I wanted to go into town more often, and that, because he was such a damn hermit, I didn't have no friends or family." She nodded emphatically. "I let him have it with both barrels. He had never allowed no one to talk to him that way before in his entire life."

I stood up. More than two hours had passed since we had first started talking. The sky was clouding over. In this part of western Pennsylvania, rain erupts suddenly, swallowing the hillsides and ravaging the roads. Besides, I was getting cold, sitting so long on that stoop. And my pants were filthy, where the old coon dog had tracked mud all over me. I walked briskly back to my motorcycle.

"He tries to be nice," she said, as she followed along behind me. "But you really can't change him. You couldn't ever change my daddy either," she added. "When you come right down to it, they was both dark and silent men."

I nodded, pulled on my helmet and kicked down on the starter. The machine cranked to life as I straddled the seat. From past experience, I knew that I couldn't wait for the right moment to leave. Otherwise I'd be waiting forever. I had to depart even while she was still in the act of talking.

She planted her foot in my path and grabbed my arm. "You know, he drove by two or three times while we was sitting here talking. He'll want to know who you are and everything was said. Hell," she said, smiling and winking, finally stepping out of the way, so that I could pull out, "I ain't telling him nothing. It serves him right."

The woman prepared herself extra special for her husband's homecoming that evening.

She went into the pump house and sponged herself down from head to toe, ran a brush through her hair a hundred times, scrubbed the grime from her fingers until the half-moons of her nails were white. Back in the house, up in the loft where they slept, she got out the nice green cotton jumper dress with the pretty yellow and white floral design and laid it out on the quilt. He had bought her the dress the day she came home. She had only taken it out of the box once, the following Sunday when they went to church.

After preparing dinner and setting the table nice and neat, she went back upstairs and put on the dress. Then she dusted herself with some fancy-smelling powder she had ordered through a magazine and gotten in the mail. She was just about ready, when his truck crackled outside on the gravel. He walked into the house. She could hear him move about downstairs, looking into the big pot on the cast-iron stove, sniffing what was for dinner. But not until he walked across the room and started up the ladder toward the loft, did she reach into the water glass on the nightstand beside their bed. Only then did she put in her new teeth.

GRIDS AND DOGLEGS

CLARK BLAISE

"I remember Pittsburgh as a city of fanatic devotions—to the teams, the schools, the districts, the personalities, the institutions—and that devotion to the city was heightened by a kind of tenderness (the Steelers and the Pirates and the Panthers were the collective doormats of their leagues); to be a loyal Pittsburgher was a test. (We were all so tough and strong and good—how come we never won? We all worked so hard and sacrificed so much—how come it never paid off?)

"Outsiders never talked about our Art Students' League and the Carnegie Museum and Library, and the fact that Buhl Planetarium had a Zeiss projector and William Steinberg found reason to stay at the podium of the Pittsburgh Symphony year after year, and that somehow or other those institutions were financed out of Pittsburgh coffers.

"History and society and the economy were tangible presences in Pittsburgh; it was the city of natural confluences. My classmates in high school included the son of the head of Westinghouse, the son of the head of the Steel Workers, and the son of Fritzie Zivic (a well-known middleweight fighter). It fed my love of the past, of science, of sports, and of the arts. I think 'Grids and Doglegs' is a pretty good testament to that love."

*   *   *

For more than fifteen years, beginning in 1966, Clark Blaise taught creative writing on the university level in Canada where, with the publication of two prize-winning short story collections, Tribal Justice *and* A North American Education, *he became recognized as one of that country's premier fiction writers. Today he is director of the writing program at Bennington College in Vermont. Although he no longer has family in Pittsburgh, he returns at every opportunity to satisfy an insatiable hunger to see the Pirates play ball.*

WHEN I WAS sixteen I could spend whole evenings with a straightedge, a pencil, and a few sheets of unlined construction paper, and with those tools I would lay out imaginary cities along twisting rivers or ragged coastlines. Centuries of expansion and division, terrors of fire and renewal, recorded in the primitive fiction of gaps and clusters, grids and doglegs. My cities were tangles; inevitably, like Pittsburgh. And as I built my cities, I'd keep the Pirates game on (in another notebook I kept running accounts of my team's declining fortune. . . . "Well, Tony Bartirome, that knocks you down to .188. . . . " the pregame averages were never exact enough for me), and during the summers I excavated for the Department of Man, Carnegie Museum. Twice a week during the winter I visited the Casino Burlesque (this a winter pleasure, to counter the loss of baseball). I was a painter too, of sweeping subjects: my paleobotanical murals for the Devonian Fishes Hall are still a model for younger painter-excavators. (Are there others, still, like me, in Pittsburgh? This story is for them.) On Saturdays I lectured to the Junior Amateur Archaeologists and Anthropologists of Western Pennsylvania. I was a high school junior, my parents worked at their new store, and I was, obviously, mostly alone. In the afternoons, winter and summer, I picked up dirty clothes for my father's laundry.

I had—obviously, again—very few friends; there were not many boys like me. Fat, but without real bulk, arrogant but ridiculously shy. Certifiably brilliant but hopelessly unstudious, I felt unallied to even the conventionally bright honor-rollers in my suburban high school. Keith Godwin was my closest friend; I took three meals a week at his house, and usually slept over on Friday night.

Keith's father was a chemist with Alcoa; his mother a pillar of the local United Presbyterian Church, the Women's Club, and the University Women's chapter; and the four children (all but Keith, the oldest), were models of charm, ambition, and beauty. Keith was a moon-faced redhead with freckles and dimples—one would never suspect the depth of his cynicism—with just two real passions: the organ and competitive chess. I have seen him win five simultaneous blindfold games, ten-second moves—against tournament competition. We used to play at the dinner table without the board, calling out our moves while shoveling in the food. Years later, high school atheism behind him, he enrolled in a Presbyterian seminary of Calvinist persuasions and is now a minister somewhere in California. He leads a number of extremist campaigns (crackpot drives, to be exact), against education, books, movies, minorities, pacifists—this, too, was a part of our rebellion, though I've turned the opposite way. But this isn't a story about Keith. He had a sister, Cyndy, one year younger.

She was tall, like her father, about five-eight, an inch taller than I. Hers was the beauty of contrasts: fair skin, dark hair, gray eyes, and the sharpness of features so common in girls who take after their fathers. Progressively I was to desire her as a sister, then wife, and finally as lover; but by then, of course, it was too late. I took a fix on her, and she guided me through high school; no matter how far out I veered, the hope of eventually pleasing Cyndy drove me back.

In the summer of my junior year, I put away the spade, my collection of pots and flints, and took up astronomy. There's a romance to astronomy, an almost courtly type of pain and fascination, felt by all who study it. The excitement: that like a character in the childhood comics, I could shrink myself and dismiss the petty frustrations of school, the indifference of Cyndy and my parents; that I could submit to points of light long burned-out and be rewarded with their cosmic tolerance of my obesity, ridicule from the athletes in the lunch line, and the Pirates' latest losing streak. I memorized all I could from the basic texts at Carnegie Library, and shifted my allegiance from Carnegie Museum to Buhl Planetarium. There was a workshop in the basement just getting going, started for teen-age telescope-builders, and I became a charter member.

Each week I ground out my lens; glass over glass through gritty water, one night a week for at least a year. Fine precise work, never my style, but I stuck with it while most of the charter enthusiasts fell away. The abrasive carborundum grew finer, month by month, from sand, to talc, to rouge—a single fleck of a coarser grade in those final months would have plundered my mirror like a meteorite. Considering the winter nights on which I sacrificed movies and TV for that lens, the long streetcar rides, the aching arches, the insults from the German shop foreman, the meticulous scrubbing-down after each Wednesday session, the temptation to sneak upstairs for the "Skyshow" with one of the chubby compliant girls—my alter egos—from the Jew-

ish high school: *considering all that,* plus the all-important exclusiveness and recognition it granted, that superb instrument was a heavy
investment to sell, finally, for a mere three hundred dollars. But I did,
in the fine-polishing stage, because, I felt, I owed it to Cyndy. Three
hundred dollars, for a new investment in myself.

Astronomy is the moral heavyweight of the physical sciences; it
is a humiliating science, a destroyer of pride in human achievements,
or shame in human failings. Compared to the vacant dimensions of
space—of time, distance, and temperature—what could be felt for Eisenhower's heart attack, Grecian urns, six million Jews, my waddle and
shiny gabardines? My parents were nearing separation, their store beginning to falter—what could I care for their silence, their fights, the
begging for bigger and bigger loans? The diameter of Antares, the
Messier system, the swelling of space into uncreated nothingness—
these things mattered because they were large, remote, and perpetual.
The Tammany Ring and follies of Hitler, Shakespeare, and the Con-
stitution were dust; the Andromeda galaxy was *worlds.* I took my meals
out or with the Godwins, and I thought of these things as I struggled
at chess with Keith and caught glimpses of Cyndy as she dried the
dishes—if only I'd had dishes to dry!

The arrogance of astronomy, archaeology, chess, burlesque, baseball, science-fiction, everything I cared for: humility and arrogance are
often so close (the men I'm writing this for—who once painted murals
and played in high school bands just to feel a part of something—they
know); it's all the same feeling, isn't it? Nothing matters, except, perhaps, the proper irony. I had that irony once (I wish, in fact, I had
it now), and it was something like this:

In the days of the fifties, each home room of each suburban high
school started the day with a Bible reading and the pledge of allegiance
to the flag. Thirty mumbling souls, one fervent old woman, and me.
It had taken me one night, five years earlier, to learn the Lord's Prayer
backwards. I had looked up, as well, the Russian pledge and gotten
it translated into English: this did for my daily morning ablutions. The
lone difficulty had to do with Bible Week, which descended without
warning on a Monday morning with the demand that we, in turn,
quote a snatch from the Bible. This is fine if one's name is Zymurgy
and you've had a chance to memorize everyone else's favorite, or the

shortest verse. But I am a Dyer, and preceded often by Cohens and Bernsteins (more on that later): Bible Week often caught me unprepared. So it happened in the winter of my senior year that Marvin Bernstein was excused ("We won't ask Marvin, class, for he is of a different faith. Aren't you, Marvin?") and then a ruffian named Callahan rattled off a quick, "For God so loved the world that he gave his only begotten Son . . ." so fast that I couldn't catch it. A Sheila Cohen, whose white bra straps I'd stared at for one hour a day, five days a week, for three years—Sheila Cohen was excused. And Norman Dyer, I, stood. "Remember, Norman," said the teacher, "I won't have the Lord's Prayer and the Twenty-second Psalm." She didn't like Callahan's rendition either, and knew she'd get thirty more. From me she expected originality. I didn't disappoint.

"Om," I said, and quickly sat. I'd learned it from the Vedanta, something an astronomer studies.

Her smile had frozen. It was her habit, after a recitation, to smile and nod and congratulate us with, "Ah, yes, Revelations, a lovely choice, Nancy. . . ." But gathering her pluckiness she demanded, "Just what is that supposed to mean, Norman?"

"Everything," I said, with an astronomer's shrug. I was preparing a justification, something to do with more people in the world praying "Om" than anything else, but I had never caused trouble before, and she decided to drop it. She called on my alphabetical shadow (a boy who'd stared for three years at my dandruff and flaring ears?), another Catholic, Dykes was his name, and Dykes this time, instead of following Callahan, twisted the knife a little deeper, and boomed out, "Om . . . amen!" Our teacher shut the Bible, caressed the marker, the white leather binding, and then read us a long passage having to do, as I recall, with nothing we had said.

That was the only victory of my high school years.

I imagined a hundred disasters a day that would wash Cyndy Godwin into my arms, grateful and bedraggled. Keith never suspected. My passion had a single outlet—the telephone. Alone in my parents' duplex, the television on, the Pirates game on, I would phone. No need to check the dial, the fingering was instinctive. Two rings at the Godwins'; if anyone but Cyndy answered, I'd hang up immediately. But with Cyndy I'd hold, through her perplexed "Hellos?" till she queried,

"Susie is that you?" "Brenda?" "Who is it, please?" and I would hold until her voice betrayed fear beyond the irritation. Oh, the pleasure of her slightly hysterical voice, "Daddy, it's that *man* again," and I would sniffle menacingly into the mouthpiece. Then I'd hang up and it was over; like a Pirates' loss, nothing to do but wait for tomorrow. Cyndy would answer the phone perhaps twice a week. Added to the three meals a week I took with them, I convinced myself that five sightings or soundings a week would eventually cinch a marriage if I but waited for a sign she'd surely give me. She was of course dating a bright, good-looking boy a year ahead of me (already at Princeton), a conventional sort of doctor-to-be, active in Scouts, Choir, Sports, and Junior Achievement, attending Princeton on the annual Kiwanis Fellowship. A very common type in our school and suburb, easily tolerated and easily dismissed. Clearly, a girl of Cyndy's sensitivity could not long endure his ministerial humor, his mere ignorance disguised as modesty. Everything about him—good looks, activities, athletics, piety, manners—spoke against him. In those years the only competition for Cyndy that I might have feared would have come from someone of my own circle. And that was impossible, for none of us had ever had a date.

And I knew her like a brother! Hours spent with her playing "Scrabble," driving her to the doctor's for curious flaws I was never to learn about . . . and, in the summers, accompanying the family to their cabin and at night hearing her breathing beyond a burlap wall . . . Like a brother? Not even that, for as I write I remember Keith grabbing her on the stairs, slamming his open hands against her breasts, and Cyndy responding, while I ached to save her, "Keith! What will Normie think?" And this went on for three years, from the first evening I ate with the Godwins when I was in tenth grade, till the spring semester of my senior year; Cyndy was a junior. There was no drama, no falling action, merely a sweet and painful stasis that I aggrandized with a dozen readings of *Cyrano de Bergerac*, and a customizing of his soliloquies . . . "This butt that follows me by half an hour. . . . An ass, you say? Say rather a caboose, a dessert. . . ." All of this was bound to end, only when I could break the balance.

We are back to the telescope, the three hundred well-earned dollars. Some kids I knew, Keith not included this time, took over the school printing press and ran off one thousand dramatic broadsheets, condemning a dozen teachers for incompetence and Lesbianism (a word that we knew meant more than "an inhabitant of Lesbos," the definition in our high school dictionary). We were caught, we proudly confessed (astronomy again: I sent a copy to *Mad* magazine and they wrote back, "*funny but don't get caught. You might end up working for a joint like this*"). The school wrote letters to every college that had so greedily accepted us a few weeks earlier, calling on them to retract their acceptance until we publicly apologized. Most of us did, for what good it did; I didn't—it made very little difference anyway, since my parents no longer could have afforded Yale. It would be Penn State in September.

I awoke one morning in April—a gorgeous morning—and decided to diet. A doctor in Squirrel Hill made his living prescribing amphetamines by the carload to suburban matrons. I lost thirty pounds in a month and a half, which dropped me into the ranks of the flabby underweights (funny, I'd always believed there was a *hard* me, under the fat, waiting to be sculpted out—there wasn't). And the pills (as a whole new generation is finding out) were marvelous: the uplift, the energy, the ideas they gave me! As though I'd been secretly rewired for a late but normal adolescence.

Tight new khakis and my first sweaters were now a part of the "New Look" Norman Dyer, which I capped one evening by calling the Arthur Murray Studios. I earned a free dance analysis by answering correctly a condescending question from their television quiz the night before. Then, with the three hundred dollars, I enrolled.

I went to three studio parties, each time with the enormous kid sister of my voluptuous instructress. That gigantic adolescent with a baby face couldn't dance a step (and had been brought along for me, I was certain), and her slimmed-down but still ample sister took on only her fellow teachers and some older, lonelier types, much to my relief. I wanted to dance, but not to be noticed. The poor big-little sister, whose name was Almajean, was dropping out of a mill-town high school in a year to become . . . what? I can't guess, and she didn't know, even then. We drank a lot of punch, shuffled together when we had to, and I told her about delivering clothes, something she could respect me for, never admitting that my father owned the store.

But I knew what I had to do. For my friends there was a single event in our high school careers that *had*, above all, to be missed. We had avoided every athletic contest, every dance, pep rally, party — everything voluntary and everything mildly compulsory; we had our private insurrections against the flag and God, but all that good work, that conscientious effort, would be wasted if we attended the flurry of dances in our last two weeks. The Senior Prom was no problem — I'd been barred because of the newspaper caper. But a week later came the Women's Club College Prom, for everyone going on to higher study (92 per cent always did). The pressure for a 100 per cent turn-out was stifling. Even the teachers wore WC buttons so we wouldn't forget. Home room teachers managed to find out who was still uninvited (no one to give Sheila Cohen's bra a snap?). The College Prom combined the necessary exclusiveness and sophistication — smoking was permitted on the balcony — to have become the very essence of graduation night. And there was a special feature that we high schoolers had heard about ever since the eighth grade: the sifting of seniors into a few dozen booths, right on the dance floor, to meet local alums of their college-to-be, picking up a few fraternity bids, athletic money, while the band played a medley of privileged alma maters. I recalled the pain I had felt a year before, as I watched Cyndy leave with her then-senior boyfriend, and I was still there, playing chess, when they returned around 2 A.M., for punch.

It took three weeks of aborted phone calls before I asked Cyndy to the College Prom. She of course accepted. Her steady boyfriend was already at Princeton and ineligible. According to Keith, he'd left instructions: nothing serious. What did *he* know of seriousness, I thought, making my move. I bought a dinner jacket, dancing shoes, shirt, links, studs, cummerbund, and got ten dollars spending money from my astonished father. I was seventeen, and this was my first date.

Cyndy was a beautiful *woman* that night; it was the first time I'd seen her consciously glamorous. The year before she'd been a girl, well turned-out, but a trifle thin and shaky. But not tonight! Despite the glistening car and my flashy clothes, my new near-mesomorphy, I felt like a worm as I slipped the white orchid corsage around her wrist. (I could have had a bosom corsage; when the florist suggested it, I nearly ran from the shop. What if I jabbed her, right *there*?) And I could have cried at the trouble she'd gone to, *for me*: her hair was up, she wore glittering earrings and a pale sophisticated lipstick that made her lips look chapped. And, mercifully, flat heels. The Godwin family turned out for our departure, so happy that I had asked her, so respectful of my sudden self-assurance. Her father told me to stay out as long as we wished. Keith and the rest of my friends were supposedly at the movies, but had long been planning, I knew, for the milkman's matinee at the Casino Burlesque. I appreciated not having to face him — wondering, in fact, how I ever would again. My best-kept secret was out (Oh, the ways they have of getting us kinky people straightened out!); but she was mine tonight, the purest, most beautiful, the *kindest* girl I'd ever met. And for the first time, for the briefest instant, I connected her to those familiar bodies of the strippers I knew so well, and suddenly I felt that I knew what this dating business was all about and why it excited everyone so. I understood how thrilling it must be actually to touch, and kiss, and look at naked, a beautiful woman whom you loved, and who might touch you back.

The ballroom of the Woman's Club was fussily decorated; dozens of volunteers had worked all week. Clusters of spotlights strained through the sagging roof of crepe (the lights blue-filtered, something like the Casino), and the couples in formal gowns and dinner jackets seemed suddenly worthy of college and the professional lives they were destined to enter. A few people stared at Cyndy and smirked at me, and I began to feel a commingling of pride and shame, mostly the latter.

We danced a little — rumbas were my best — but mainly talked, drinking punch and nibbling the rich sugar cookies that her mother, among so many others, had helped to bake. We talked soberly, of my enforced retreat from the Ivy League (not even the car stealers and petty criminals on the fringe of our suburban society had been treated as harshly as I), of Keith's preparation for Princeton. Her gray eyes never left me. I talked of other friends, two who were leaving for a summer in Paris, to polish their French before entering Yale. Cyndy listened to it all, with her cool hand on my wrist. "How I wish Keith had taken someone tonight!" she exclaimed.

Then at last came the finale of the dance: everyone to the center of the floor, everyone once by the reviewing stand, while the orchestra struck up a medley of collegiate tunes. "Hail to Pitt!" cried the president of the Woman's Club, and Pitt's incoming freshmen, after whirling past the bandstand, stopped at an adjoining booth, signed a book, and collected their name tags. The rousing music blared on, the fight songs of Yale and Harvard, Duquesne and Carnegie Tech, Penn State, Wash and Jeff, Denison and Weslyan . . .

"Come on, Normie, we can go outside," she suggested. We had just passed under the reviewing stand, where the three judges were standing impassively. Something about the King and Queen; nothing I'd been let in on. The dance floor was thinning as the booths filled. I broke the dance-stride and began walking her out, only to be reminded by the WC president, straining above "Going Back to Old Nassau," to keep on dancing, please. The panel of judges—two teachers selected by the students, and Mr. Hartman, husband of the club's president— were already on the dance floor, smiling at the couples and poking their heads into the clogged booths. Cyndy and I were approaching the doors, near the bruisers in my Penn State booth. One of the algebra teachers was racing toward us, a wide grin on his florid face, and Cyndy gave my hand a tug. "Normie," she whispered, "I think something wonderful is about to happen."

The teacher was with us, a man much shorter than Cyndy, who panted, "Congratulations! You're my choice." He held a wreath of roses above her head, and she lowered her head to receive it. "Ah—what is your name?"

"Cyndy Godwin," she said, "Mr. Esposito."

"Keith Godwin's sister?"

"Yes."

"And how are you, Norman—or should I ask?" Mr. Wheeler, my history teacher, shouldered his way over to us; he held out a bouquet of yellow mums. "Two out of three," he grinned, "that should just about do it."

"Do what?" I asked. I wanted to run, but felt too sick. Cyndy squeezed my cold hand; the orchid nuzzled me like a healthy dog. My knees were numb, face burning.

"Cinch it," said Wheeler, "King Dyer."

"If Hartman comes up with someone else, then there'll be a vote," Esposito explained. "If he hasn't been bribed, then he'll choose this girl too and that'll be it."

I have never prayed harder. Wheeler led us around the main dance floor, by the rows of chairs that were now empty. The musicians suspended the Cornell evening hymn to enable the WC president to announce dramatically, in her most practiced voice, "The Queen approaches."

There was light applause from the far end of the floor. Couples strained from the college booths as we passed, and I could hear the undertone, ". . . he's a brain in my biology class, Norman something-or-other, but I don't know her. . . ." I don't *have* to be here, I reminded myself. No one made me bring her. I could have asked one of the girls from the Planetarium who respected me for my wit and memory alone— or I could be home like any other self-respecting intellectual, in a cold sweat over *I Led Three Lives*. The Pirates were playing a twi-nighter and I could have been out there at Forbes Field in my favorite right-field upperdeck, where I'm an expert . . . why didn't I ask her out to a baseball game? Or I could have been where I truly belonged, with my friends down at the Casino Burlesque. . . .

"You'll lead the next dance, of course," Wheeler whispered. Cyndy was ahead of us, with Esposito.

"Couldn't someone else?" I said. "Maybe you—why not you?" Then I said with sudden inspiration, "She's not a senior. I don't think she's eligible, do you?"

"Don't worry, don't worry, Norman." I had been one of his favorite pupils. "Her class hasn't a thing to do with it, just her looks. And Norman"—he smiled confidentially—"she's an extraordinarily beautiful girl."

"Yeah," I agreed, had to. I drifted to the stairs by the bandstand, "I'm going to check anyway," I said. I ran to Mrs. Hartman herself. "Juniors aren't eligible to be Queen, are they? I mean, she'll get her own chance next year when she's going to college, right?"

Her smile melted as she finally looked at me; she had been staring into the lights, planning her speech. "Is her escort a senior?"

"Yes," I admitted, "but *he* wasn't chosen. Anyway, he's one of those guys who were kept from the Prom. By rights I don't think he should even be here."

"I don't think this has ever come up before." She squinted into the footlights, a well-preserved woman showing strain. "I presume you're a class officer."

"No, I'm her escort."

"Her *escort?* I'm afraid I don't understand. Do I know the girl?"

"Cyndy Godwin?"

"You don't mean Betsy Godwin's girl? Surely I'm not to take the prize away from that lovely girl, just because – well, just because *why* for heaven's sake?"

The bandleader leaned over and asked if he should start the "Miss America" theme. Mrs. Hartman fluttered her hand. And then from the other side of the stand, the third judge, Mr. Hartman, hissed to his wife. "Here she is," he beamed.

"Oh, dear me," began Mrs. Hartman.

"A vote?" I suggested. "It has to be democratic."

The second choice, a peppy redhead named Paula, innocently followed Mr. Hartman up the stairs and was already smiling like a winner. She was a popular senior, co-vice-president of nearly everything. Oh, poise! Glorious confidence! Already the front rows were applauding the apparent Queen, though she had only Mr. Hartman's slender cluster of roses to certify her. Now the band started up, the applause grew heavy, and a few enthusiasts even whistled. Her escort, a union leader's son, took his place behind her, and I cheerfully backed off the bandstand, joining Cyndy and the teachers at the foot of the steps. Cyndy had returned her flowers, and Mr. Wheeler was standing dejectedly behind her, holding the bouquet. The wreath dangled from his wrist.

"I feel like a damn fool," he said.

"That was very sweet of you, Normie," Cyndy said, and kissed me hard on the cheek."

"I just can't get over it," Wheeler went on, "if anyone here deserves that damn thing, it's you. At least take the flowers."

I took them for her. "Would you like to go?" I asked. She took my arm and we walked out. I left the flowers on an empty chair.

I felt more at ease as we left the school and headed across the street to the car. It was a cool night, and Cyndy was warm at my side, holding my arm tightly. "Let's have something to eat," I suggested, having practiced the line a hundred times, though it still sounded badly acted. I had planned the dinner as well; *filet mignon* on toast at a classy restaurant out on the highway. I hadn't planned it for quite so early in the night, but even so, I was confident. A girl like Cyndy ate out perhaps once or twice a year, and had probably never ordered *filet*. I was more at home in a fancy restaurant than at a family table.

"I think I'd like that," she said.

"What happened in there was silly — just try to forget all about it," I said. "It's some crazy rule or something."

We walked up a side street, past a dozen cars strewn with crepe.

"It's not winning so much," she said, "it's just an embarrassing thing walking up there like that and then being left holding the flowers."

"There's always next year."

"Oh, I won't get it again. There are lots of prettier girls than me in my class."

An opening, I thought. So easy to tell her that she was a queen, deservedly, any place. But I couldn't even slip my arm around her waist, or take her hand that rested on my sleeve.

"Well, I think you're really pretty." And I winced.

"Thank you, Norman."

"Prettier than anyone I've ever —"

"I understand," she said. Then she took my hand and pointed it above the streetlights. "I'll bet you know all those stars, don't you, Normie?"

"Sure."

"You and Keith — you're going to be really something someday."

We came to the car; I opened Cyndy's door and she got in. "Normie?" she said, as she smoothed her skirt before I closed the door, "could we hurry? I've got to use the bathroom."

I held the door open a second. *How dare she,* I thought, that's not what she's supposed to say. This is a date; you're a queen, my own queen. I looked at the sidewalk, a few feet ahead of us, then said suddenly, bitterly, "There's a hydrant up there. Why don't you use it?"

I slapped the headlights as I walked to my side, hoping they would shatter and I could bleed to death.

"That wasn't a very nice thing to say, Norman," she said as I sat down.

"I know."

"A girl who didn't know you better might have gotten offended."

I drove carefully, afraid now on this night of calamity that I might be especially accident-prone. It was all too clear now, why she had gone with me. Lord, protect me from a too-easy forgiveness. In the restaurant parking lot, I told her how sorry I was for everything, without specifying how broad an everything I was sorry for.

"You were a perfect date," she said. "Come on, let's forget about everything, OK?"

Once inside, she went immediately to the powder room. The hostess, who knew me, guided me to a table at the far end of the main dining room. She would bring Cyndy to me. My dinner jacket attracted some attention; people were already turning to look for my date. I sat down; water was poured for two, a salad bowl appeared. When no one was looking, I pounded the table. *Years of this,* I thought: slapping headlights, kicking tables, wanting to scream a memory out of existence, wanting to shrink back into the stars, the quarries, the right-field stands—things that could no longer contain me. A smiling older man from the table across the aisle snapped his fingers and pointed to his cheek, then to mine, and winked. "Lipstick!" he finally whispered, no longer smiling. I had begun to wet the napkin when I saw Cyndy and the hostess approaching—and the excitement that followed in Cyndy's wake. I stood to meet her. She was the Queen, freshly beautiful, and as I walked to her she took a hanky from her purse and pressed it to her lips. Then in front of everyone, she touched the moistened hanky to my cheek, and we turned to take our places.

WHERE ARE OUR M.I.A.'S?

ROBERT TAYLOR, JR.

"The campus where I teach sits upon a hill above the Susquehanna River, a river that is equal to its lovely name. I grew up in Oklahoma City; rivers in that part of the country are modest, frequently only the ghosts of rivers. I must have dreamed of rivers such as the Susquehanna; it is better even than the Mississippi. And there is comfort living in a river town, even though that river can rise and travel well beyond its banks on occasion, forcing us to depart for higher ground. I cannot explain this comfort. Mostly, I never see the river; but I know it is there and remember its heritage, the logging, the canals, and think fondly of its passage from the mountains to the Chesapeake.

"To the west of Lewisburg, in Buffalo Valley, are large, productive farms, many Amish, and east is coal mining country, serene ridges giving way to slag heaps, grim gray towns that remind one all is not well in the world. That country interests me. Travel twenty miles from Lewisburg and you come to Mt. Carmel and a string of towns, including Centralia, where smoke seeps from the ground, and you seem to have journeyed to another, perhaps truer, world. Knowledge of this world is as much with me as knowledge of the river. Geography thus blesses me twice."

*   *   *

Short story writer Robert Taylor, Jr., who teaches at Bucknell University, is co-editor of West Branch, a magazine of poetry and fiction. "Where Are Our M.I.A.'s?" originally appeared in Kansas Quarterly.

LINDA ZARKOSKIE WAS a nice girl, willing to work hard for advancement. These days, of course, you didn't dare hope for too much for fear that you then would not be able to bear losing everything. Wanda Smolok, Linda's friend and co-worker at the Pulaski Street Pizza Hut, said that you *would* lose everything, no matter how hard you worked or hoped. Loss was the rule of life. Wanda, Linda thought, was a little weird, but you had to like her when you saw the way she moved so swiftly and directly from one point to another, balancing the trays of thick-crusted pizzas and tall cokes and heavy mugs of light draft Schmidt's, and the way she talked so boldly of her sexual preferences. Older men, she said, were much to be preferred over the younger ones. Linda was interested in this idea. How old, she wanted to know. At least thirty, Wanda said. Her current "companion" was thirty-two. The owner of a white GTO convertible, he also sang alto falsetto in a Kingston rock group called "The Gathered Moss," all of which put him really in a whole other class from these punks of eighteen or nineteen who, with such a swagger, boasted of what they could not deliver. Of course, Linda admitted, if he delivered what he promised, why then he must be some guy.

Linda's boyfriend, a twenty-one-year-old shoe salesman named Martin Klinger, delivered what he promised, sure, but then he promised so little! At first she thought him shy, but soon enough saw that he was actually a common arrogant male trying to seem the strong silent type. He *was* silent—but strong? Well, she had once dated a weight-lifter whose muscles bulged and were so hard all over him that when he held her close she thought of cantaloupes. Martin Klinger, soft, his skin loose on bones that did not even seem firm enough, brought to mind tomatoes. Yet she liked him all right. Sometimes he surprised her with a witty observation—of course, he'd had plenty of time to think about what he was going to say! And he was very polite and her mother liked him because he was so quiet and appeared so harmless. She supposed that, after all, she would do no better and had recently begun to encourage him to take little freedoms with her body. He was slow to get the point. The thought of Wanda with her thirty-two-year-old rock singer inspired her to be bold. Here, silly, she had said, guiding his hand beneath her blouse. The shock in his face had amused her. He was *so* pure! She was beginning to lose heart.

About this time Wanda offered to fix her up with a friend of her "old man." Linda only hesitated an instant before saying sure, why not, what did she have to lose.

They agreed to double date.

The first thing that struck her about Stanley Dubczek was his height. It was as though the extra years he had on her were matched by extra inches. Both hands deeply pocketed, he stood before her at the door of her parents' house, and she felt very tiny. Then she noticed his eyes, light blue, her favorite color, the color of the walls of her room. She did not ask his age. She would guess maybe he was almost thirty. He had served in the armed forces in Vietnam, he told her (in the car now), but did not know whether he had actually killed anybody. You often fired into darkness, at targets more audible than visible. They—the enemy, the Cong, the Charlies—made terrible noises once they wanted your attention. Otherwise they were quiet and treacherous, everywhere but nowhere, and so you got to where you hated silence more than anything else.

She listened with interest, intrigued by the idea of those terrible jungles and what it would be like to stalk and be stalked. You could be jumped on from behind at any moment and have a sharp jungle knife plunged into your stomach. A jungle knife was like a butcher knife, only longer and shinier. It would flash in the moonlight.

They were parked at the end of a dirt and gravel lane atop Bald Mountain, overlooking the entire Wyoming Valley. You could see the lights of Scranton, the lights of Wilkes-Barre, lights all along the river, the network of boroughs seeming endless, with dark spots interspersed throughout—the slag heaps, black mounds of coal waste piled up in some places as high as small mountains, regular and smooth.

Did she come here often? he asked.

Not really. She was afraid of heights. He laughed and with a deep mellow voice told about his sensations in the airplane that had taken him to Vietnam. She kept losing the sense of his words, instead catching onto some unspoken meaning flowing dark and swift around and through the words, feeling, it seemed, the very sensations he must have felt while lying awake surrounded by all that beautiful dangerous jungle in Southeast Asia.

Then he was holding his hand right up to her face, as though desiring her to smell or taste it.

"Go ahead," he said. "Look it over real good. I'm not ashamed of it."

God! two fingers, the index and the middle, were missing.

"Go ahead. Feel the stumps."

She forced herself to do it. They were very smooth.

"That's enough!" he said, withdrawing the hand. Also he withdrew the arm that had held her close to him and moved away from her, pushing his hand again beneath his leg and looking out the window.

"Where'd they go?" he asked in a hoarse whisper. The fingers? No— of course he meant Wanda and Merrit. She was sure that she didn't know. In the bushes maybe. Lying beneath a tree. Not far, you could be sure about that. He laughed. Did she ever have the feeling, he wondered, that people were always avoiding her? Now *she* laughed. You mean, she asked, like when people move to the other side of the carseat? He stopped laughing. This was serious. He meant, he said, the feeling of being left out, standing at the end of a long line, watching doors close in front of you, seeing people drive off, people you cared for who did not wave as they drove by, passing you in their sleek cars when you were afoot and weary. He edged closer to her as he talked; she felt drawn to him. He was so strange, after all. *Unique*, she would say, describing him to Wanda. As far as the other girls went, she did not think she would mention his missing fingers, unless they seemed genuinely interested. And then only in an offhand manner. *Offhand!* God. A *casual* manner. She would put no emphasis on it at all, skipping right away to the blueness of his eyes, his impressive height, his dangerous career in foreign jungles.

What would it be like to make a complete break in your life? Just imagine how it would be to say to Mr. Gerald Seigel, "I quit," and hand him your red apron. Oh, but she could never do it. What would they all think of her, Mary Ann and Doris and Anita and Wanda? What would she think of herself? And what would she do in place of the job, where would she go? Even in California there would be

Pizza Huts. She saw herself traveling all that distance, then, in desperation, putting on the apron again.

Suddenly Stanley Dubczek was putting his arm around her, then kissing her very hard, thrusting his tongue into her mouth. She thought of Martin Klinger. What would he think about this! Pressed up against her side of the car, the door handle hard and blunt like the handle of a knife in the small of her back, she felt his hand, his good hand, fall warm and swift against her breast and squeeze as though she might be a sponge he wished to test for resilience. Gently, she whispered, gently, please. He seemed to have calluses on the tips of his fingers and touched her too long in some places, not long enough in others, like a machine programmed to satisfy some other woman—in the end breaking down altogether. No apologies. He asked her if he compared favorably with other men she had known. Quite favorably, she said. Better than most. He offered her a cigarette.

"In Saigon I knew a lot of women."

He leaned back in his corner of the seat, his legs spread wide apart, his almost fingerless hand resting atop his crotch, that hand looking for all the world, she thought, like a sadly misshapen potato, pink, a new potato with a few straggly white roots. It was easy to listen to other sounds and still get the drift of his stories. She listened for some signal, some clue to Wanda's whereabouts. Cicadas were chirping madly, leaves rustling, twigs snapping, life all around her, crawling and creeping insect life and animal life. How ever would she manage in a jungle! Saigon would be no better: rickshaws, opium dens, scurrying little yellow people. Like Hong Kong. Like Tokyo, Shanghai, Peking. No, Peking would be different, austere, cold, gray because of the sad-faced communists. The women—the women in Saigon, he said, were friendly and warm. They did not cheat you. They were small but firm of flesh and loved American clothes, loved everything American, painted their faces skillfully and treasured American movie magazines. They made you feel important, "like you were somebody," somebody bigger and smarter than you were, with influence and special privileges. He took a deep breath.

"We let them beat us. Us! The most powerful nation on this earth— losers. Why? How in hell did it happen? Can you explain it to me? They beat us! We're the losers—"

There was a sudden thrashing sound from the area where she had imagined Wanda and Merrit to be.

"What's that!" he whispered. "What *is* that?"

He leaned down, slid from the seat and kneeled on the floor, peering over the edge of the window. It was nothing, she said, just Wanda and Merrit enjoying themselves. She saw that he was actually very frightened—right here on Meatskin Ridge, in the heart of Luzerne County! Hey, she said, this isn't Vietnam. He gave a little laugh, but pushed down the door lock and rolled up the window—good thing Merrit hadn't put the top down!

"Ever hear him sing?" he asked.

She guessed that he meant Merrit. She hadn't. She didn't go to dances much, she explained. Well, she should hear him sing sometime. Quite a voice, that guy! If only *he* could sing like that—why, if he could sing like that guy sang, *nothing else would matter!*

He grew calm. He talked about his past, the good times he'd had with his uncle, hunting in the mountain forests up in Sullivan County. It was so clean in those woods, he said, so clean and fresh. You'd really have to have been there to understand just how clean and fresh it was on those frosty mornings in the woods so long ago.

He made it sound lovely. She thought she might after all be able to fall in love with him.

2

Two weeks passed. No phone call, nothing at all from Stanley Dubczek. She had nothing to say to the other girls. She avoided Wanda. On her nineteenth birthday Martin Klinger brought her roses and took her to the Hotel Genetti for dinner and dancing. To her surprise, The Gathered Moss provided the music. Merrit, Wanda's older man, wore tight velvet pants with sequined cuffs, the white tips of his patent leather boots protruding like little half-moons flattened by dark clouds. He clapped the palm of his hand against a tambourine as he sang, his teeth flashing brilliantly in the stage light. His voice was high and shrill, a quavering whine. He appeared not to recognize her.

The days seemed a blur of cheese yellows and tomato reds, an endless chanting of engagements and impending engagements and broken engagements, of weddings, honeymoons, tragic separations. Anita had high hopes and Doris was depressed and Mary Ann was so distracted one day that she ran into the salad bar, bruising her thigh and dropping hot cavatini into the thousand island dressing.

The big Grant's store in the center next door went out of business. And all the time her mother was urging her to go to college and get into secretarial science. If you want to get ahead these days, she kept saying, get yourself as much education as you can.

Around Halloween, three months after their date, Stanley visited her at home. It was a Saturday, the wind blowing sodden yellow leaves up against the windows of her mother's house, and Stanley called about two o'clock to say that he was coming. I'm not alone, she said, immediately thinking what a silly thing to say. Her mother asked her, as soon as the phone was back in its cradle, if she would *prefer* being alone.

And so Stanley came, behaved as though he was accustomed to doing this, almost convincing her that he really was, as Wanda had once put it, a very nice guy. Certainly her mother thought so. He's really very nice, she said, watching from the window as he drove away in his fifteen-year-old car. They had talked about nothing. He had only asked her questions about her work, commenting on how fortunate she was in having a Saturday afternoon off. Then came a series of questions about her friends, her "favorite recreational activities." It was, she later thought, as though he had decided on these categories of conversation in advance; she imagined him choosing them from a list in a book on winning friends. He certainly was not in the least bit self-conscious about his hand this time. He kept waving it in front of her as he spoke, so that she had the feeling that the real subject of their conversation, that which remained unspoken, was indeed fingerlessness, what it meant to lose one's fingers while fighting an unseen enemy in dark foreign jungles while girls like her languished and blossomed in warm homes oceans away.

Monday Wanda told her she had heard that Stanley had lost his job, and Linda realized that she had not even known where he worked. She had the idea that surely he must receive a generous pension from the government because of his missing fingers. According to Wanda, he had been driving a delivery truck for Baer's Beer Depot and had been accused of secreting away beer for his own use, leaving cases behind bushes in vacant lots and coming back later in his own car to get them. The trouble was, Wanda said, as often as not when he went back to get the case he found that someone else had beat him to it. So he had to put aside more than he originally needed in order to accommodate the thieves, and his boss of course noticed the sudden heavy losses and fired him on the spot, giving no notice.

She told herself that it was a good thing their relationship had not developed. Surely he would be in jail one of these days. Or worse. Her mother said the same, lamenting the waste of his "niceness," of his good manners and his neat appearance.

Then, on the eve of Thanksgiving, he showed up again, all smiles and with a huge frozen turkey in his arms. Although her family's turkey had been bought several days ago, a fifteen-pounder, she tried to be polite. He had a friend who was working for a meat processing plant, he explained, and could get the birds cheap. Her mother took the turkey straight to the Amana and shut it up—no doubt thinking about Christmas—then ushered her father upstairs.

Nice parents, Stanley said. His were dead. He'd been raised by a cousin of his mother's in Pittston who liked her own children best.

She made him a cup of instant coffee, wishing, in spite of herself, that he would talk again of his experiences in the jungles of Vietnam— though not, please, of the girls of Saigon. She caught herself staring at his hand. How *had* he lost those fingers? She would never ask it, though.

He had a dream, he said, and that dream was to go into politics. This country was on the decline. People had lost faith in their leaders. Leaders did not deserve to lead, having no faith in the nation. This was not the America of old, not the land of the free, home of the bold conquerors of a wild and savage continent.

He sipped the coffee rapidly, as though he had craved it. You'll burn your tongue, she said. How pink and full his lips were, and how small his chin was, almost dainty! And those lovely light blue eyes. Politics! *Sure.* He was too idealistic, though.

She never saw him again. When she tried to call him to invite him to share the turkey with her and her family on Christmas Day, she was told that his number had been disconnected. Once she thought she saw him ride by the Pizza Hut on a motorcycle, a big chrome-plated Harley Davidson with white streamers on the handlebars, but she couldn't be sure.

About three weeks into the new year she found in the mailbox an envelope addressed to her with Stanley's name in the corner, but no return address. She opened it and unfolded a mimeographed sheet, thin yellow paper with bold red ink used for the message and a black ink border around the edges.

WHERE ARE OUR M.I.A.'s?!

Beneath the bold-faced headline was a brief editorial reprinted from a prominent newspaper taking the President to task and calling on the nation to rise up from its bed of apathy. *Otherwise we would never know whether these brave men were truly dead, or only lost.* She immediately pictured wild-eyed men, their uniforms ragged, boots unlaced, beards grown thick, wandering the muddy roads of Vietnam, looking for their camp, begging food from suspicious villagers who would pretend to understand no English. Hundreds, thousands of them, inadvertently left behind, declared *Missing-in-Action!*

Nowhere on the sheet did she find a personal message from Stanley.

Then there was a Valentine's Day card, with no return address but postmarked London, England, an American card, the kind children exchange at school. Where on earth had he gotten it? Why was he in England?

Wanda said he had probably lost his mind.

By Easter her former boyfriend Martin Klinger started coming around again. He told her he was beginning to think that selling shoes was not so bad after all. You could get promoted to assistant manager if you kept at it long enough.

Sure, Martin!

When she thought about Stanley she remembered mostly his light blue eyes, the calmness they conveyed. Also the enemy, the Charlies that blended into lush green leaves, seemed somehow to have gotten into her mind. In lulls at the Pizza Hut she sat on the high stool behind the cash register and, gazing through the thick plate glass window, saw small yellow-skinned men peering back through at her. At times like this she found she longed for Stanley, so strong and with such lovely blue eyes, the protector of the Vietnamese. In England he would learn to be a gentleman, would gain enough self-confidence so that he would no longer be ashamed of his hand. And, no longer dependent on Saigon prostitutes, he would come to know ways to please mature women.

Going on twenty, she considered herself a mature woman now.

3

Spring gave way to summer. Trees everywhere were heavy with their leaves, and scraggly shrubs even appeared on the slopes of the slag heaps she had to pass on her way to work. It was late in June when she heard news of Stanley's fate. She heard it on the radio, almost dropping the dish she was drying, quickly turning up the volume. She couldn't believe her ears. Stanley! They were talking about Stanley Dubczek! He was dead. No, not dead yet—only sentenced to die. What on earth! He had gone to Angola—wherever that was—to fight for the cause of freedom and now was being held captive by the enemy revolutionary government, accused of being a mercenary!

Dear God. Stanley, a mercenary with his poor hand the way it was! And now he would lose his life.

The next day his picture was in the paper, an old picture taken when he was in high school, his eyes smaller, his smile forced, hair very short. She clipped the picture and put it in an envelope, placing the envelope in a drawer, beneath her good black slip. All that week she thought about him constantly. *We're the losers*, he'd said. How true!

No, she told Wanda, this man was *not* a fool! Anita and Doris understood better. She told them the story of how he had brought her family a turkey for Thanksgiving, of the children's Valentine mailed from London, and they were very interested.

By the end of the week news about Stanley dwindled to almost nothing. And then there was nothing at all; the editorials expressing outrage stopped. She wrote a letter to the editor protesting this obvious lack of responsibility, including in her letter generous quotations from the flyer Stanley had sent her so many months ago. Courage and idealism were the themes of these quotations. Also sacrifice. The letter was printed and then she received in the days that followed a number of personal replies. So there *were* people who cared! She was invited to join several organizations devoted to telling the truth about our government's capitulation to world Communism. All of these letters and pamphlets she put in one large manila envelope, the envelope itself going into her drawer, the same one that contained the photograph of Stanley, beneath the black slip. Every evening when she came home from work she took out the two envelopes. She looked at Stanley's picture and she read each pamphlet carefully, underlining key phrases with the same red-ink ballpoint pen she used at work to take orders with. What she read continued to shock her. Eisenhower a Communist! The Beatles part of a worldwide plot hatched in the early 1920s with the full cooperation of Lenin! Who would have thought . . . all so new, so strange.

Four weeks after the news of Stanley's arrest and impending execution there was still no further word of his fate. About this time she received a phone call from a man who explained that he had mailed her a quantity of literature and would like to come by her house and have a discussion with her. Her parents being home, she said yes.

The doorbell rang at about nine-thirty. She had taken the manila envelope from her drawer and brought all the pamphlets to the kitchen table, laying them out in an attractive manner, and, rising to answer the door, she now made a few last-minute adjustments, straightening the top edges so that the pamphlets together formed a large square that resembled from a distance a small patchwork quilt in which the primary colors were black and white. The television in the next room was very loud. She didn't think her parents even heard the bell. No matter. This was *her* business. She brushed lint from her skirt and moistened her lips, then touched the cold doorknob just as the bell rang a second time.

He stood in the shadows on the stoop, tall and broadshouldered, the features of his face not distinguishable in the dark. She had the sensation, for an instant, that it was Stanley himself, returning to her as mysteriously as he had left. She caught herself looking at his hands, and, as if to lend credence to her fanciful illusion, he stood to one side, not facing her directly, so that one arm could not be made out. But it was only an instant, and then she caught herself. His name, he announced, was John Schmidt; he had talked to her earlier on the telephone. She remembered then to click on the porch light and invite him inside. She caught her breath as he turned toward her. His right sleeve! It seemed to hang loose by his side. An armless man! But no. She was wrong. He seemed whole.

This way, please.

He was dark, with shiny skin and small eyes and a mouth and nose jammed together in what seemed his face's darkest corner. The breadth of his shoulders, she now saw, had more to do with pads than with bone structure or muscles; it was an old-fashioned sportcoat that he wore, the kind she imagined her father might have worn long ago, dark gray with narrow lapels and really a lot of padding in the shoulders. Yet he was not old, not even middle-aged, perhaps not yet thirty. There was something boyish about his face—perhaps the shininess or the small features—even though his dark hair, combed straight back and oiled, had begun to thin at the temples. His hands, large but somehow frail, dangled from the wide sleeves of the heavy gray coat as though sewn onto the fabric for an interesting decorative effect.

She felt strangely excited. *Unusual* was the word she settled on for him. In his small eyes she saw great reserves of caution, mixed with steely determination. Very *masculine* eyes that made her want to serve him coffee.

He wanted first of all to express his sincere condolences over her tragic loss.

Quickly she directed his attention to the arrangement of pamphlets on the table. His eyes opened wide then:

"We're not alone," he said.

He sat down and ran his fingers over the letters. She went after the coffee, then joined him, sitting opposite him at the table, and with due solemnity they began to discuss the poison that was flowing so freely into their once-clean lives. It was a state of emergency that they lived in. He hinted of well-equipped armies, militia men as in days of old, on call.

She came to see, as the evening progressed, that there was fire in his eyes, and although he didn't kiss her goodnight he did clasp her hand warmly and look at her meaningfully. The real passion, she knew, would come later. Much after all had to be deferred, much sacrificed. Defeat, she would explain to Wanda, came only to those who had ceased to struggle. The stakes were very high. She would mention the frightened look in the eyes of the many Vietnamese refugees, who were everywhere these days, walking the streets in search of God knew what. Not just jobs. Lost kin, some said. Something important, anyway, something that in transit—perhaps out of carelessness or a lack of proper vigilance—they had lost and wished now with all their hearts to find.

COMFORT STATIONS

John Griesemer

"I had an uncle who, a couple of generations ago, left Pennsylvania to homestead in Montana. I thought that was wonderful: the one real pioneer in our family. But soon he gave up the ranch and came home to Pennsylvania, the story goes, and that always bothered me: our family couldn't cut it in the great American West. Then, a couple of years ago, I went to a wedding in the valley where my uncle used to live, and I saw the neat farms, the gentle hills, the well-cared-for richness of the place, and I realized the eminent sense of my uncle's return from the sub-zero winters, the dying range cattle, and the twenty miles between neighbors out there in Montana. He had enough wisdom to remember his home place and to say, for him anyway, it was better."

*   *   *

John Griesemer lives in New York City, where he works as an actor, off-Broadway, and in film, as a screenwriter. His three-and-a-half hour mini-series, "The Voyage of the Mimi," aired in the fall of 1984 on the Public Broadcasting System. "Comfort Stations" originally appeared in West Branch and was subsequently listed in Best American Short Stories 1983 and The Pushcart Prize VIII (1983).

T HE SUMMER MY parents parted ways, Eisenhower's heart was on the mend, I had just turned thirteen, and my grandfather was visiting us all the time. I was spending long hours in the abyss of our lawns, lying low, feeling dwarfed by grasshoppers and the prospect of divorce. My grandfather, who finally had enough of my swoons, decided in mid-July it was time to get me out of the suburbs and into the heartland. We went to what we called our family farm.

It wasn't really the family farm because it was rented by my grandfather's brother's daughter and her husband, but it was in Pennsylvania Dutch country near the village where my grandfather was born, and it was the only farm ever held by any member of our family.

The trip, I could tell, was all for my own good. My younger brother and sister were staying with my mother's parents in Rye while our mother and father stalked through their eroded attachments and did their lawyers' biddings. It had been a spring and early summer runneled with bitterness for our family. All of us children felt smaller for it. Sometimes mother would not be living at home; sometimes neither of our parents was there, and we would spend days and nights with our grandfather in his still house with its ticking clock and bonsai tree in the pool of sunlight on the dining room table.

All of this went on for just several weeks, but it seemed to last for seasons, and I was glad when my grandfather stopped by one evening and announced the trip to Pennsylvania.

"They'll be haying this weekend," he said. "We can make it like an old-fashioned motoring trip in the country. We'll see the sights. Aunt Gillian said she'd like to go. What do you say?"

"Yes."

And I rose from the grass as if surfacing from the sea.

I rode in the front seat of Grandfather's Buick, the one with the real portholes in the front fenders. Grandfather drove and Aunt Gillian rode by herself in the back.

I had been to the family farm two or three times before for summer holiday picnics in better times. We would load the family—Mother, Father, we three children, Aunt Gillian and my grandfather—into the Buick and drive from Connecticut, across the George Washington Bridge, out through New Jersey on Route 22 all the way to Pennsylvania. There would be singing and spats among the restless young ones on the way out, and cramped slumber amid the smells of manure and grass and the boxes of fresh eggs and vegetables on the way home.

The Buick felt eerily spacious on this trip, though, with only the three of us in it, and I could smell the odors of the old people even with the windows rolled down. My grandfather exuded starch and witch hazel; Aunt Gill breathed a strange combination like turned carnations and anise.

Grandfather was a bald man with bright blue eyes. He looked like Ike, whom he admired openly. Though he had only one lung, having lost the other to mustard gas and tuberculosis in World War I, he was spry enough to dance a jig sometimes after supper at our house, which he visited at least once a week even in happy times.

Aunt Gill was frail, a lover of birds. She was the widow of an Uncle Russ whom I never met and whose portrait, stern and dark, hung in her living room and looked down forbiddingly on the mint dish and doilies. My grandfather had married Gill's sister, and Aunt Gill, the frailest of the family, was the only sister still alive. She and my grandfather each lived alone in houses about a half mile apart in the town next to ours.

"*Wie gehts*, Samuel?" my grandfather asked after a long stretch of silence in the car during which we had listened to a New York radio station fade away, had passed into Pennsylvania, gone by the Dixie Cup factory in Easton with its mammoth paper cup water tower, and moved out into farmland. The names on the exit signs must have triggered his German.

"Fine," I said.

"*Gut!*" he said and laughed. I always answered in English, he said.

We passed the Kutztown exit, and my grandfather told me the word *Kutz* means vomit in Pennsylvania Dutch.

"Oh dear," said Aunt Gill. Grandfather laughed.

He went on to say that *Krankeit* means sickness, and he wondered if the newscaster knew how much his name sounded like the German word for poor health.

The ride was dappled with small talk like this. To this day, I am sure my grandfather was every bit as confused as I about the dissolution of the marriage that should have been the intersection of our lives. We were on far ends of an unbecoming covenant, and it seemed all we could do was look on and chat as things fell apart. We all felt diminished by my parents; how my grandfather and Aunt overcame it, I do not know, but I have my ideas.

My grandfather was naming the varieties of grains and grasses in the fields we passed when we saw the sign.

KEYSTONE AMERICA

it said in red and white

PENNSYLVANIA'S OLDEST
AND THE NATION'S BEST
MINIATURE VILLAGE
(NEXT EXIT)

A chain link fence separated it from the highway. Its only approach was from an access road off the exit ramp a mile beyond. The road doubled back and skirted a weedy archery range with three disintegrated targets that looked like the battle flags of a massacred army. There was a miniature golf course in slightly better repair amid a sycamore grove—the 18th hole's windmill still turned. In the center of an empty gravel parking lot was a low, poorly painted white building about fifty yards long.

My grandfather insisted that a visit to the miniature village should be part of the trip. His was a discreet enthusiasm because Aunt Gill had been on the lookout for "a comfort station" for the past ten miles. On other trips to the family farm, we had always bypassed Keystone America because there were too many of us and never enough time. But this trip, my grandfather said, "We've got all the time in the world."

We parked the car and went through the front door into a curio shop choked with key chains, drinking glasses, decals, car deodorizer baubles and postcards with pictures of hillbillies swinging on outhouse doors waving "Greetings from Ma and Pa in PA!"

There was a large nickel-plated cash register on the center counter, and my grandfather strode up to it to pay our admission. The register was so large it was obscuring whoever was sitting behind it. My aunt asked for "the comfort station," and a girl's voice said, "To the left once you're inside. There's only one. No one else is here, though, so it's empty." The voice had a musical ring to it, a Pennsylvania Dutch upward trip at the end of each sentence.

My grandfather and aunt went through the entrance to the exhibit, but I stayed a moment in the shop just to see who it was they had been talking to. I turned a postcard rack, and it made a squeaking laugh. The girl stood up behind the counter.

"Well, I *thought* they had bought three," she said. "I didn't see you."

She had red hair that she had pulled back into a pony tail. Her eyes, wide set, were green, but later, when I was closer to her, I could see they were flecked with tiny sparks of bronze. She pointed at me with a pale hand, then pulled it back and touched the side of her finger to her lipsticked mouth. She was wearing a patterned skirt, but she had on a man's Army fatigue shirt with the name "Diefenderfer" stenciled on the pocket. I guessed she was about a year older than I.

"Don't you want to go in?" she asked.

"I will," I said. "I thought I'd look around here first."

"Sure," she said and sat back down. She rattled the pages of a magazine, but I could see from a quick glance she was watching me through the glass of an exhibit case.

I strolled around the curio shop feeling dumb for not going right into the exhibit, for being under the girl's scrutiny. I looked at a sign over the door my aunt and grandfather had gone through.

EVERYTHING ACCURATE

the sign said in red letters

EXCEPT FOR ONE THING.
CAN YOU FIND IT?
IF YOU CAN FIND THE
ERROR, WE WILL
REWARD YOU A FREE
GIFT FROM THE
THE GIFT SHOPPE.
CAN YOU FIND THE ERROR?

I walked up to the cash register.

"I found the error," I told the girl.

"What?" she said. "Say, you haven't even been in there yet. Go on."

"No. It's on the sign," I told her. "The word 'the' is there twice. It says, 'the the gift shoppe.'"

She sighed.

"Well, you hit the jackpot. What do you want for your gift?"

I didn't know. I asked if I could pick something on my way out.

"Pick whenever you want. I got all the time in the world," she said.

I tapped the cellophane envelope of a pine tree deodorizer. In what must have been the first conversation I started all that sulking summer, I asked her age.

"Sixteen," she said, not bothered at all by the question which suddenly had seemed inept to me. "You?"

"Fifteen," I lied. "Almost sixteen. I turn sixteen in a couple of months."

"You look younger," she said.

"I'm not," I said.

"Looks can be deceiving, right?" she said and giggled a little. "That's what Donald says: 'Looks can be deceiving.' Donald said that when he put up that sign there. He thought it would be a good gimmick. It's an old proofreader's test. He learned sign painting in the Army. Donald's my husband. He runs this place. He took it over last year when his father died. His father had a miniature village in Germany before World War II. It was destroyed. Bombs."

"You're married?" I asked.

"Sure."

"How old is your husband?" I asked.

She tucked her chin and looked at the name on her shirt.

"Donald? Nineteen. He got out of the Army last year. He owns this place. We're going to put it back on its feet again. We got plans. We're going to have kids, and we're going to build a whole amusement park like the one he saw in Denmark when he was in the Army. Like this."

She pointed to the scratched top of the display case where, under the glass by the cash register, there were a half dozen snapshots of the Tivoli Gardens in Copenhagen.

"Donald's out painting a new billboard for us in Easton. Sure you don't want to pick a gift?"

"No," I told her, "not right yet."

"Say, did you see the billboard in Easton? Is that why you're here?"

"Well, no," I said. "I didn't notice it."

"Must be he doesn't have it done yet," she said. "He's a 'slow and steady.' Me, I'm a 'fast and furious.' I move into things quick. Ask my mother about the wedding. Lord. What are you?"

"Pardon?"

"'Slow and steady' or what?"

"I don't know."

She squinted at me as if trying to read the face of a faraway clock. "I'd say . . . Hell, I don't know either. Boy, I'm just jabbering."

She sat back down in her chair and popped open the magazine. She smiled at me once before she began reading again.

I went through the door, leaving the curio shop with all its glass and sunlight behind, and I stepped into the modulated light of a room which was about the size of a low-ceilinged gymnasium. There was a railed gallery going around the perimeter.

The gallery looked over a miniature world so crowded with minutely detailed and varied terrain it made my eyes ache. It shimmered with movement. Aunt Gill was down at the far end looking at tiny sloops turning on a mountain lake. My grandfather was standing near a cityscape with white skyscrapers that went up to his waist. Between us there were villages and hamlets with twinkling lights and little roadways with moving traffic. Trains curved through ravines and across trestles, pulled into stations and switched onto sidings. Semaphores winked yellow, green and red. There was even a traveling circus circled in a field outside a small town at my feet.

The display ran automatically, a sign said. The intricacies and expansiveness of the exhibit seemed to bespeak a supreme self-delight, as if this master-work, spinning along in precise grace, could actually have felt pride in itself.

My aunt, my grandfather and I were all leaning on the railing in different parts of the gallery staring into the pivoting and swiveling wonder that spread before us.

"Want to see something?" a voice said behind me.

It was the girl from the curio shop. She tapped me on the shoulder and touched her finger again to her lips.

"There's no other customers, so Donald wouldn't mind. I can show you my favorite part of the exhibit. Come on."

She plucked once at my shirt sleeve and turned to open a door hidden in the wall. I stepped in behind her, and she closed the door. We went down several steps and through a portal.

"This is under the whole damn thing," she said. "These are the guts of the little world."

I crouched down on my knees and looked through a labyrinth of two-by-four braces diagonally supporting a layered ceiling that was the underside of the exhibit. A few bare bulbs illuminated the plywood and plank catacombs. There were wires taped in bundles running through the crawlspaces which had pieces of old carpet on the floor where access could be obtained only on hands and knees. Labels and measurements were penciled on the lumber in German in an engineer's delicate cursive. Sevens were crossed and nouns capitalized.

"Donald learned how to run the whole thing from his father," she said, "and now Donald's teaching me. It's all pretty automatic. Once you get it started, it can go by itself all day."

She began to crawl down one of the passages. I could see tunnels going off to one side or the other. Some tunnels had bulbs dangling from their ceilings, others were passages into darkness and had flashlights hanging on nearby beams for use in repair work.

"You could get lost down here," I said.

"Not me," the girl said. "I remember every tunnel by heart. I could do this with my eyes closed."

She stopped and thumped a bulge in the ceiling with her fist.

"We're under the lake here," she said. "We're headed for the mountains."

We had to crawl lower under the lake, almost on our bellies.

"I like it down here," she said. "I come here sometimes to get away."

She stopped crawling, cocked her head down and looked back between her breast and her arm.

"You know, you were pretty quick to pick up that mistake. A lot of people don't even *see* the sign."

She started crawling again.

"People just come and go," she said. "That is, *if* they come, they go. Mostly they don't even come. Business ain't so hot. But I got to help Donald, if you know what I mean. You got a girlfriend?"

"No," I said.

"Ever have one?"

"No."

"No? Well, then you wouldn't understand, I guess."

"I understand," I said.

"Yeah?" she said, considering it. "Well, maybe you do. And maybe you don't. It would be nice if you did."

She twisted on her haunches and sat down facing me. A bare bulb shone between us. She stuck out her hand.

"Clarice," she said.

"Samuel," I said. We shook on it.

She began to crawl again. We lumbered down the passage until we came to an unevenly vaulted chamber that rose higher than our heads. We could stand up with room to spare.

Clarice pulled a crate over from the shadows and told me to stand on it. She stood there with me. From the crate, I could look out several peepholes.

"We're inside the mountain," she said. "We're looking out the mine shafts of the silver mine."

Tiny bucket loaders turned in front of each portal, but I still could see across most of the exhibit. By being inside the mountain, I felt an almost dizzying sense of participation in the movements of the display. I touched the inside wall of the peak to steady myself on the box.

Through the mine shafts, I could see the entire south end of the miniature land. I saw the city spread out and evolve into a small suburban scene. I saw the countryside rolling all the way to where tractors plowed wide fields in an irrigated desert. I followed the course of rivers up into the high country around me where sheep grazed on meadows that spread out below me like skirts, and tiny cable cars went up into the crystal escarpments of replicated ice on a peak next to ours.

"Those your folks?" I heard Clarice ask. She was looking at my grandfather and aunt, who now were standing close together on the gallery.

"My grandfather and my aunt," I told her. "They aren't my parents."

Then, from out of the clear blue, I said, "My parents are overseas. They are both ambassadors. They each have their own embassy. We are on our way to visit them. The government is paying for everything."

"Oh," she said.

She asked me where my home was and I told her West Point in the winter, and in the summer we traveled. My grandfather, I said, inspected farms.

"What's he inspect them for?" she asked.

"Plagues," I said.

"*Who* for?" she asked.

"The government," I said. "My whole family is connected with the government one way or another. You notice how much my grand-father looks like President Eisenhower?"

"Oh yes," she said.

"Well, they're related somehow. Distantly."

"Boy," she said.

"When I join the Navy, I'll go right in as an Ensign First Degree."

"Oh," she said again. "Donald was in the Army, you know. He got out a private first class."

"That's a good rank," I said. Somehow, I was telling her all of this with a steady, calm tone of authority.

"You sure you don't have a girlfriend?"

"Positive," I said. "I travel too much." And this time I made it sound like the sad, single tolling of a bell at dusk. Outside the mountain, in fact, the lights were dimming automatically on the exhibit to simu-late nightfall. The illumination coming through the mine shafts was turning rust and purple. Other lights around the exhibit were going on too. A tiny aircraft beacon on a neighboring peak flashed red and green through the apertures of our mountain.

Clarice sat down by my feet on the crate. She wrapped her arms around her knees and faced away from me as she talked.

"Just think," she said, "nobody knows where you are. I think that a lot when I sneak in here and look out at customers. They look right at me and don't see me."

I was still standing and watching the exhibit through the holes. I saw my grandfather point to something on our mountain, and I saw my aunt nod her head. In the back-lighting from the curio shop, I could see my grandfather's arm go around her shoulder, and I saw his head bend toward her cheek and stay there. She moved her head back and forth a little to feel his lips on her skin. I stood in the center of the mountain watching them.

I wanted to call to them to stop, but all I could do was hold onto the mountain's inner walls for support and listen as the trains scratched their way around the circuits, water puttered in plastic tubes, and all the wires whispered with voltage.

"People never know you're in here," Clarice said. "Nice, huh?"

"Yeah," I said, still steadying myself.

"Hey, your grandfather's never found any plagues yet has he?"

"Never," I said.

"That's good," she said. "Well, I didn't believe what you said anyway. About embassies and West Point and stuff. That was a spoof, yes?"

"Yes," I said.

"Well, good," she said. "I don't really want to know anything about you, you know. So promise me you won't tell a thing."

"You know too much already," I said.

She giggled and stood up and looked out the shafts with me. I could feel her sway a little as she caught her balance, and I could smell the faint but pleasant gift shop odors in her hair and clothes.

"I come in here to think," she said. "I do my thinking in here or in the front door to the shop. I look out at this world, or I look out at that world."

She traced around one of the openings with her finger. The faint outer light showed she had lacquer on her nails that matched the color on her lips. Each nail was a small, chewed-down oval of red.

"I like the idea you come from all over, even if it isn't true. I come from no place but right here," she said.

She turned toward me. She brushed the side of my face with her hand. Then she leaned forward and kissed me on the lips.

"Nice in here, huh?" she said.

"Look," I whispered. "You're married."

My finger nervously dug into the plaster, making little rains of dust, and I thought of my grandfather and aunt outside in the exhibit. I remembered what I'd last seen them doing.

"I know," Clarice said. "But we aren't telling anybody anything are we? And no one knows you're here. Me either."

"Donald?"

"—doesn't know," she said. "And won't. Cross my heart."

She leaned toward me again, but I skittered back on the crate. I think I may have whimpered a plea.

She straightened up and turned away. She frowned to herself and nudged her forehead into the plaster.

"Aw, look," she said, "forget it. I'm just crazy. This place makes me crazy."

She looked blankly out the mine shaft. She smiled as something on the gallery caught her eye.

"Well," she said, "at least *they're* having some fun in this place."

"Don't look at them," I said. "Please."

She turned to me for an explanation, and when I said nothing, she stepped down off the crate and flicked at its corner with the toe of her shoe. I stayed on the box. My grandfather still had his arms around my aunt. I looked away from the portals.

"Maybe I'd be crazy anyplace," Clarice said. "This world. That world. We've only just been able to keep this place running. Barely. Donald's father built it all. We just keep it going. That's about it. I crawl in here, and I think I can't live here forever. So, I go sit in the door of the shop and look at the highway. I think, Is this what I want? Him and me and all these whirligigs? I come in, I go out, and all I do is feel old and young all at once. You get what I mean?"

My head was fluttering with all the sounds of the machinery and of her voice: the upward trip, the puttering and scratch. Illumination from the exhibit bore in through the mine shafts, and the geometry of light beams made the chamber seem like the inside of a magician's sword box.

Clarice reached for my leg.

"Come down here," she said.

"No," I said. My throat was hopelessly dry.

"Just to talk,' she said.

"You're married," I said.

She tugged at the back of my knee, trying playfully to make my leg buckle.

"Come *on*," she said.

"No," I said loudly. "Please." And I yanked my leg away from her.

She stood up with her fists on her hips.

"Boy, I don't *get* you at all," she said. "I thought you were something, but I think you're just a kid."

"And what does that make you?" I said.

"Gone," said Clarice, and she ducked under the mountain's rim and out of the chamber.

I yelled for her, then I heard my aunt and my grandfather calling me from the exhibit gallery. I could hear Clarice crawling away through a tunnel as the old people called my name.

I drove my fist at the side of the mountain I'd been holding for support. I stunned myself by smashing my way right through the plaster and wire mesh. I heard a splashing sound of glass breaking above me and the crack of thin pine below as the slats on the fruit crate under my feet gave way.

"Jesus Christ," Clarice said. There was a scuffle, and she stuck her head back into the chamber. "Are you nuts?"

She backed off and ducked again into the exit tunnel.

I shouted angrily for her to return, but she yelled back, "Forget it." And she threw a switch that plunged the interior of the mountain and all the passages into darkness. She scuttled toward the exit no slower than before because she knew the way, as she said, by heart.

I struggled to get free and tripped off the broken box. My arm was caught in the mountain and my hand was above ground in the miniature world, clutching at fake rocks. I had pushed my fist through a small glacial tarn high on the peak and had broken the blue-tinted mirror glass. Chicken wire and plaster dug into my skin. I tried to hold still. I had made tiny cuts on my hand, and blood was beginning to trickle down my arm. I yelled for help.

Between my shouts, I could hear my grandfather and aunt calling for assistance, and I heard footsteps running down the gallery. I stopped calling and hung free, dangling inside the mountain in pitch darkness waiting for rescue.

Donald came and got me. He must have arrived back while Clarice was under the exhibit with me. He was a lean young man with a blond crewcut. He was wearing a T-shirt, Army fatigue pants and a fatigue cap. He was spattered all over with red and white sign paint.

He grabbed me by the waist, lifted me up to loosen the plaster, and eased my arm through the crater I had made. He switched on the lights under the exhibit, the ones Clarice had turned off.

"What the hell," he grunted as he lifted, "were you doing?"

"I'm sorry," I said.

"You cut? Yeah, you are. C'mon."

"I'm sorry."

He didn't even bother to look at the hole.

"How the hell did you get down here?" he asked.

I realized Clarice must not have told him anything. I said I had just wandered down, and I apologized again.

"Never the hell mind," he said. "But didn't you know you don't belong down here?"

"Yes," I said, and I told him I just wanted to see how things worked.

"Well, now you know," he said. "Come on." And he took me to the employees' restroom where he showed me a first aid kit. He inspected my hand.

"No bad cuts," he said. "Fix yourself up."

He left me alone. I washed off and put a half dozen band-aids on the tiny slices.

When I walked through the gift shop, Clarice was back behind the cash register. My grandfather was telling Donald he'd pay for damages.

Donald said forget it—it was only a cosmetic mirror his father had stuck on the mountain years ago. Donald said he wanted to make a more realistic lake anyway.

"Guess he just panicked down there is all," Donald said, smiling at me. I looked away, out to the turnpike.

My grandfather started to ask of me, "How—?" when Clarice interrupted from behind the register, "Don't you want your free gift for being so smart?"

I didn't say anything, and Donald asked Clarice, "Did he catch the trick sign?"

"He caught it all right," she said. "Here's your prize."

She leaned across the case and put a flashlight in my bandaged hand. The side of the light said, "GREETINGS FROM KEYSTONE AMERICA."

"So's you don't get lost in the dark," she said.

By telling me to say thank-you to the nice girl, my aunt unwittingly inflicted the final humiliation, and Clarice must have sensed it. She relented.

"It's all right, really," she said to my aunt, but she was looking at me. "It's all right."

I led the way out the door, and the old people followed.

I worked hard that whole weekend with my Uncle Edward and his hired man in the hay fields. The weather was hot and dry—perfect for haying. My grandfather and aunt sat on the farmhouse porch while Aunt Rebecca brought well water in milk bottles to us in the fields.

No one asked me about my cuts or what happened under the miniature world, and I didn't say a word.

I could tell they were all pleased I was enlivened by the labor. The work pleased me too: the tug of the hay bales' weight on my shoulders, the size and substance of the cattle and other farm animals around us, the slap of a handle in my palm when my uncle passed me a tool. In the evening I sat tired and content on the farmhouse porch where the members of my family talked in low voices of crops and acreage.

I sat silently among their rocking shadows and watched the spun patterns of fireflies and starlight.

On the way back to Connecticut, I rode alone in the back seat. My grandfather and aunt were together up front. We were passing Keystone America on the far side of the highway when my aunt was looking, once again, for a comfort station.

"Can't use that place," my grandfather said. "It's for going the other way."

He told my aunt to keep her eyes peeled for something on our side of the road, and he went back to reciting the species of grains and grasses. He did it in German this time, his memory refreshed by a visit to his homecountry. I could see through the crack between the seats he and my aunt were holding hands.

My foot had found the flashlight on the floor of the car. I had left the gift there all weekend. As we passed the white building amid the sycamore grove, I could see a man in a T-shirt painting archery targets on the newly mown grass of the range. In the door of the curio shop I could see Clarice's red hair and her fatigue shirt. She was looking across the empty parking lot, through the link fence, out to the highway. Our car, one of many, glided eastward through the grain fields on its quest for a comfort station.

I pressed the light to the window and flicked it on and off. It was a patternless signal, but that was all right. The girl in the door never moved. She was watching a world of whirligigs and probably never saw the passing light that was outshined by a westering sun which was going the other way.

THE STUDENT

MYRON TAUBE

"I was down in Florida recently, and I was bored. I was bored by the weather—always nice; I was bored by the landscape—always flat; I was bored by the architecture—always late McDonald's or early Winky's. When we flew over Pittsburgh, my heart skipped a beat at the beauty of the grayish, reddish, greenish hills and valleys and slate-colored rivers. And there is nothing quite like coming out of the Fort Pitt Tunnel at night, on the one side, the hills of suburbia, the sprawling scratchiness of something that really has no definition of itself, no real existence without the city, and SHAZAM! there it is: the city. Talk of Paris as the city of lights? Pick a cool spring evening—or a cold winter night—or any evening that is dark (don't go when it's a full moon, for even Pittsburgh has things that come out only when the moon is full), and go up to Mt. Washington and look at our city of light. We who know these things aren't often moved by the beauty around us. But show them to foreigners and watch them ooh and aah—and take pictures and send you copies."

*　　*　　*

Myron Taube was born in New York City, but moved to Pittsburgh in the middle sixties to teach writing and literature at the University of Pittsburgh, where he has remained. His short stories have appeared in many prestigious magazines and journals. "The Student" first appeared in the University of Missouri's University Review.

I ALWAYS WANTED to go to college. I guess it's because my cousin Ellen Fenstermacher and other girls were going. Her poppa is Dr. Fenstermacher, over in Topton. Everybody in the family knew she'd go to college, because everybody in Uncle Fenstermacher's family did go to college—to Muhlenberg, or Lehigh, or State College. Cousin Erwin and my cousin George are in graduate school already. And Aunt Emma, Uncle Fenstermacher's wife, even went to State when it was still the normal school. So nobody thinks it's so strange for cousin Ellen to talk about going to medical school.

But my poppa is a farmer, and nobody in my family ever went to college. My two older brothers didn't even finish high school, but went out and got their own farms after they farmed with poppa a while. So I tried hard to convince poppa.

I guess the college thing has been going on for years. I was always reading. We didn't have much of a library in town, but I read everything in the school library. I never read those movie magazines, or those true confessions or hair-do magazines, but I liked the stories and articles in *Life* and *Seventeen*. I remember once cousin Ellen lent me all her Nancy Drew books, and her brother George lent me his Tom Swift books that had belonged to his father, but I didn't like them as much as the Nancy Drew books. Momma always used to say, "She's always reading; I'll be getting her soon eyeglasses."

"She must be getting very smart," poppa would say.

"I don't notice."

"Well, just so long she does her chores. She ain't too smart for that?"

Momma laughed. "No, she does them."

"Good. Sometimes people get so smart they can't figger out which end to sit on anymore." Then poppa would fold his arms and hold his corncob pipe in one hand and puff up at the ceiling. "You still know which end is up?"

I'd have to look up and say, "Yes, poppa."

Then he'd grunt as if he wasn't so sure.

We didn't have many books in the house. We got the *Farmer's Almanac* every year, and we had a book on engine repair. We got the Sears-Roebuck catalogue every six months, but we didn't use it so much since papa built the indoor toilets. And mamma gets the *Reader's Digest*. The funny thing is, while poppa makes fun of me reading, he's always reading his bulletins from the Agriculture Department in Washington. Every morning he reads the reports from the produce market in Philadelphia and the livestock markets in Lancaster and Chicago. One day I asked him why he made fun of me reading and did so much reading himself.

"What do you read, anyway? You read stories?"

"Yes, novels—a lot."

"They don't tell you nawthing. I read the reports; they tell me something."

"What do they tell you?"

"They tell me the weather forecast. They tell me the crop prices, the crops going to market. They tell me when to spray and what to spray. So they tell me something how to do and something how to do it. When you know something how to do it, you do it. And you can't complain. Do your stories tell you something to do and something how to do it?"

"No, poppa, that's not the sort of thing I read."

"Well, maybe you'll read someday the right book, you'll find which end is up."

When I was a junior in high school, I started asking poppa if I could go to college. Usually he just sat there and smoked his pipe. Or he'd wipe his face with his red bandanna and then stuff it back in his overalls. Then he'd grunt at me. "You wanna go to collitch, eh?"

"Yes, poppa."

"Why?"

"I think I'd like to be a school teacher."

"You don't haff to be a school teacher."

"No, but I'd like to."

He puffed away. "You'd like to."

"Yes, poppa."

He grunted again and opened a farming magazine. I waited, because I knew he was never through just because he stopped talking. "How much do you like to?"

"Very much, poppa."

Then he puffed on his pipe, and he looked away, and then he stood up and hitched up his overalls. "We'll see how much," he said, and went outside to work on the tractor.

The next day at dinner I asked poppa if he thought about what

I said, and he looked up from his potato soup. He has a very rugged face, all tanned from the sun, and his neck looks like cracked leather. Sometimes he squints at me. "I don't hold that girls should go to collitch."

"Why, poppa?"

"It makes them lazy. They don't work no more."

"Oh no, poppa—it lets them get better jobs."

Poppa grunted. "You'll get a better job?"

"Oh yes, poppa. I could teach."

"That's better?"

"Oh yes, poppa."

"Better than being a farmer?"

"It's different for a girl, poppa."

"What would you teach?"

"Grade school, maybe. They need teachers, poppa, and I could teach in Kutztown or Topton."

"Your momma didn't go to collitch," he said, and the way he said it, I knew that was the end of that conversation.

Once I had a long talk with Uncle Fenstermacher, and he asked what was wrong with poppa.

"Well, he just don't believe that girls should go to college," I said.

"Why do you want to go?" Uncle Fenstermacher was always interested in why things happened, as though people acted the way they do the same way diseases act the way they do, because there's a germ that causes it. "What's bugging you to go to college?"

"I don't know, Uncle. I thought it would be nice to get more schooling. I don't want to go to medical school, like Ellen, but if I go to State College I could teach school for a little bit before I get married and start having children."

"You thinking of moving out of the area?"

"Oh, I don't care. I could teach in Kutztown or Topton. But poppa won't listen to me anymore. He said if I talk about it anymore, he'll shut me up in the old barn."

Uncle Fenstermacher laughed. "He's just pig-headed."

I never heard anybody talk about poppa like that before, and I was surprised. "Don't say that."

"Why not?"

"It's not right to talk about my poppa like that."

"Well, it's not right for him to act like that either."

I had never really thought of it that way.

"Well, Etta," he said, "I'll try to talk to your father about it and see if he won't change his mind."

A couple of weeks later I went over to see Ellen, and her father called me into his office. "I spoke to your father," he said.

"He didn't tell me."

"No. He doesn't talk much." Uncle Fenstermacher fingered one of those things with a flashlight on it that he looks into your ears with. "Well, he said he really doesn't think you want to go to college."

"Did he say that?"

"And he thinks girls should stay at home with their mothers."

"He always says that. Did you tell him a girl can go to a college in her home town and still help around the house?"

"Oh, yes," he laughed. "I told him my daughter was going to college, and he said, 'Cousin, you plow your field and I'll plow mine. And don't tell me what manure to use.'"

"Oh, he gets me so mad."

Uncle Fenstermacher laughed. "I guess he's just another dumb Dutchman."

That remark sort of upset me. I know a lot of people call us dumb Dutchmen, but it was funny to hear Uncle Fenstermacher say it, because he's a Dutchman too, just like us. It's mostly the outsiders who call us that. But they don't know us too well, I guess. Besides, poppa isn't dumb. If he doesn't want me to go to college, that's no reason to call him dumb. Or because he's a farmer, because I know he's got a lot of money in the bank and he's a good farmer.

He's not a dairy farmer, like most of the farmers around. In fact, poppa doesn't have any animals on the farm, not even chickens. Momma used to keep chickens, but poppa said he wouldn't lift a finger to care for them, so after a while momma gave them up. Now we get all our eggs down the road, from Siegfried or Moyer, and our milk too.

It isn't that poppa doesn't like animals. We have lots of cats and dogs always running around. But poppa always says, "I don't have to keep feeding animals all the time, paying out for feed, when they don't do any work. You pay for the starter mash, for scratch, for corn, and how long do you feed a chicken before it starts layin'? Same with a horse. You feed the horse, you bed it down, she don't work for you all the time, but you gotta feed it all the time. My first farm, I signed a note to buy a team of horses and one of them broke down with the wind colic, so I had to work with one horse. But I still had to feed the sick horse. And in the winter time, I gotta feed both, and they don't do no work." That's the way poppa talked, and he was one of the first farmers around here to have a tractor. "I don't have to feed it if it don't work," he always said.

That's why poppa went into vegetables. Every year he contracts with the Campbell soup people, and he plants all sorts of things they put in soup, like celery and tomatoes and potatoes and peas and beans and okra, and stuff like that. He's got a barn full of bushel baskets for the vegetables. He hires migrant workers to pick the stuff, and then he sends the bushels down to the rail head.

It's really beautiful to look at the fields the way poppa has them laid out. He plants from late in April, and he's always out there, cultivating or fertilizing. By June it all stretches out in parallel green lines. The different fields are set off with markers, and sometimes they're set at angles with each other.

When you see it from the hill in back of the farm, it looks like different patterns laid out on the ground. And the one thing poppa always hopes for is rain. He likes long, steady, two or three-hour rains, not the heavy thunder-showers. "Ach," he once said, "a big rain, it ain't worth more than a thousand dollars. But a long rain, put five thousand in the bank for every hour."

Sometimes, I remember, when I was a little girl, we'd walk over the hill behind the house, and poppa would tell momma what he wanted to do to the place. How he'd put in a cesspool and get rid of the outhouse. And he did. One fall, after the crops were in, poppa worked with some of the cousins and put in the cesspool. He had a regular plumber put in a flush toilet on the second floor, with the bedrooms, and one on the first floor right off the playroom near the dining room.

I remember we'd always walk around on Sundays when poppa didn't work, after we came back from church, and he'd talk about what he wanted to do. He said how he'd like to buy up some of the land around, and always, in a few years, he did. He kept talking to old man Dietrich about selling the place next to us, and he did too.

I remember, every four or five years poppa would sign papers with some neighbor and then farm his land. Sometimes he bought it. Poppa started with ten acres, he said, and now he has over three hundred. Poppa isn't so dumb.

Anyway, when I was a senior, I asked poppa again about college. He just grunted a little. "You got the money?"

"No," I said. "But I'd like to go, poppa."

He puffed on his old corncob pipe. Poppa never gives a quick answer, but when he says something, you can't change his mind. You could hit him on the head with a hammer when he says something, but you won't change what he says. So you just got to get him to say what you want him to in the beginning, because if you don't, he'll never change his mind.

He just kept puffing. "We talked about it."

"That was last year, poppa. Now I'm older, and I'll be graduating in June."

"I ain't changed."

"But I've changed, poppa. I'm older, and I want to go even more."

"I don't believe it." That meant he didn't think women should go to college.

"But cousin Ellen goes."

"Her poppa's a doctor."

"So mine's a farmer."

"So I didn't go to collitch. I didn't do so bad."

"But I want to go."

"How much?"

"A lot."

"Your momma didn't go. And my poppa didn't go. Why should you?"

"Your poppa didn't have a tractor, and his poppa didn't have a tractor, but you got a tractor."

"That's a nevermind."

"No it's not. It's the same thing. You don't want me to do it because you didn't or grandpa didn't."

"Yah. It was OK grandpa didn't go, it was OK I didn't go, so it's OK you don't go."

"But it was OK for grandpa to have a horse, but you don't have a horse. You got things they didn't have. Why don't you let me have something you didn't have?"

He looked up at the ceiling and puffed his pipe. I felt like a wound-up spring, waiting for him to say it was OK. Hoping he would.

But he didn't. All he said was, "I said a girl should learn to cook."

I got so mad, I exploded. "Oooh, you're just a . . . a . . . a pig-headed dumb Dutchman!"

When momma rang the supper bell, I came down from my room and saw there was one place less at the table. "If she don't like the way her poppa runs this house, she don't have to eat his food," my poppa said. When he was mad at us, he always called us he or she, not by name. I knew he was still mad. After he hit me, I ran upstairs and locked my room, and I thought he'd maybe calm down, but he didn't. And I knew I better apologize or there'd be no living in the house.

But I also knew I better wait until morning before I apologized, because he'd ask me if I thought about it long enough, and if I wasn't making a mistake by apologizing too quickly, just like I made a mistake by talking too quickly. And he'd ask if missing supper had anything to do with it, and just how much. So I knew I better give it a lot of thought, and I went back upstairs.

At breakfast I was really hungry, and I helped momma. When poppa came in, I sat down at the table, but he ignored me and drank a glass of milk.

Then momma said, "Etta wants to say something."

Poppa grunted and wiped his mouth on the red and white checkered towel momma got once in a big box of soap. "Well?"

"Poppa, I'm sorry I insulted you last night."

He grunted and cut into his fried eggs. "Better you think a little before you talk."

"I'm sorry, poppa."

"Just because you want to go to collitch don't make you so smart you can call your people names."

"I know."

"Think a little. And maybe, after you think, before you talk, better you should bite your tongue."

I nodded, but I didn't say anything, because he was a little bit right.

Then I graduated, and I didn't have anything to do. I thought of taking a night course in typing, so I could get a job in an office. I wrote to some correspondence schools. I saw their ads in the magazines: "Learn Stenography at Home." "Learn Typing at Home." I even sent away to one school that advertised: "Study law at home. Begin a new career. . . ." Maybe I'd become a lawyer instead of a teacher. I saw myself standing in front of the jury, pleading with them: "Ladies and gentlemen of the jury: Would you send this poor man to jail just because he refused to let his daughter go to college? I beg you, have mercy. The man broke no law; he is a good man. Please, please, don't send him to jail."

And then I turned away and took off my veil and my lawyer's outfit and said, "Have mercy, for I am his daughter, and I have long since forgiven him."

And then momma started to cry, and poppa hugged me, and the judge banged with his little wooden hammer, and the jury shouted, "Let him go, let him go!"

But I read all the brochures, and all the courses cost money, and I didn't have that much. Oh, I had a little, from when I did baby-sitting for some of the college faculty that lived in the country. And sometimes I worked on Saturday in the farmer's market. But I really didn't try very hard, because I just didn't need much money. I didn't need a car, because I had a bike that I rode everywhere. A good one, too, with three forward speeds, and hand brakes, and a speedometer.

So most of the time I stayed around the farm, and helped momma with the cooking, or I helped poppa with the farming. In August I helped harvest the carrots. Then poppa put in a crop of alfalfa that he'd bale and put in the barn to sell in the winter for silage. In September I helped poppa and the boys with the apples. We put hundreds of bushels in the barn. Then I helped momma with canning. We always kept some of the fruit and vegetables and momma canned it for the winter. That was a lot of work. But it didn't make any money for me.

Then I got a part-time job at a drive-in, but that didn't last very long. So most of the fall and early winter I spent around the farm, waiting, reading, feeling a little sorry for myself.

At Christmas I saw cousin Ellen and talked about school. And the old desire came back: I wanted to go to college. I had wasted so much time. I was nineteen already. If I didn't get into Saturday classes for January, I'd have to go over the summer. And in September I'd be

twenty. I was being left behind. I could have made something of myself, but now I'd end up a farm wife.

I thought of writing the school and seeing what courses they had
on Saturday. I asked momma if I could go on Saturdays, if I had a
job during the week. She said she'd talk to poppa. That night I lay
in bed thinking what life would be if I got married to some farmer.
I didn't know who, just anybody. What else was there? Then I heard
them talking in their bedroom. They always did their talking alone—
when we weren't around. I knew they were talking about me, and I
imagined them holding my life in their hands, judging what was to
become of me. But then they started talking louder, and poppa was
excited. I had never heard him shouting at momma before, and momma
was defending me.

"But she wants so much to go," momma said.

"So much, so much. How much? I ask her how much, she got no
answer. What she wanna go for?"

"Cousin Ellen goes."

"Cousin Ellen goes because cousin Ellen wants to go. Why she want
to go? Because cousin Ellen goes ain't good enough for me. I do something because I want to do something, not because somebody else does
something, I should do it. Maybe I'm a dumb Dutchman, but I ain't
crazy."

"She didn't mean it. Don't you forget anything?"

"I don't forget nothing, so I don't have to learn so much over again."

"She wants to learn something, so she want to go to collitch."

"I didn't go to collitch, you didn't go to collitch, the boys didn't
go to collitch. You see something wrong with the boys, or with me,
or with you? Maybe we ain't good enough people?"

"That ain't why she wants to go."

"Then there ain't no reason."

"She wants to be a teacher."

"She says. So I ask her, How much, she got no answer. She don't
want to be nothing. First you want to be something—*then* you go to
collitch. What did she want? Did she want hard enough to work? How
much money did she save? Nothing. When I want a property, I work
hard for it. Does she work hard? In collitch, you think they let you
fool around all the time? You think she'll go work hard in collitch?
No. She don't work hard for collitch to go there, she don't work hard

when she get there. Better she learn how to cook and take care of a house. I don't need no lazy girls to send to collitch."

"All right, all right. Don't shout so loud. I'll tell her in the morning."

"I'll tell her. I don't need no lazy girl in collitch. Let her learn how to work."

I heard their light go off, and they whispered a little, and then it was quiet. I lay in the darkness, and my eyes burned with shame. Looking at me like that, poppa was right. I didn't do anything. I had made no action. I could have done something. I could have gotten a job. I could have held onto the part-time job at the drive-in. If I had wanted to go to college bad enough, I would have worked hard, and it wouldn't have mattered what I felt then, if I really wanted it. I could have gotten a job in the diner. I could have worked as a waitress in the Glockenspiel.

I thought of all the things that I could have done, and each one was a stone on my heart. I had shamed myself, and I had shamed poppa. I had made him feel I was lazy, worthless. What a proud man poppa was, proud of all he had done, and all the boys had done, and he had never gone to college, and was proud that what he had wanted he had achieved.

He had worked hard. And he must have felt that I was a failure. I was. I was nothing. What is a person apart from what he does? I could not have been a worse sinner if I committed a sin, for I had done nothing.

The tears flowed slowly down my face. I hoped poppa still loved me. I wouldn't say anything to him tomorrow. I wouldn't talk about college anymore. I'll get a job and I'll earn my tuition, and I'll decide later if I want to go on Saturdays, or during the summer, or in September.

But I'll have the money. I'll show poppa how much I want to go to college, not just talk about it. I had been the dumb Dutchman, not poppa. I had many lessons to learn, before I was ready for college. But I would study hard, beginning tomorrow, when I got the job.

ELEGY TO THE CARLTON HOUSE HOTEL

ROY McHUGH

"By birth, I'm an Iowan. I went to Coe College in Cedar Rapids, finishing in 1940, and then started working for the Cedar Rapids Gazette. I covered sports. After thirty-eight months in the army and another year at the Gazette I hooked on with The Pittsburgh Press in 1947. Pittsburgh's only attraction for me then was the fact that it had major-league professional and college teams, and I had decided to be a sports writer. But year by year Pittsburgh looked better and better. I liked the hills and the rivers and the steel mills, the distinctiveness of the neighborhoods, the kinds of people who lived in them, the cultural variety, the cross-breeding of big city and small town. When Scripps-Howard asked me to go to Indiana in 1961 to be sports editor and columnist of the Evansville Sunday Courier & Press, I resolved to stay at least a year—but not more than two years. I came back to Pittsburgh in twenty months."

*   *   *

Roy McHugh wrote a sports column for The Pittsburgh Press from 1963 to 1972, and was then appointed columnist-at-large. He wrote poignant, exciting, journalistic prose poems, such as this elegy to the Carlton House Hotel, three times weekly until his retirement ten years later.

F ROM A DISTANCE, the Carlton House never looked better than in the instant or two before its collapse.

It stood there proudly, wired for destruction, while the hand on the plunger hesitated. A moment of prayer, so we are told, preceded the execution.

If a blindfold had been offered, I think the Carlton House would have refused it. Watching on television, I felt a surge of admiration for the sixteen stories of egg-yolk-colored brick. The manner of its departure gave the Carlton House dignity. Its past may not have been glorious, or even laudable, but at the end there was something like stateliness.

The Carlton House went before its time. That is often pathetic. On the other hand, it was all in one piece. There would be no sordid spectacle of undressed walls, beaten to the ground by a demolition ball. The Carlton House died with its boots on.

Its descent into rubble was timed at five seconds—and also at seven seconds. Take your choice. The building ejected a few puffs of smoke and then it caved in on itself, gently assuming the lotus position.

When the dust cleared away, surprisingly little remained. The dust was more impressive than the debris so neatly piled underneath. The dust looked as ominous as the mushroom cloud over Hiroshima. The debris made it evident that there was less to the Carlton House than met the eye. The sum of its parts exceeded the whole.

Khrushchev stayed there, and Lassie too, but at best it was never a legendary hotel. Its memory will endure for those last seven seconds— or was it five? The Carlton House said goodbye to Pittsburgh with a style it could not have attained in any other possible way.

It became a metaphor then for impermanence and fragility. In time Gibraltar will crumble, the Rockies may tumble; anything less substantial is apt to vanish at the blink of an eye. As the Carlton House subsided with an eerie serenity, "here today, gone tomorrow" took on the flavor of understatement.

In a different sense, the Carlton House is a casualty of the throwaway society. It was built to outlast its builders, yet a boardroom decision condemned it after twenty-eight years.

Not that Pittsburgh has lost an architectural masterpiece. Still, couldn't Renaissance II proceed with a little less wastefulness?

My personal recollections of the Carlton House are meager. In the lobby one day, two men were talking about an acquaintance, and the dialogue went like this:

"What's Mel doing now?"

"Burning down buildings."

As the person of whom they spoke passed in front of them on his way out the door, the second man said to him, "When are you gonna have another fire?"

A fragment of conversation that outlived the bricks and the mortar.

The Carlton House was finished in 1952. Now it makes way for the Dravo Building. If something made way for the Carlton House, offhand I couldn't tell you what it was.

INNOCENCE LOST

· MIKE VARGO

"*This was Mike Vargo's first article for the publication,*" *according to Terry Fackler,* *former publisher of the now defunct* Pennsylvania Illustrated, *where* "*Innocence Lost" first appeared.* "*Mike came to* Pennsylvania Illustrated *as an assistant editor along with Editor Pat Minarcin, both formerly with Pittsburgher Magazine. Both Pat and Mike arrived at my house a week earlier than their employment contracts started, because of the news of the accident at Three Mile Island. At 2:00 A.M. the night of the accident, the three of us violated the curfew in Middletown, and stood in front of the awesome cooling towers with their blinking red lights.*

"'*By tomorrow every reporter in the world will be here to do this story, how can we do it for* Pennsylvania Illustrated *so that Three Mile Island will be remembered when we publish two months from now?' That was the question of the night, standing in the warm red glow of an island that might have gotten much, much brighter.*"

* * *

Today Fackler runs his own typesetting company, while Vargo, a freelance writer in Pittsburgh, is working on a book about nonconformity in American society.

1. In the Beginning . . .

AT KUPPY'S DINER in the heart of Middletown, the morning began, as usual, with the smell of coffee. The seven a.m.

gang was there, as usual—John Garver and Bob Reid and seven or eight other guys lined up at the counter on stools, cracking the usual jokes. Behind the counter serving up coffee and breakfast was Carl Kupp himself, as usual. Everything as usual.

That's the kind of town Middletown is, you might say—a town where the commonplace is commonplace. It's an old town, founded in 1755, before the nation was. Some families have been there for eight, nine, ten generations, never having seen a good reason to leave. It's a pleasant town, gathered in the lap of a line of old hills that slope gently down to the Susquehanna.

Solid, conventional, all but unchanging—these are the thoughts that come to mind as one surveys Middletown, and wanders through its streets, from the suburban-style developments on the hillsides, to the old Victorian section in the center of town, to the frame houses down on the riverbank. For the most part, the people are that way, too—why, up at Middletown Area High School, if you don't show up for class conventionally tidy and dressed, you just might get reprimanded and sent home.

Perhaps Middletown is that way because it can afford to be that way; there is very little unemployment here. What with the Fruehauf trailer plant on one edge of town, Bethlehem Steel upriver and a host of other businesses nearby, jobs are plentiful and the economy is stable. So stable that nearly all of the young people find work straight out of high school; only ten to fifteen percent go away to college.

All of which only serves to heighten the sense of continuity Middletown has. A favorite expression, for instance—and it's not just the oldtimers who say it—is "I was born and raised in Middletown; I live in Middletown; and I'm going to die in Middletown." Thirty years ago Bob Reid played football for the Middletown High Blue Raiders. His nickname back then was Bird. Now Bob Reid teaches at Middletown High, and last year his son played football for the Blue Raiders. The boy's nickname: Bird.

The name fits the town—All-America, Our Town, Middletown. Even the morning gang at Kuppy's is steeped in ritual. To wit: John Garver, a forty-year-old office machine salesman, has been coming to Kuppy's every morning before work since he got married, seventeen years ago. Each morning he indulges in the same morning-gang routines: Jockeying for a seat at the counter. Fighting good-naturedly for a section of the single newspaper that finds its way into Kuppy's ("Where's the sports, damn it?"). And trying to get an argument started, a little seven a.m. eye-opener to go along with the coffee. "Kuppy, you're nothing but a hash-slinger," Garver will say. "You never did anything in your life tougher than break an egg." (Neither, he might add, did Kuppy's father or his grandfather, who started the diner in 1933.)

To which Kuppy might reply, drawing himself up with dignity in his white apron. "At least I'm an honest businessman, John. Not a Communist like you." The gang started calling Garver "The Communist" when he came out against the Vietnam war. They sent him a sympathy card when Nixon was elected President.

The gang at the diner loves to kid one another. When summer vacation comes, and Bob Reid the schoolteacher finally gets to sleep late in the morning, the gang will phone him at seven a.m. "Hey Reid! Get your ass out of bed and get to work." Or when Reid walks in the door of the diner there might be mutterings of "Well, well, here comes the big shot"—because Reid, in addition to teaching school, serves as mayor of Middletown, a job for which he is paid $150 a month.

. . . Yes sir, good old Bob Reid and John Garver and all the boys, every morning at seven a.m. in Kuppy's Diner. It's a good feeling to start the day with something you can depend on.

The gang in Kuppy's that morning had no way of knowing that anything was wrong at the nuclear power plant. The plant is three miles away from the center of Middletown.

But around the bend and down on River Road, the tree-lined road that runs along the north bank of the Susquehanna past Three Mile Island, employees driving in for the daylight shift at the plant knew something was up right away. Before they even got to the plant gate, as soon as they came in sight of the cooling towers, they could see there was no vapor rising from them. Not a wisp. That meant that once again the Unit 2 reactor had "tripped"—that is, automatically shut itself down because of a malfunction somewhere. (The other reactor at the plant, Unit 1, was already down for routine refueling and maintenance.)

If you were a repairman driving to work at Three Mile Island, those dead cooling towers were a sight you didn't like to see. It probably meant another long day (or days) of scrambling around to get Unit 2 started up again while nervous managers looked over your shoulder and worried out loud about the money the company was losing. It seemed Unit 2 was always breaking down, ever since they'd first fired it up a year ago. About once a month, on the average, down she went. You could count on it. People at the plant were starting to talk about the thing as if it had a mind of its own, as if it didn't want to run.

An early-morning traffic jam built up along River Road. Gate guards weren't letting anyone drive across the narrow bridge to the island. At last the long line of cars started to move—but very slowly, because a sorting process was going on at the gate. Only "essential personnel" were being allowed across the bridge. "Nonessential personnel"—secretaries, clerks, and the like—were waved away and told to drive down the road to the observation center.

The Three Mile Island observation center is a little white building that was built on the shore for tourists and visitors. Tour groups could come there and see videotape presentations on nuclear energy, and get pamphlets on it. Then they could go up to the observation deck and look out across the channel at the Three Mile Island Nuclear Generating Station itself, with its massive gray cooling towers rising majestically, as the newspapers like to say, above the waters of the Susquehanna.

On this morning, though, the observation center filled up with nonessential personnel. They wandered in, greeted one another, shook off the stiffness of a long sit in traffic. The atmosphere was that of a fire drill at school—a little excitement, a little bit of a holiday feeling, but with a tiny edge of apprehension. Some of the nonessential personnel remembered a training film they'd seen, which said the observation center would be the rallying point in case of a serious emergency. This was the first time they'd been sent to the observation center.

Finally a company official made an announcement: *There's been a small radiation leak, possibly, nothing serious. We're working to find out what's wrong. More details later.*

But no details were forthcoming. Every half-hour or so, the word was: *No change. Stand by.* After a while people stopped listening to the announcements. It was turning into a party. Coffee was being served. *Hey, where's the coffee? Boy, I wish we had some donuts. Got a cigarette? Mine are in my desk on the island.*

In a trailer parked beside the center, a secretary brought out a deck of Tarot cards and began telling fortunes. *Here is your card: the Hanged Man. Fear death by water.*

Meanwhile, out on the island, in the Unit 2 control room, a different and much less relaxed kind of party was in progress. The guests of honor were four men named Craig Faust, Ed Frederick, Bill Zewe, and Fred Scheimann. They should've gone home hours ago, but so much was happening they couldn't seem to tear themselves away.

Faust, Frederick, Zewe and Scheimann were the night-shift control room crew assigned to Unit 2. And a solid crew they were. All of them sober guys, family men, veterans of the nuclear Navy. Frederick was twenty-nine, while the rest were in their early thirties—young enough to be quick on the stick, yet old enough to use mature judgment. Just the kind of guys you want at the controls of a nuclear power plant. After an earlier malfunction at Unit 2, one that had been brought under control, the plant manager had said he was glad Faust, Frederick, Zewe and Scheimann were the ones on the job when it happened.

Controlling a nuclear power plant is like piloting an airliner. Most of the job is fairly routine—takeoffs, landings, in-flight corrections—but you've got to be ready at any second for the big one. Airline pilots train regularly on an electronic simulator that duplicates actual flying conditions—including emergencies—so they'll know precisely, instinctively, what to do in case, say, an engine catches fire. Likewise, control-room personnel at nuclear power plants train on a simulator that duplicates operating conditions—including emergencies. Faust, Frederick, Zewe and Scheimann were scheduled to go down to the Babcock & Wilcox Company simulator in Virginia soon for a week of testing in mock emergencies. Instead, on this morning, they got the real thing.

It started at four a.m., in the dead of night. While the river was dark, and Bill Whittock was sleeping quietly in his bedroom on the far shore, Craig Faust, Ed Frederick and Bill Zewe sat in the fluorescent daylight of the Unit 2 control room. Before them stretched the Unit 2 control panel, several feet high and about as wide as a tennis court, filled with instruments and gauges. One moment everything was running smoothly. And then the next, it was not.

Suddenly, alarms started sounding and lights began flashing—not just in one section of the panel, as they usually do when there's a malfunction—but all over the place, a steady rain of shots to return all at once. "Oh, my God," Ed Frederick said as the alarm sequence spread. "This is a classic." Whereupon Frederick and Faust took up stations before the panel and swung into action. Zewe stood behind them, supervising. In a moment, Scheimann (who had been out of the room on an errand) came dashing back through the door to position himself in front of the panel, too. Together the four worked quickly and calmly, responding as they'd been trained to.

But for some reason which the men couldn't understand, the reactor didn't respond as *it* was supposed to. Both of the reactor's cooling systems began overheating badly. Something was wrong down there, and nobody could figure out quite what. . . .

Actually, two things were wrong down there that the men didn't know about.

One: A pump in the secondary cooling system, the system which propels the unit's turbine, had conked out. Backup pumps had kicked on automatically, as they should have. But the valves on these pumps were closed, as they shouldn't have been, a detail which rendered them useless.

Two: Within seconds, pressure started building in the primary cooling system, the system enclosing the reactor, and a relief valve popped open, as it should have. But instead of closing again as soon as the buildup was relieved, the valve stuck open—as *it* shouldn't have.

Results: Water stopped circulating in the secondary cooling system, and water was spilling from the primary cooling system.

Fact: Without water circulating through *both* systems, a reactor gets terribly hot in a hurry.

Prognosis: Bad.

And then something went wrong in the control room. Even though water was pouring out of the primary cooling system, a gauge showed that pressure in that system was continuing to build. The gauge climbed up, up, up off the scale. The men took one look at it and promptly shut off the urgently needed flow of replacement water that the unit's computerized safety system had been sending in.

Temperatures went screaming up. More alarms were going off on the control panel. Faust, Frederick, Zewe and Scheimann were dutifully throwing switches, turning dials, checking gauges and everything was still wrong, wrong, wrong.

Then someone noticed that the valves in the secondary system were shut. Surprise!

Then the pressure gauge for the primary system came back on scale — and went waaay down, of course. Surprise, surprise.

And then complications set in. The water pouring out of the stuck relief valve had been running into a holding tank, filling it to bursting, and now it blew a seal and started to flood the floor of the reactor building. Water, radioactive water everywhere. All in the wrong places.

On and on the men worked. Unit 2 was misbehaving in such complex and unpredictable ways that the men began to doubt their own perceptions — at one point they pulled out manuals and leafed through them to see if they had memorized their procedures correctly. They had.

Deep in the core of the reactor, where the pellets of uranium fuel lie carefully sheathed, it became very hot indeed. Physical and chemical changes of the most undesirable sort were taking place. In the control room, the computer printed out a line of question marks for core temperature. Around daybreak the men called for help, and help started to arrive in the person of chief electrical engineer Richard Bensel and others.

Were the men scared? Not of dying, no; they never were. For weeks afterward they would insist to friends and neighbors that there was never any real threat to human life.

But they were deeply concerned with what *was* indisputably transpiring — damage to the reactor. It is not surprising that this was their first concern. When someone entrusts you with a $700 million piece of equipment, you feel a certain sense of responsibility. You like to be able to bring it back in one piece.

Not once during those agonizing early-morning hours did the control room crew attempt to notify public authorities outside the plant that a potentially dangerous situation had developed. They couldn't have, even if they'd thought of it — federal Nuclear Regulatory Commission regulations say that a control room crew cannot notify the public of an emergency without corroboration from at least two outside sources. But by 7:30 that corroboration was available —

the control room was full of worried MetEd management people. And at 7:30, they notified Civil Defense that Three Mile Island was in trouble.

2. The Uncertainty Principle

Bob Reid, the mayor of Middletown, left Kuppy's Diner about 7:30 a.m. "So long, big shot," the gang called after him. "See you tomorrow." He drove up Union Street, past the still-closed shops of the business district, to Middletown Area High School, a sprawling modern building on the outskirts of town. There Reid teaches civics and government to ninth graders.

Students who are considered potential troublemakers are often placed in Reid's class; he gets along with them just fine. He is known as a teacher who can control things without being a tyrant. With an easy, measured voice, no-nonsense eyes and a six-foot-one ex-athlete's frame, he has what is known in the trade as presence. The middle-age paunch that has settled on him only seems to lend further dignity. He wears it as if he's earned it.

It's fun for the students to learn government from the mayor. "Hey Mr. Reid," they'll say, "how come there's a law here against hanging out on the street corner? Don't we have a constitutional right to peaceably assemble?"

"Sure," Reid will answer, "but not all of you are peaceable. And when somebody starts hollering and waking up Mr. Jones and Mr. Green, then you're violating Mr. Jones' and Mr. Green's right to peace and quiet. You've got to remember we're all in this together."

On this morning Reid stopped in the office on his way to class. As he was sorting through some papers the phone rang. It was Butch Ryan, the senior radio dispatcher at the borough police station.

"Bob, they had an accident down at the island," Ryan said.

"An accident? What kind of accident, Butch?"

"I don't know. Dauphin County Civil Defense just called, and they said it's an 'on-site emergency.' That's all I've got."

Reid agreed with Ryan that while this sounded rather mysterious, it might be important, something that maybe the mayor should be on hand for. After getting an assistant principal to take his classes, Reid drove downtown to the borough hall. He walked into the police station where he found Ryan, a burly ex-fireman who is also Middletown's volunteer Civil Defense director, sitting behind the glass partition at his L-shaped dispatcher's desk. George Miller, the police chief, was there too.

No further word yet from county Civil Defense. So Reid slid a chair over to the dispatcher's console, and they sat and waited for another call. Ryan had a TV and a radio turned on, from which they caught bits and snatches of news. It provided little more than what CD had said: Metropolitan Edison, operator of the power plant, had declared an on-site emergency. It was possible that some radioactivity had leaked to the atmosphere. No details, no word of any immediate danger to people off-site.

As the matter didn't seem particularly urgent, police chief Miller got tired of waiting and returned to his office. There was important work to be done that morning on a string of burglaries that had been troubling the town. A young man had been going around knocking on doors of houses. If someone was home he would ask for directions to a local restaurant; but if no one answered, he would break into the house and help himself. One of Miller's detectives, Don Foreman, had isolated a suspect—a student at Middletown High, unfortunately. Now Foreman was here at the station, and warrants had to be made out for searching the boy's house and picking him up.

Meanwhile, townspeople began calling the police station. They'd heard the news; they had relatives working at the power plant, or they had friends working there, and they wanted to know what was going on.

So did Bob Reid. *If the situation is serious,* he thought, *why isn't anybody telling us about it? And if it isn't serious, why did Civil Defense bother to call us in the first place?*

At ten o'clock Reid telephoned Three Mile Island. The line was busy. When he finally got through, fifteen minutes later, the operator told him they didn't have any information there. She suggested he call Blaine Fabian at Metropolitan Edison headquarters in Reading. Fabian, who is MetEd's director of public relations, was in a meeting when Reid called. His secretary took a message.

At eleven o'clock Jack Guerin, one of Fabian's assistants, returned Reid's call. "Can I help you with anything?" Guerin asked.

Reid said he had a town of about eleven thousand people here, right next to Three Mile Island, and he'd like to know what was up.

Guerin explained that there had a been a malfunction in the secondary cooling system at Unit 2, and that it had caused coolants to build up in the reactor containment building. But there were no injuries, and no radioactivity had escaped to the atmosphere.

"That's great," said Reid, relieved. "Thank you very much." He hung up. George Miller and Butch Ryan were watching him. He relayed the information about the malfunction and the coolants, and told them there was nothing to worry about. "And now *I'm* going back to school," he said.

Reid strolled out of the station, slid behind the wheel of his car, and started the engine. As the radio came on, a newscaster was saying that radioactive particles had escaped into the atmosphere from Three Mile Island this morning. Reid sat there for a while with the engine idling. Then he turned it off and walked back to the station.

Back inside, Reid learned that Ryan and Miller had heard the same thing on their radio. So began their first taste of the now-notorious phenomenon of "conflicting information." In the space of a few minutes, two supposedly responsible and well-informed men – a utility-company executive and a newscaster – had told them two entirely different things. Either one of them was lying, or one of them didn't know what he was talking about. Both prospects were equally disturbing.

And most disturbing of all was the prospect that radioactive particles might be floating down on Middletown at that very moment. Ryan brought out a geiger counter – Middletown Civil Defense had kept some around since the nuclear plant was built – and carried it outside. He took readings in the station parking lot, then walked up and down the street with it. The instrument didn't register much of anything. For the time being, at least, the air was clear of radioactivity.

But not of uncertainty. Bob Reid felt his head spinning. He walked into his mayor's office, a sparely furnished room with a steel desk, across the hall from the dispatcher's room. Closing the door behind him, he sat down to digest what had happened.

Maybe the radio report was wrong, he thought. *You can't believe everything you hear in the news.* Yet it's hard *not* to believe what you hear in the news. And the more Reid thought about it, the more he became convinced that MetEd's Jack Guerin was the one who'd been wrong. The thought that MetEd might've been lying intentionally about the release of radioactivity made Reid furious: *Not only did they lie to me, but I had to call them for the privilege of being lied to.*

. . . Yet he couldn't be sure. And there was no way he *could* be sure. He didn't know how to get the truth himself, nor did he know how he'd even recognize it if he did get it. Moreover, he wasn't certain what the truth might mean. If, for instance, there had been a radioactive release from the island, Reid couldn't know whether it might be dangerous, or whether another release might be in the offing, or whether anything else—anything *worse*—could yet happen. Or what in the world he, as mayor of Middletown, could do about anything anyway.

For the fact was that nothing in Bob Reid's background had prepared him for this. He was a schoolteacher. A Middletowner. All his life he had functioned in an environment where there were rules, where you could depend on things. Now he found himself in a situation where you couldn't depend on anything at all.

The truth about the Three Mile Island incident descended gradually on Bob Reid that day.

Throughout the afternoon he heard more radio and television reports of the morning's radioactive discharge from Three Mile Island. The more he heard, the more he felt certain that the news people were right, and that MetEd's Guerin had been wrong.

Then at four o'clock Guerin called back. "Bob, I want to update our conversation of eleven a.m.," Guerin said.

"Yeah, I think you should," said Reid coldly.

Guerin said he'd had the wrong information earlier. There had indeed been a release.

"Yeah, I heard about it," Reid said evenly. "On the radio. Right after you called me." There wasn't too much more Guerin could say.

Now it was confirmed. But there was a further revelation yet to come.

About 5:30, Reid heard that the wind had shifted since earlier in the day—now it was blowing from Three Mile Island toward Middletown. So he requested another check of the area with geiger counters. Don Foreman, the detective, happened to still be at the police station, finishing his report on the burglary case. Incriminating evidence had been found in the suspect's home, the boy had been apprehended, his unhappy parents spoken with.

Foreman took a geiger counter in his hand and walked into the street beside the police station. Reid walked alongside. Both men watched the needle on the geiger counter climb—slowly, hypnotically, like the second-hand on a watch. It didn't climb very far, but it climbed and stayed there. Reid felt a chill run the length of his back. *Here* was truth.

3. A 132-pound Fullback and the Fear of Fire

Later news that evening was reassuring. Police officers and CD volunteers whom Reid had sent out to other parts of Middletown with geiger counters phoned in their readings. Most of them were negligible, nothing above normal background-level radiation. And the six o'clock news on television reported that the reactor at Three Mile Island had apparently been stabilized, though its condition wasn't certain.

At seven o'clock Bob Reid took his customary evening ride through the streets of Middletown in a police patrol car. Reid, a man of habit, rides shotgun in a patrol car every Monday, Tuesday, and Wednesday night from seven to nine. He believes in being a "visible" mayor, and feels that these rides help get him out on the streets among the people, keep him in touch with the town. It also gives him a chance for a leisurely bull session with a certain friend of his, a policeman named Earl Anderson.

As Reid and Anderson rode through Middletown that evening, talking over the day's events, the image of that needle on Don Foreman's geiger counter kept creeping back into Reid's mind.

It hadn't been an especially big deal, Reid kept telling himself— the reading hadn't been that high, after all, and it might even have been a fluke. But the needle was *real*; it wasn't a news report. You could see it, you could see it climb. It was like the difference between seeing the Burning Bush and reading about it in the Bible.

The day's other events had made Reid angry, confused, perplexed, worried. But seeing the slow sweep of that needle had triggered a more basic emotion—simple, raw fear.

One thing to understand about this man Bob Reid, the mayor of Middletown, is that he is not a man who scares easily. Several weeks after the Three Mile Island incident, on South Union Street in Mid-

dletown, the state erected a billboard that reads, "Pennsylvania—
We're Tough." Bob Reid is probably the kind of Pennsylvanian they
were thinking about when they dreamed up that slogan.

Bob grew up poor, or as he likes to put it, more diplomatically,
in "a family that was not wealthy." His dad immigrated to Middletown from North Carolina and worked two jobs—one at the old Win-
croft Stove Works, one in a salvage yard. There were eight kids in
the family. As soon as he was big enough, young Bob started hustling
for money himself, washing cars, scrubbing floors and stocking shelves
at a grocery store, and—prophetically—passing out campaign hand-
bills for local politicians.

When Bob got to Middletown High School he joined the football
team. He stood six-foot-one and weighed 132 pounds. He was a fullback. Actually, he didn't get much playing time; the coach was afraid
to use him. "I can't put you in there, Reid," he would say. "They'll
break you up."

After high school Reid wanted to go to college but there just wasn't
enough money. So he drove a truck, worked odd jobs, and played
some sandlot football. Then one day he heard from a buddy at North
Carolina A&T University. "We need defensive ends," the friend said.
"I told the coach I knew a guy up north who was six-one, 190. He
has an athletic scholarship for you."

Reid went down to North Carolina A&T carrying, oh, 165 pounds.

The coach said, "You don't look like you weigh 190."

Reid said, "Don't I?"

There was a scrimmage the next day. Playing defensive end, Bob
Reid made fifteen unassisted tackles.

He played football at A&T for two years, and boxed at 156 pounds.
When the school's scholarship program was cut he transferred to Shippensburg and got his degree. After a hitch in the Army he found his
way back to Middletown—of course—taught school, raised a family,
and ran for borough council and won. Two years ago he ran for mayor.
His opponent, Harry Judy, was the incumbent and a popular man.
Reid, a black man in a town with a black population of maybe four
hundred out of eleven thousand, running against an incumbent, won
by eighty-nine votes.

A tough customer, then, this Bob Reid. But a slightly scared customer, that Wednesday evening. Reid had never worried about the
power plant at Three Mile Island before. In fact, its opening had got-

ten him interested in nuclear energy, stimulated him to do some reading on the subject. So he'd pored through some science books in the
school library—nothing very extensive, to be sure, but he'd learned
the basics. He knew what gamma rays are, and what they could do.
He knew that a civilian nuclear plant contained far more fissionable
material than was in the atomic bomb at Hiroshima. He knew that
E equals mc^2, and that c is a very large number. Now, riding in the
patrol car through the streets of Middletown and looking out the windows at the rows of houses, it occurred to him for perhaps the first
time to imagine those staggering mathematics applied to the squares
of this very small, finite town.

When Reid got home he learned that MetEd was holding a press
conference the next morning in Hershey. Company president Walter
Creitz and Vice President Jack Herbein would be there. Reid decided
he'd be there, too, and get the word on this business straight from
the top.

At eleven o'clock, with his wife Priscilla already in bed, Bob Reid
went through his nightly going-to-bed ritual. He shaved and shined
his shoes. He laid out his clothes for the next day, picking his best
three-piece pinstripe suit for the press conference.

Then he walked through the house, making sure that the plugs
were pulled on all the electrical appliances—the television, the toaster,
the record player, all the lamps. He tried the burners on the stove,
to see that the pilots were lit. He tried the oven, too. One more thing
to understand about Bob Reid is that tough as he may be, he is ob-
sessed with the threat of fire in the night. He has smoke detectors and
heat sensors in every room in the house. "It's only good sense," he tells
his friends. "Next week, don't buy a case of beer, buy a smoke detec-
tor. It's the height of foolishness to let something catch you unawares
in your sleep and burn you up."

Finally, his inspection complete, Reid climbed into bed. He has
always been a light sleeper, but he had an especially hard time sleeping that night.

4. Getting Ready for the Big Time

Thursday morning, after arranging for someone else to take his
classes again, Reid drove up to Hershey with George Miller. Miller

was in uniform, dapper with his starchy-white chief's shirt and black pants, and Reid in his pinstripe.

The press conference was at the Hershey Motor Lodge. All the media were there—ABC, CBS, NBC, New York, Washington, San Francisco, lights, cameras, everything. Reid hadn't been expecting this. "Whoa, this is big stuff," he whispered to Miller. "And here we are, two country boys."

Reid and Miller sat at the edge of the audience. Neither of them had seen a major press conference before. The proceedings, Reid thought, proved less impressive than the setting. MetEd's Herbein, the principal speaker, insisted over and over that the Three Mile Island situation was under control and posed no danger to the public. The press, meanwhile, seemed to Reid to be behaving rather poorly. A microphone stood in the center aisle, from which reporters were supposed to address their questions. But nobody used the microphone; they all just fired away from their seats, ten or fifteen of them at once. It was turning into a shouting match.

Reid was getting angry. He stood up and walked to the empty microphone. "I'm Mayor Bob Reid of Middletown," he announced.

Instant silence. Then suddenly, every light and camera in the house swung onto Bob Reid. "I thought I was going to get mugged," he said later. But he went on and spoke his piece. He wanted to know why it had taken so long to notify his borough of the nature of the accident. "We were the ones most affected, and yet we were the last to know," he said. "We had no way of knowing what the extent of the danger was. And right now we still have no way of knowing."

He concluded, "I'm upset and I'm angry." And he looked it.

Jack Herbein, somewhat taken aback, launched an explanation: MetEd was trying itself to evaluate the situation, and that took time, and so forth. Logical enough, maybe, but Reid was unsatisfied. Finally Creitz cut in: "We're sorry," he told Reid. "We're sorry."

Reid walked away from the mike. A crowd of reporters swarmed after him, but he hardly noticed them. He was steaming.

Driving home with George Miller, Reid acknowledged that not much had been settled at Hershey, except for these things: This was definitely big stuff, definitely the big time. It might not be over yet. And nobody was going to tell them what would happen, because maybe nobody knew.

As they rode along, Reid's anger subsided and a more rational concern presented itself—namely that Middletown, just three miles from a hot nuclear power plant, did not have an evacuation plan.

Reid and Miller and Butch Ryan had been talking about it for months. They'd been worried not about TMI, primarily, but about the danger of a chemical spill on the railroad tracks through town. To get eleven thousand people out of town in a hurry you needed routes, procedures, buses, ambulances, pickup points, dropoff points, personnel assignments—a solid plan. And they didn't have it.

Granted, if something happened most Middletowners would manage to clear out on their own, in their cars. But even then there would be incredible traffic jams. And what about people whose cars broke down or ran out of gas, or who didn't have cars? Or old folks living alone? What about people who wouldn't want to leave?

There was Henry, for instance, an old Pennsylvania Dutchman who lived alone on Social Security. Henry couldn't read or write, and he hadn't been out of Middletown in twenty years. He stayed home all day and watched the soap operas on TV. Henry thought the people in the soaps were real. "How can those people afford to dress like that and have houses like that?" he once asked a friend. "They're never *working.*"

What happens when you try to tell Henry that it's time to evacuate, that he'll get too many millirems?

In the Unit 2 control room at Three Mile Island, the situation was indeed still being evaluated, as Jack Herbein had said. A throng of specialists was congregating. Specialists from MetEd; specialists from its parent company, General Public Utilities; specialists from the Nuclear Regulatory Commission; specialists from Babcock & Wilson, builders of the reactor.

A lot of good questions were being raised. One big one concerned the exact extent of the mess the reactor had made of itself. MetEd announced that possibly one percent of the fuel assemblies in the core had been damaged. Some NRC people thought it was closer to fifty percent. Some B&W people thought there was no damage at all.

Another good question was who was supposed to be in charge. At one point a MedEd operator walked into the control room and, seeing an NRC man near his chair, asked, "What do you want me to do?" The NRC man threw up his hands. "Hey, I'm not here to give orders," he replied. "I'm just here to watch."

Sometimes it got so crowded in there that you could hardly turn around, and everybody had a different recommendation to make, it seemed. The men who knew the reactor best—the operators like Zewe and Frederick and Faust and Scheimann who had piloted this machine and understood its every quirk—were being pushed into the background, and occasionally were being used as mere messengers. On more than one occasion, someone like Zewe had to argue forcibly against an ordered adjustment because the outsiders were recommending things that might well have complicated the situation further.

In Middletown on Thursday, apprehension was beginning to build. It was obvious, from the media attention being given the TMI accident, that this was no ordinary shutdown. And then there were little things that added to the unease—like the fact that townspeople who held nonessential jobs at the plant still were not being allowed back on the island, that every so often a police officer could be seen checking radiation levels with a geiger counter, that Bob Reid had now missed classes at Middletown High two days in a row. Middletown being a close-knit place, bits of information like this were quickly noted and duly passed on, with all possible interpretations.

Nevertheless, there was virtually no disruption of the town's normal routine. Not very much serious talk about the physiological dangers of radiation, not much individual planning for the possibility of a forced evacuation. When George Miller got home that afternoon, for example, his wife barely bothered to ask for news about Three Mile Island—despite the fact that she'd already had her allowable dose of radiation for the year through medical X-rays.

Then again, Middletown never *had* been very concerned about radioactivity from the plant at Three Mile Island. When MetEd announced it was building the plant in 1966, a lot of folks saw it as an improvement over the utility's old coal-fired Crawford plant, at the lower end of Middletown, which dumped soot and coal dust over cars, porches, and everything else. To others, the nuclear plant's construction meant vital new income for a town recently stung by the closing of Olmsted Air Force Base nearby.

There were complaints while Three Mile Island was going up—but they were mostly complaints about the out-of-town construction workers MetEd had brought in. Those construction workers got drunk, drove their cars all over the place, didn't keep their apartments clean, and came and went at all hours. They . . . intruded. "They just weren't Middletown people," one woman remembers. "They didn't live here; they didn't have a stake in the town.

But nobody worried much about low-level radiation or nuclear waste storage or the danger of a large-scale accident. Jack Herbein told reporters that at one meeting with Middletown area residents, what the people wanted to talk about most was MetEd's plan for building a river recreation area on an unused part of Three Mile Island. Not about nuclear safety.

5.   Black Friday

Friday morning at Kuppy's Diner. John Garver was doing a slow burn, waiting for Bob Reid to show up. Garver was one of the few Middletowners who *had* been concerned about the safety of the power plant. In the past, he'd often tried to lecture the gang at Kuppy's on the subject. The gang, experienced kidders that they are, had quickly learned that all you had to do if you wanted to get Garver really steaming was get him started on radioactivity. "It's invisible death!" he would say while they chuckled. "It'll come and get you and you'll never see it; you'll never hear it. Silent death."

But suddenly "silent death" didn't seem like such a melodramatic joke any more. The previous night had been a tense one at the Garver household. John, his wife Bonnie, and John's dad—seventy-year-old John Sr.—live together in John Sr.'s house on Park Circle, at the top of Middletown. They can see Three Mile Island from their windows. They'd all been feeling jumpy because, as Dad had observed, it was getting to the point where he held his breath every time the news came on TV or radio. And when the news did come on Thursday evening, it had featured the earlier press conference at Hershey, with Bob Reid confronting MetEd's Herbein and Creitz and not getting much satisfaction.

Now Bob Reid in person walked into Kuppy's. "Hey, Bob," Garver said. "That was a pretty nice answer that Walter Creitz gave you yesterday. 'We're sorry.'"

Reid sat down. Garver kept at him: "Is that all they had to say? 'We're sorrr-ry.' Wasn't that a hell of an answer?"

"I didn't like it any better than you did," said Reid. Reid was feeling a little rocky. He'd stayed at the office late the night before to work, but he'd not gotten much done. He'd spent a lot of time answering phone calls from reporters all over North America. And the night had been another bad one for sleeping. Maybe today, he thought, things would settle down and Middletown could go back to business as usual.

No such luck. Over at Three Mile Island they had been juggling hot water, drawing reactor coolant off into a drain tank. Now pressure was building up, and to relieve it they would have to vent some steam. The water was radioactive, so naturally the steam would be too. But there didn't seem to be much choice. You could vent the stuff now, or sit on it until something burst. So they vented it. In the air directly above the plant, a light plane with monitoring equipment picked up a radiation reading of 1,200 millirems, the equivalent of some forty chest X-rays all at once.

The Nuclear Regulatory Commission—and the media—would describe it as an "uncontrolled" release of radioactivity. MetEd's Jack Herbein insisted all along that it was a *controlled* release. And of course it was controlled, in the sense that it was deliberate. An operator turned a dial, released just-so-much steam, then turned it off. But in another sense—that if MetEd had had their druthers, they certainly would rather not have done it at all—well, in that sense, it was uncontrolled.

A matter of semantics. But a most critical one, because very soon thousands of startled people would hear on their radios that something "uncontrolled" was going on at Three Mile Island.

Bob Reid got the news at about ten past nine that morning. He was giving a test to his second-period class when he was summoned to the office for a phone call. It was the borough police station again.

Reid hung up the phone and said to assistant principal Russ Eppinger, "I gotta go." He could barely stand still.

"What *happened?*" asked Eppinger.

"There's a new on-site emergency."

Bob Reid, former 132-pound fullback now hampered by bad knees and a middle-age paunch, burst out the doors of Middletown High and sprinted across the parking lot. "Hey, look at Mr. Reid go!" hollered a kid from a window. "Mr. Reid, I didn't know you could run so fast!" another kid shouted.

Reid hopped in his car and drove through a stop sign and down the road, into "Black Friday," the day of the Big Fear.

The news of an uncontrolled radioactive release was enough in itself to spread panic. Then at ten a.m. the governor's office advised people within ten miles of the plant to stay indoors, with windows shut and air conditioners off.

The governor acted after consulting with the NRC in Washington. It was considered a necessary precaution. The announcement was carefully phrased to avoid creating undue alarm. Yet its impact was tremendous. The implications of what it left *unsaid* were so sinister.

"Don't go outside? What the hell do they *mean*, don't go outside? What's *out*, outside?"

Likewise:

"Within ten miles? What do they have at ten miles, a brick wall? What if I'm within 10.1 miles? Or eleven? Or twenty?"

And oh yes—while the governor did not order an evacuation, he said that people should be ready for one, just in case.

Thus began the great Friday morning panic. These were some of the highlights:

☐ A lot of people simply got in their cars and drove away as fast and as far as they could, heading for grandma's place in the country, for the Howard Johnson's in Allentown, for the Jersey shore, for Florida. . . . *Gas. Gotta get gas and money.* Long lines, frantic lines, at gas stations and banks.

☐ Banks. In York, twelve miles from Three Mile Island, a woman went into a bank and withdrew $100,000 in savings bonds, not wanting to leave them behind to get contaminated.

☐ In Harrisburg, someone set off an air-raid siren. Office workers and people on sidewalks scrambled about, not knowing whether to head for the road out of town or the basement of the nearest large building. *Do I run or do I hide?*

On the floor of the state House of Representatives, the siren's shriek brought a shocked moment of absolute silence – a rare event in those quarters.

☐ In Camp Hill, a couple hurried into a real estate office and said they wanted to sell their house right away, before property values dropped.

☐ At Herbert Hoover Elementary School north of Harrisburg, Barb Taylor, a fourth-grade teacher, calmed her frightened children as best she could. Then she went down the hall to help comfort a fellow teacher who was going to pieces. When Ms. Taylor came back, she found the children writing their wills. One girl left her stuffed animals to her cousin, except for Paddington the Bear. She asked to be buried with Paddington. Another girl wrote simply, "My bed go to my sister Susie. And my soul go to heaven."

At Middletown High, transistor radios cleverly concealed in book bags and purses carried the word to the student body almost before the dust had cleared from Mayor Reid's quick departure. Classes went on as scheduled, though, and there was little panic. But there was a good bit of leaving. Students simply walked out, either on their own or to be picked up by parents. No one bothered to stop them.

The Fruehauf trailer plant off Route 230, straddling the borough of Middletown and Lower Swatara Township, is the largest tractor-trailer factory in the world. It is also, by consequence, probably the noisiest. On Friday morning all production lines in the sprawling factory buildings were going full-tilt, cranking out trailers with an incessant whomping of metal-stamping machines and a clatter of rivet guns. There were some nine hundred workers on the premises, and all those in the production buildings were wearing safety-prescribed earplugs. Not a chance of getting the news by radio down here.

The news came to Fruehauf through administrative secretary Bonnie Garver, sitting upstairs at her quiet desk outside plant manager Tom Fleming's office. Around ten o'clock the Lower Swatara police chief called and asked to talk to Fleming. Bonnie put the call through. But soon as she set the receiver down she thought, *Wait a minute. Why would the police chief be calling for Mr. Fleming?*

Bonnie took a radio from a drawer, turned it on and sure enough, that was it. *Stay indoors . . . keep windows closed . . . Three Mile Island . . .* Her heart racing, she phoned John at work and told him.

"Are you serious?" was all John could say.

She said she was. John said he'd keep in touch. Bonnie hung up and went out in the hall. People were milling around; the word had spread—in the offices. Now it had to be spread to the rest of the factory.

Bonnie caught the assistant plant manager coming out of his office. It was apparent that he had heard. "We've got men fixing the roof," Bonnie Garver told him. "You'd better get them down."

The repairmen were ordered in from the roof, and other employees working outdoors were quickly herded inside. Supervisors also were alerted to the governor's announcement. But production and assembly line workers, since they were already under cover, weren't notified at all. They kept on riveting and hammering and feeding their cutting and stamping machines, immersed in a sea of noise, probably the only people in all of Dauphin County unaware that Three Mile Island was running "uncontrolled" and Black Friday had arrived.

Eventually, though, the news began to get around. A few workers, mostly women, asked to leave to go to their families. Then there were moments of consternation as supervisors pointed out that people were being told to stay indoors—and that's where they all were. Company policy didn't say anything about leaving your shift under such circumstances. A few left anyway.

But by far most of them stuck to their posts. Fruehauf was indoors, and Fruehauf was making trailers.

Upstairs in the office, Bonnie stayed at her desk. There was no question, really, of the plant manager's secretary leaving at a time like this. If there were further developments at TMI, she reasoned, the front office at Fruehauf would hear about them as soon as anyone. Meantime she would hold onto reality—hold onto normality—as long as she could.

For Bob Reid, reality and normality were quickly slipping out of reach. After leaving the high school, he'd gotten to the police station about quarter after nine. There he heard the same old story: "On-site emergency. That's all we got, Bob."

Reid was no longer in the mood to sit around waiting for phone calls and newscasts. He drove down River Road to Three Mile Island, bringing with him Howard Noel, a Middletown mailman and Civil

Defense volunteer who'd had training with radiation-monitoring devices. Noel was packing a Middletown geiger counter.

Reid pulled off the road in front of the observation center, which by now was serving as off-island headquarters for the many teams of specialists that had been brought in. The grassy lot behind the center was filled with trailers fitted out as mobile laboratories, conference rooms, and equipment centers—"Trailer City," it came to be called. Reid had figured this was the only place he'd get some straight talk. So, apparently, had about one hundred reporters and cameramen who now stood seige along the apron of the road in the hazy morning sun.

Both the observation center and Trailer City were under guard. Reporters couldn't get in; neither could Reid or Howard Noel. But Noel with his geiger counter soon found himself surrounded by curious reporters asking whether he worked for MetEd.

"No," answered Noel, "I'm with the mayor here." Now it was Reid's turn to be surrounded. This was a nightmare—he'd come to ask questions, not answer them.

The reporters did, however, tell Reid that MetEd would soon be holding a press conference at the American Legion Hall back in Middletown. Thinking he might find some answers there, Reid decided to go.

When Reid walked into the Legion Hall he found it packed with around two hundred members of the media, stewing under the heat of their own lights. He also found John Garver there.

After hearing of the emergency from Bonnie, Garver had left his office—which was in Harrisburg, several miles away—and driven *into* Middletown to check on his dad. Then he'd come here to see for himself a real, live MetEd press conference.

"Now they've done it to us," Garver said softly, shaking his head. "Now they've really screwed us, Bob. I can't believe it. Now they've really gone and done it to us."

Reid and Garver watched Jack Herbein mount the platform in front of the blazing lights. Herbein, a ruggedly handsome man, had been described by the press as looking more like a tough cop or a prizefighter than a corporate executive. Now, having been through a two-hour pummeling just the day before at the Hershey press conference, he looked like an overmatched heavyweight entering the final rounds.

No, said Herbein, the maximum emission above the plant was 350 millirems, not 1,200 as the airborne monitoring team had reported. No, it was not uncontrolled, it was done on purpose. No, it was not dangerous to health, not by the time it settled to the ground. No, he didn't think an evacuation was necessary. Yes, there might be more radioactive emissions. No, he couldn't say for sure. . . .

"Ain't this the shit?" Reid asked Garver.

Garver replied that he didn't believe a word of it. Reid admitted he didn't either. The reporters clamored for more. They were standing on chairs and tables, almost climbing over one another's backs.

Garver turned to Reid and muttered, "Now it's between MedEd and the press. And we're caught in the middle."

6. A Sinking Ship?

Friday afternoon brought a second wave of fear. Around 12:30, Governor Thornburgh came on the air with a new announcement: Pregnant women and preschool children within a five-mile radius of the plant were to be evacuated as a precautionary measure, they being the most susceptible to harm from low-level radiation.

This announcement, like the earlier one about staying indoors within a ten-mile radius, set artificial limits that one could hardly expect people to observe:

"Preschool children? What about my first-grader? Or my second-grader? . . ."

And like the earlier announcement, this one had a sinister unspoken message:

"Women and children? Women and children first? What is this—a sinking ship?"

Maybe Three Mile Island *was* on the verge of going down with all hands, according to further news that trickled out. There were reports of a "bubble" in the reactor, a bubble full of potentially explosive hydrogen. A hydrogen explosion: Visions of the *Hindenburg*. And the NRC in Washington was talking about the risk of a meltdown. Few people knew yet exactly what a meltdown was, but the word itself was evil. Visions of massive concrete cooling towers turning liquid and shiny.

At the Middletown borough hall, it was time to act. George Miller had all his policemen called in for duty. School buses were brought to the borough hall for pregnant women and children who had no private transportation.

Bob Reid came hustling in; he and Miller conferred. Since there would be empty homes in Middletown tonight, there was potential for looting. They decided it would be best to put the town under curfew.

And here, even here in the face of chaos, the old Middletown streak of business-as-usual surfaced: Reid and Miller at first discussed a 7:30 p.m. curfew. Then Reid said, "No, let's make it nine o'clock. The stores are open till nine." Nine o'clock it was.

Fire trucks and squad cars roamed the streets of Middletown announcing the curfew over loudspeakers—the same loudspeakers they used in normal times to announce bake sales and car washes.

At Reid's request, one other item was added to the curfew announcement—anyone caught looting and attempting to flee would be shot. Reid maintains to this day that he was in dead earnest at the time, while George Miller says the order was "strictly for public consumption." At any rate, Miller told his men, "Don't you dare shoot anyone."

With the governor's announcement, with the increasingly ominous news from the plant, with the loudspeaker trucks prowling the streets, many folks who were Middletown-born and Middletown-bred and lived in Middletown all their lives began to think that it might not be a good idea to die in Middletown.

In his police journal for Friday afternoon, George Miller described the scene with wonderful terseness, writing:

"At this time, some of the people of the town took it upon themselves to leave."

When notice of the partial evacuation came over the radio in the offices of the Fruehauf trailer plant, manager Tom Fleming called Bonnie Garver into his office. This news *would* have to be carried to the workers in the factory. Transmitting a complex message to hundreds of workers at once—workers who are wearing earplugs and operating ferociously noisy equipment and can't *hear* you—requires an intricate process.

Fleming dictated a memo containing details of the evacuation notice. Bonnie typed it up, shakily, misspelling a word or two. (Fleming told her not to worry about it.) Then she had copies run off and distributed to clerks. And the clerks went down into the factory, carrying the memo wordlessly past the hammering machines, to dozens of foremen. Each foreman waved his workers together. In all the corners of the Fruehauf plant, workers stopped machines, set down rivet guns and hand tools, removed earplugs, and gathered in knots to hear their foremen read the message.

Quite a few workers left the plant immediately. Company policy on leaving had been relaxed since morning. Still, enough stayed through till quitting time to keep the plant rolling. The remainder of the day shift left at 2:30. They hadn't done badly at all. On a normal day, the Fruehauf day shift turns out about sixty trailers. Today, on Black Friday, they'd turned out fifty-six.

But things changed with the evening shift. Three hundred people had been due in at 2:30. Twenty-three reported for work.

Bonnie Garver stayed on until 5:30, working with manager Fleming in the nearly empty plant. Then she picked up her purse and, wondering what she would find, stepped into the world outside for the first time since early that morning.

It was quiet, so quiet everywhere, the way it is when it snows. Yet it was warm and muggy—there'd been a temperature inversion that day, and the air seemed heavy to her, she felt as if a huge hand were pressing down the sky.

Bonnie drove home through empty streets, past quiet houses and vacant driveways. Some of the people had taken it upon themselves to leave.

When Bonnie got home, John was there to greet her. He hadn't been there long, having returned to work himself that afternoon. Bonnie went to the kitchen and started to fix supper. She noticed her hands were shaking. Very strange; she couldn't stop them. She was fumbling, spilling things, dropping pots and pans, clanking and clattering until at last she *threw* some silverware across the kitchen. That seemed to help.

Supper was eaten to the accompaniment of two televisions and a radio. The news was full of meltdown talk, and while all the reports insisted that the possibility of a meltdown at Three Mile Island was very remote, they also described in great detail what a meltdown would be like—how the reactor core would melt and slump to the floor of the containment, how it would melt through the floor and breach the containment, and how there was no recourse for breach of containment.

John and Bonnie and Dad reviewed their own evacuation plan. If necessary, Bonnie's sister in Philadelphia had offered to put them up indefinitely. Now Bonnie began to wonder how long "indefinitely" might be.

After supper she took out a list she'd made of things to bring along in the event of evacuation. She made a few additions—sheets and towels, in case they had to set up housekeeping in an apartment somewhere; and business clothes for her and John, in case they had to go hunting for new jobs.

Lists, lists—the conference room a few steps away from the Unit 2 control room back on Three Mile Island was sprouting lists. All of them outlined approaches for bringing the reactor back under control.

The NRC's Harold Denton, who had been introduced to the nation a short while earlier by a tense Governor Thornburgh, was now poring over these lists, asking questions and receiving recommendations. The bubble was the paramount concern now; it had to be reduced before anything else could be done.

And so late that night, as the people of Middletown tried with varying degrees of success to sleep, Denton and the rest of the on-site NRC staff approved a series of experiments designed to find out whether the bubble's size could be manipulated. Then even these were stopped when someone pointed out that the experiments might trigger another hydrogen explosion down in the reactor (one such explosion had occurred already). And back everyone went to making lists.

At the far end of Middletown, Bob Reid was lying in bed feeling miserable. For the third night in a row, he was having trouble sleeping. This night, in fact, was the worst one yet. It seemed that every time Reid managed to doze off, a passing car would touch its brakes for the stop sign outside his house, and the flicker of red brake lights through the curtains would wake him up.

7. Meet the Press

Middletown began Saturday with another round of press conferences. First MetEd held its farewell performance in the American Legion Hall, abdicating all further TMI communications to the NRC. Then the NRC opened at the borough hall, introducing Harold Denton live.

Saturday was also the day that every publication which hadn't yet done so sent a reporter to Middletown. The descent of the press upon Middletown had become almost as big a phenomenon as the accident itself. One estimate placed the total number of reporters in town at around three hundred; there may have been many, many more. They were everywhere. They jammed the restaurants and lined up at the phone booths and swarmed over the streets, grizzled old vets in baggy pants, natty young ones in tweed blazers, pretty TV newswomen with scarves around their necks. Every single one of them wanted to find out *exactly* what was going on, and to find out *fast*.

It quickly became apparent that they faced an almost impossible task. For one thing, "what was going on"—the really good stuff, the crisis and the high-level decision-making—was mostly going on inside the plant. Inside thick concrete walls, on an island surrounded by chainlink fence a quarter-mile from shore, and the only way to get there was through a gate and across a narrow bridge, and there were armed guards at the gate. So what you could do, if you were a reporter, was stare out across the water and think about how awesome the plant looked with its massive cooling towers rising majestically above the Susquehanna. Or, if you were a TV reporter, you could do a stand-up in front of the plant, with its massive cooling towers rising majestically above the Susquehanna.

For another thing, what was going on was extremely complex. A very, very complicated machine had come down with some very baffling problems. There were dozens of possible ways to fix these problems, and every one was intricate. Whether anyone even *knew* what was going on was problematic.

And for still another thing, most of these three-hundred-odd reporters—like most of the rest of us—didn't know too much about nuclear power. So there you had it. The uneducated in search of the inexplicable. And the whole world—literally the whole, wide, teeming world—was depending on these reporters to understand what was going on.

Those news people who did know something about nuclear energy—science writers and the like—soon found themselves giving crash courses for their colleagues. A common sight in Middletown was a group of reporters crowded around a *savant* as he leaned on the fender of a car, drawing diagrams on a notepad to explain the difference between the feedwater system and the primary cooling system, or some other such subtlety. Learning in the streets. You squeezed yourself into the crowd and fired off as many questions as you could:

"What exactly is a rem?"

"It stands for 'roentgen equivalent, man.' It's the amount of radiation that produces the same effect on a human being as one roentgen of X-ray or gamma ray."

"Aha. And a millirem is a thousand rems?"

"No, it's a thousandth of a rem."

"Is that constant or does it add up?"

"What?"

"In other words if you're getting one millirem an hour for 24 hours, is that one millirem a day or 24 millirems a day . . . ?"

Then, armed with your newly acquired knowledge, you waited for some official to come down from the island and hold a press conference. At the press conference you squeezed in and waved your arm and hoped that the PR man standing next to the speaker would point to you to acknowledge your question. And you only got one question; then the PR man would point at someone else who was waving and shouting. While this procedure did provide some semblance of order—giving everyone in the room who waved his arm at least a fighting chance—it made it very difficult to sustain a line of questioning. At MetEd's farewell conference, for instance, a series of reporters had just about managed to pin down Jack Herbein on one of the fine points concerning the hydrogen bubble. Then the next reporter asked, "Mr. Herbein, what do you think this incident will mean for the future of the atomic power industry?"

It wasn't only technical information the reports were after. They focused on the people of Middletown, too. Suddenly, for a Middletowner to go out on the streets was to face the almost certain prospect of being accosted and poked and prodded. *What do you think of the NRC? What do you think of the job they're doing? Are you staying or leaving? What about your children? Your grandmother? What do you think? How do you feel?*

. . . How do you feel, Middletown? The world wants to know. The New York Times *wants to know.*

The New York Times, in fact, wanted to know with great precision how Middletown felt. *The Times* became the first publication to use the now-standard TMI degree-of-uptightness scale when it reported that farmer Richard Alwine was "concerned" but not "worried," whereas Alwine's neighbors, the Lytles, were "worried, but not frightened."

The next most popular question, after "How uptight are you?", was "How do you feel about MetEd?" At one point during the week after the accident, CBS decided to put that question to Bob Reid. To help it look laid-back and natural on camera, they decided to do it in Kuppy's Diner.

So they set up a few lights behind the counter at Kuppy's, and turned them on. The cameramen got behind the counter with his camera, and the sound man with his tape recorder and his microphone, and the technician with his slate (Excuse me, Mister Kupp), and the interviewer squeezed in there too. Bob Reid was sitting at the counter dressed in his Sunday best.

The slate clicked. The camera was rolling. The question came, loaded and portentous: *Mister Reid, do you still have faith in MetEd after this incident? Will you trust them again in the future?*

"No. I don't think so," said Reid very blandly, very tiredly. A little *too* laid-back and natural.

"We'd like to do that again," said the interviewer.

Again the slate, again the camera, again the question, the same as before. And again Bob Reid said, "No, I don't think so." As if it were the sort of question he'd been asked all his life. *Another cup of coffee, Bob? Nah, no thanks. Trust MetEd! Nah, no thanks.*

"We'd like to do it one more time," said CBS. "We want to get it exactly right."

They did it two more times, and twice more—No, Bob Reid didn't think so. Finally CBS moved off to talk to some other patrons down the counter. Bob Reid shook his head. "They were gonna keep doing

it until they made me angry," he said. "They wanted to see anger."
He laughed.

Reid would communicate, but he would not perform. And beyond
a certain threshold, he would not even communicate. During one in-
terview, a reporter was trying mightily to get Bob Reid to talk about
himself. Finally the reporter asked point-blank, "What kind of man
are you, Bob? How would you describe yourself?"

"Oh, hell, I can't describe myself," Reid laughed. "A man can't
describe his own self. That's like asking a skunk to describe his own
smell."

Three Mile Island has been written about as a twenty-first century
disaster in a nineteenth century town. To the extent that that is true,
the encounter between the media and Middletown was also an encounter between the twenty-first and nineteenth centuries: A corps
of highly analytical reporters examining a town that hardly knows
what a psychiatrist looks like, a town where people are not used to
the modern pastime of thinking about how they think.

8. Saturday Night Action

What Middletowners knew how to do was act. On Saturday at
the borough hall Bob Reid, George Miller and the others were finishing their evacuation plan. They had traffic routes laid out; they
had pickup points established. Police assignments were worked out.
They had buses at the ready with tires and oil checked and fuel tanks
full — and National Guard trucks at the local armory standing by to
back up the buses.

That should have made everyone feel better. But something awful
was still bothering Reid, something Miller and Butch Ryan knew too,
but which none of them would speak of, even among themselves.
Through Civil Defense, Ryan had been told that if an evacuation were
ordered, Middletown would have two and a half, maybe three hours
to pull it all off. And there were probably still some eight thousand
people left in Middletown — plus tens of thousands of others in eight
thousand neighboring towns who'd also be on the move if an evacuation order came down.

Why just three hours? Was that how long a meltdown took? My God,
thought Bob Reid, *we just can't get them all out that fast.*

Saturday night over supper the Garvers watched another NRC news conference starring Harold Denton. Like most other Middletowners, the Garvers approved of Denton, found his bedside manner soothing.

"Now here's someone who looks like an ordinary guy," John said.

"Not like those goddamn know-it-all snobs they got down there at MetEd."

"It's his eyes," Bonnie said. "Look at his eyes."

After supper the Garvers talked to one another in reassuring tones: Maybe they had things under control down there. Nothing's going to happen after all; maybe we won't have to leave. Yesterday was the crisis, and if nothing's happened yet. . . .

BRRROOOOOOOMMMM.

There was no mistaking that sound. TMI blowing off steam. Bonnie had heard it other times down by the river, but this was the first time it'd ever been so loud way up here at the house, a couple of miles from the plant. With the sound roaring in their ears, the Garvers ran to the window and looked down the valley at TMI. Nothing happening, no steam. Then they saw what it was—in the sky above the house a mammoth airplane was heading into Harrisburg airport, a C-130 transport loaded (as they learned later) with lead bricks and emergency repair equipment for the power plant. There would be several more that evening.

After that the screws began to tighten again. Bonnie was tense; John noticed that she avoided standing or sitting in front of the windows that faced TMI. The phone was ringing with calls from friends and relatives who were leaving town, or had already left, and who were telephoning to exchange out-of-town addresses and numbers. When the callers said good-bye it was always with an air of finality: "Take care, now. We love you. God bless you." BRRROOOOOOMMMM.

John's dad retreated to his rooms downstairs. Bonnie came in to say hello and found him sitting alone, wringing his hands.

Bonnie's mother called from Philadelphia with disturbing news. A television station there had just broadcast a bulletin that a hydrogen explosion might be imminent inside the Unit 2 reactor. (The report later proved false.) "I want you to get my daughter out of there," she told John.

Bonnie went to the bathroom and soaked in a hot tub.

Then as she was dressing she got a call from her friend Jean Baumbach, who lives on River Road near the TMI entrance. Jean was terrified. "I called to tell you we're leaving," she said, her voice shaking. "There's a terrible commotion down here, and I don't know what it's all about, and I'm not going to stay to find out." In the background over the phone Bonnie could hear sirens, horns, truck engines, loudspeakers.

That did it. There was no more reality or normality worth holding onto. Time to pack up. Bonnie went to tell John, and found out he'd spontaneously decided the same thing.

Bonnie dragged out the biggest suitcases they had and opened them on the bed. Into them she emptied whole dresser drawers that had been strategically loaded for just such an operation.

In a short while they were packed and driving through Middletown in the night. It was like joining a secret procession. Every few blocks they saw headlights go on in another dark driveway, and another car would pull out and ease onto the street, riding low with the weight of a Middletown family and its possessions.

At Three Mile Island, the decision-makers had sifted through all their lists one last time, and settled upon a series of steps that they hoped would finally begin moving the reactor toward a safe cool-down. The trucks that had so terrified Jean Baumbach, and in turn had so frightened Bonnie, were ferrying in equipment for use in these steps— pipe, lead brick, hardware and all manner of heavy artillery for the fight against the hydrogen bubble. The equipment kept coming throughout the night. In the morning the small army of technicians on the island would begin readying it for deployment.

9. I Keep Waiting for a Voice

As the Garvers drove down the Turnpike to Philadelphia Saturday night, Bob Reid finally set his worries aside and gave in to fatigue. That he'd have only three hours for an evacuation still bothered him, but he was beginning to enjoy a sense of relief over having prepared as much as he and the others possibly could. Nobody was going to catch Middletown unawares in its bed now. So Reid could sleep the sleep of the just—and the very tired.

Sunday morning Reid dressed in casual clothes and put on his son's

Middletown High football jacket. National television be damned – if the world saw him in a Middletown football jacket, that was just fine. The jacket said "Bird" on the front, and that was just fine too, because he was the Big Bird – remember?

At the borough building the only news on the power plant was that conditions remained stable. It wasn't encouraging, exactly, but it would do for now. In the main hall, volunteer firemen were setting up hundreds of chairs. For the President, they said – Jimmy Carter was coming today. Reid laughed. A reporter had told him the previous night that Carter would be in Middletown, but he still didn't believe it. He'd heard enough rumors in the past few days to make him very skeptical. Then he walked into the police station and saw a couple of tall strangers in suits talking to George Miller. Secret Service. Jimmy Carter *was* coming. The President himself.

Out on the street a crowd was already gathering. As Bob Reid walked out of the borough hall and down the street, taking a little pre-Presidential stroll to collect himself, he knew that the eyes of that crowd were on him. They were watching him the way the passengers in an airliner watch the flight attendant when the plane hits turbulence – watching and looking for signs, to see if he was worried, to see how bad the trouble was, to see if they were going to land safely. And Reid knew his role: Maybe he couldn't land the plane for them, but he could sure as hell smile when he walked down the aisle.

He put on his game face and smiled and waved and joked his way down the street, picking out familiar faces and talking to them. After you've lived in Middletown for forty-six years most of the faces *are* familiar, so his progress was rather slow. Here were a couple of former students, young guys who worked in town now. "Hey, how you doing? You scared?" Reid asked them.

"Sure we're scared," they grinned.

"Huh," snored Reid. "Bad as you were in school? Bad as you were? Didn't think *you* were scared of nothing." And so on down the street.

As he moved along, Reid realized that he wasn't putting on an act at all, that it wasn't an effort to smile for the troops, the way it had been for the last few days. Though that red-hot reactor was still sitting out there in the river, he really *did* feel good, and he wasn't sure why. Maybe it was because he was back in his element here, working the streets and talking to the folks, instead of putting on three-piece suits

and haggling with utility executives and reporters. Maybe it was because he'd finally *done* something—put the evacuation plan together—
after days of stumbling around wondering what was happening. Maybe
it was because he'd decided earlier that morning to send his family
away for the duration of the crisis—a decision that had been weigh-
ing on his mind. Or maybe it was because the President was coming,
and it was beginning to feel a little like a holiday. Or maybe it was
simply because, after days of sweating about the fire in the night, it
still hadn't caught him. He was still alive, man, still here.

The President came to Middletown. He toured the nuclear plant,
wearing his yellow radiation boots, and he came to the borough hall
and made his speech. Dick Thornburgh followed him to the microphone and announced that Pennsylvanians were made of stern stuff.
Reid watched from his favorite press conference vantage point, the
back of the hall. As usual, he did not seem overly impressed with the
official goings-on. After Jimmy Carter was gone, a reporter cornered
him and asked, *Mr. Reid, when you saw the President of the United States
standing right here in your borough hall, what did you think?*
"How short he was," Reid answered.
As Jimmy Carter headed for Washington, Bob Reid took his post-
Presidential stroll down Union Street. He went into the Hy-Lo market
and bought a couple of boxes of JujyFruits, his favorite candy. On
his way back to the office, he stopped for a few minutes on the corner,
popping JujyFruits, talking to passersby, and—as was his custom—
offering pieces of the candy to anyone who wanted them.
The newspapers reported that there was an atmosphere of courage
and hope in Middletown that Sunday afternoon. They attributed it
to the President's visit, and to the soothing presence of Harold Denton, but what they did not mention was that if you could walk down
Union Street in the middle of the worst nuclear crisis in American
history and see the mayor of Middletown standing on the street corner, dressed in a Middletown High football jacket, passing out candy,
as usual, you had to believe—for that brief moment you just had to
believe—that somehow everything was going to be all right.

"Bonnie! What's wrong with you?"
That same afternoon, Bonnie Garver was a hundred miles away

from Middletown, in Philadelphia, out shopping with her sister. They were walking through an indoor shopping mall. Muzak was playing over the loudspeakers, water was tinkling in a little fountain, and it was all very pleasant and very safe.

But all of a sudden Bonnie had a funny look on her face, and her sister was holding her by the arm and asking what was wrong.

"I know what it is," Bonnie said after a moment. "It's the music."

"What?"

"The music on the loudspeakers. I keep waiting for a voice to come on and tell us something awful."

10. Suitcases and Bad Dreams

As it turned out, things *were* all right in Middletown, more or less. The next morning, Monday morning, Harold Denton announced that the dangerous hydrogen bubble in the Unit 2 reactor had been reduced practically to nothing. The reactor began cooling down; the crisis passed. By the end of the week most of the people who had left Middletown were back home.

Martin's men's store on South Main Street did a brisk business that week in "I Survived Three Mile Island" T-shirts. In Kuppy's Diner, Bob Reid spotted one of these shirts on a teenager who had evacuated with his family during the emergency. "Get out of here with that shirt," Reid kidded him. "You didn't survive Three Mile Island. You ran! You should have a shirt that says 'I *Ran* From Three Mile Island.'"

But Middletown didn't really "survive" Three Mile Island; Middletown was rescued from Three Mile Island. Things did not turn out all right because Middletowners are made of stern stuff and hung in there (though they are, and they did). Nor did they turn out all right because the mayor was able to stand on a street corner in a Middletown High football jacket, passing out candy, as usual, in the middle of the worst civilian nuclear crisis in American history. The bubble disappeared and things turned out all right because of the concentrated efforts of some of the most highly skilled engineers and technicians in the free world, along with, as Denton said, a little bit of serendipity.

Middletown was saved by modern technology—which is like the spouse who helps you with all the problems you wouldn't have if you hadn't gotten married in the first place.

And in the long run, some Middletowners may discover that they were not saved. The long-range effects of the radioactivity they were exposed to will be studied carefully for years. Estimates of the doses the townspeople received have already been revised upward several times.

Then there are the psychological effects of the incident. Two months afterward, some people in town still slept with packed suitcases close by their beds. Others continued to have trouble sleeping at all, though there were fewer who woke up in the middle of the night screaming. And a lot of people still think every little rash is a symptom of radiation poisoning.

Dr. John Barnoski—a family physician in Middletown who does a good bit of mental health counseling as part of his practice—believes there have been more subtle manifestations as well. "A lot of people were very *quietly* upset by TMI," Barnoski explains. "They didn't run around crying about it, okay? But these are the kind of people it shows up in later, in other ways. Marital problems, problems with their teenage son, whatever. Things that normally wouldn't bug them are bugging them now. There is definitely an increase in tension in the town . . . You can see it everywhere."

Remember that billboard on South Union Street, the one that says, "Pennsylvania—We're Tough"? Somebody's gone and ripped a big piece out of it, right down the middle.

SHILLINGTON

JOHN UPDIKE

The author of more than two dozen novels, collections of stories, essays, and poems, including the "Rabbit Trilogy," (Rabbit Run, Rabbit Redux, Rabbit is Rich), John Updike was born in Shillington, near Reading, in 1932. He has lived in England, attending the Ruskin School of Drawing and Fine Art; New York, as a staff member of The New Yorker *magazine; and Massachusetts, in Beverly Farms, where he lives and writes today. This description of growing up in Shillington is an excerpt of a much longer essay Updike wrote in 1962 for an anthology,* Five Boyhoods, *edited by Martin Levin.*

Environment

THE DIFFERENCE BETWEEN a childhood and a boyhood must be this: our childhood is what we alone have had; our boyhood is what any boy in our environment would have had. My environment was a straight street about three city blocks long, with a slight slope that was most noticeable when you were on a bicycle. Though many of its residents commuted to Reading factories and offices, the neighborhood retained a rural flavor. Corn grew in the strip of land between the alley and the school grounds. We ourselves had a large vegetable garden, which we tended not as a hobby but in earnest, to get food to eat. We sold asparagus and eggs to our neighbors. Our peddling things humiliated me, but then I was a new generation. The bulk of the people in the neighborhood were not long off the farm. One old lady down the street, with an immense throat goiter, still wore a bonnet. The most aristocratic people in the block were the full-fashioned knitters; Reading's textile industry prospered in the Depression. I felt neither prosperous nor poor. We kept the food money in a little recipe box on top of the icebox, and there were nearly always a few bills and coins in it. My father's job paid him poorly but me well; it gave me a sense of, not prestige, but *place*. As a school-teacher's son, I was assigned a role; people knew me. When I walked down the street to school, the houses called, "Chonny." I had a place to be.

Schools

The elementary school was a big brick cube set in a square of black surfacing chalked and painted with the diagrams and runes of children's games. Wire fences guarded the neighboring homes from the playground. Whoever, at soccer, kicked the ball over the fence into Snitzy's yard had to bring it back. It was very terrible to have to go into Snitzy's yard, but there was only one ball for each grade. Snitzy was a large dark old German who might give you the ball or lock you up in his garage, depending upon his mood. He did not move like other men; suddenly the air near your head condensed, and his heavy hands were on you.

On the way to school, walking down Lancaster Avenue, we passed Henry's, a variety store where we bought punch-out licorice belts and tablets with Edward G. Robinson and Hedy Lamarr smiling on the cover. In October, Halloween masks appeared, hung on wire clotheslines. Hanging limp, these faces of Chinamen and pirates and witches were distorted, and, thickly clustered and rustling against each other, they seemed more frightening masking empty air than they did mounted on the heads of my friends—which was frightening enough. It is strange how fear resists the attacks of reason, how you can know with absolute certainty that it is only Mark Wenrich or Jimmy Trexler whose eyes are moving so weirdly in those almond-shaped holes, and yet still be frightened. I abhorred that effect of double eyes a mask gives; it was as bad as seeing a person's mouth move upside down.

I was a Crow. That is my chief memory of what went on inside the elementary school. In music class the singers were divided into three groups: Nightingales, Robins, and Crows. From year to year the names changed. Sometimes the Crows were Parrots. When visitors from the high school, or elsewhere "outside," came to hear us sing, the Crows were taken out of the room and sent upstairs to watch with the fifth grade an educational film about salmon fishing in the Columbia River. Usually there were only two of us, me and a girl from Philadelphia Avenue whose voice was in truth very husky. I never understood why I was a Crow, though it gave me a certain derisive distinction. As I heard it, I sang rather well.

The other Crow was the first girl I kissed. I just did it, one day, walking back from school along the gutter where the water from the ice plant ran down, because somebody dared me to. And I continued to do it every day, when we reached that spot on the pavement, until a neighbor told my mother, and she, with a solemn weight that seemed unrelated to the airy act, forbade it.

I walked to school mostly with girls. It happened that the mothers of Philadelphia Avenue and, a block up, of Second Street had borne female babies in 1932. These babies now teased me, the lone boy in their pack, by singing the new song, "Oh, Johnny, oh Johnny, how you can love!" and stealing my precious rubber-lined bookbag. The queen of these girls later became the May Queen of our senior class. She had freckles and thick pigtails and green eyes and her mother made her wear high-top shoes long after the rest of us had switched to low ones. She had so much vitality that on the way back from school her nose would start bleeding for no reason. We would be walking along over the wings of the maple seeds and suddenly she would tip her head back and rest it on a wall while someone ran and soaked a handkerchief in the ice-plant water and applied it to her streaming, narrow, crimson-shining nostrils. She was a Nightingale. I loved her deeply, and ineffectually.

My love for that girl carries through all those elementary-school cloakrooms; they always smelled of wet raincoats and rubbers. That tangy, thinly resonant, lonely smell: can love have a better envelope? Everything I did in grammar school was meant to catch her attention. I had a daydream wherein the stars of the music class were asked to pick partners and she, a Nightingale, picked me, a Crow. The teacher was shocked; the class buzzed. To their amazement I sang superbly; my voice, thought to be so ugly, in duet with hers was beautiful. Still singing, we led some sort of parade.

In the world of reality, my triumph was getting her to slap me once, in the third grade. She was always slapping boys in those years; I could not quite figure out what they did. Pull her pigtails, untie her shoes, snatch at her dress, tease her (they called her "Pug")—this much I could see. But somehow there seemed to be under these offensive acts a current running the opposite way; for it was precisely the boys who behaved worst to her that she talked to solemnly at recess, and walked with after school, and whose names she wrote on the sides of her books. Without seeing this current, but deducing its presence, I tried to jump in; I entered a tussel she was having with a boy in homeroom before the bell. I pulled the bow at the back of her dress, and was slapped so hard that children at the other end of the hall heard the crack. I was overjoyed; the stain and pain on my face seemed a badge of initiation. But it was not. The distance between us remained as it was. I did not really want to tease her, I wanted to rescue her, and to be rescued by her. I lacked—and perhaps here the only child suffers a certain deprivation—that kink in the instincts on which childish courtship turns. He lacks a certain easy roughness with other children.

All the years I was at the elementary school the high school loomed large in my mind. Its students—tall, hairy, smoke-breathing—paced the streets seemingly equal with adults. I could see part of its immensity from our rear windows. It was there that my father performed his mysteries every day, striding off from breakfast, down through the grape arbor, his coat pocket bristling with defective pens. He now and then took me over there; the incorruptible smell of varnish and red sweeping wax, the size of the desks, the height of the drinking fountains, the fantastic dimensions of the combination gymnasium-auditorium made me feel that these were halls in which a race of giants had ages ago labored through lives of colossal bliss. At the end of each summer, usually on Labor Day Monday, he and I went into his classroom, Room 201, and unpacked the books and arranged the tablets and the pencils on the desks of his homeroom pupils. Sharpening forty pencils was a chore, sharing it with him a solemn pleasure. To this day I look up at my father through the cedar smell of pencil shavings. To see his key open the front portals of oak, to share alone with him for an hour the pirate hoard of uncracked books and golden pencils, to switch off the lights and leave the room and walk down the darkly lustrous perspective of the corridor and perhaps halt for a few words by an open door that revealed another teacher, like a sorcerer in his sanctum, inscribing forms beside a huge polished globe of the Earth—such territories of wonder boyhood alone can acquire.

The Playground

The periphery I have traced; the center of my boyhood held a calm collection of kind places that are almost impossible to describe, because they are so fundamental to me, they enclosed so many of my hours, that they have the neutral color of my own soul, which I have always imagined as a pale oblong just under my ribs. In the town where I now live, and where I am writing this, seagulls weep overhead on a rainy day. No seagulls found their way inland to Shillington; there were sparrows, and starlings, and cowbirds, and robins, and occasionally a buzzard floating high overhead on immobile wings like a kite on a string too high to be seen.

The playground: up from the hardball diamond, on a plateau bounded on three sides by cornfields, a pavilion contained some tables and a shed for equipment. I spent my summer weekdays there from the age when I was so small that the dust stirred by the feet of roof-ball players got into my eyes. Roof-ball was the favorite game. It was played with a red rubber ball smaller than a basketball. The object was to hit it back up on the roof of the pavilion, the whole line of children in succession. Those who failed dropped out. When there was just one person left, a new game began with the cry "Noo-oo gay-ame," and we lined up in the order in which we had gone out, so that the lines began with the strongest and tallest and ended with the weakest and youngest. But there was never any doubt that everybody could play; it was perfect democracy. Often the line contained as many as thirty pairs of legs, arranged chronologically. By the time we moved away, I had become a regular front-runner; I knew how to flick the ball to give it spin, how to leap up and send the ball skimming the length of the roof edge, how to plump it with my knuckles when there was a high bounce. Somehow the game never palled. The sight of the ball bouncing along the tarpaper of the foreshortened roof was always important. Many days I was at the playground from nine o'clock, when they ran up the American flag, until four, when they called the equipment in, and played nothing else.

If you hit the ball too hard, and it went over the peak of the roof, you were out, and you had to retrieve the ball, going down a steep bank into a field where the poorhouse men had stopped planting corn because it all got mashed down. If the person ahead of you hit the ball into the air without touching the roof, or missed it entirely, you had the option of "saving," by hitting the ball onto the roof before it struck the ground; this created complex opportunities for strategy and gallantry. I would always try to save the Nightingale, for instance, and there was a girl who came from Louisiana with a French name whom everybody wanted to save. At twelve, she seemed already mature, and I can remember standing with a pack of other boys under the swings looking up at the undersides of her long tense dark-skinned legs as she kicked into the air to give herself more height, the tendons on the underside of her smooth knees jumping, her sneakered feet pointing like a ballerina's shoes.

The walls of the pavilion shed were scribbled all over with dirty drawings and words and detailed slanders on the prettier girls. After hours, when the supervisors were gone, if you were tall enough you could grab hold of a crossbeam and get on top of the shed, where there was an intimate wedge of space under the slanting roof; here no adult ever bothered to scrub away the pencillings, and the wood fairly breathed of the forbidden. The very silence of the pavilion, after the daylong click of checkers and *pokabok* of ping-pong, was like a love-choked hush.

Reality seemed more intense at the playground. There was a dust, a daring. It was a children's world; nowhere else did we gather in such numbers with so few adults over us. The playground occupied a platform of earth; we were exposed, it seems now, to the sun and sky. Looking up, one might see a buzzard or witness a portent.

The Movie House

It was two blocks from my home; I began to go alone from the age of six. My mother, so strict about my kissing girls, was strangely indulgent about this. The theatre ran three shows a week, for two days each, and was closed on Sundays. Many weeks I went three times. I remember a summer evening in our yard. Supper is over, the walnut tree throws a heavy shadow. The fireflies are not out yet. My father is off, my mother and her parents are turning the earth in our garden. Some burning sticks and paper on our ash heap fill damp air with low smoke; I express a wish to go to the movies, expecting to be told No. Instead, my mother tells me to go into the house and clean up; I come into the yard again in clean shorts, the shadows slightly heavier, the dew a little wetter; I am given eleven cents and run down Philadelphia Avenue in my ironed shorts and fresh shirt, down past the running ice-plant water, the dime and the penny in my hand. I always ran to the movies. If it was not a movie with Adolphe Menjou, it was a horror picture. People turning into cats—fingers going stubby into paws and hair being blurred in with double exposure—and Egyptian tombs and English houses where doors creak and wind disturbs the curtains and dogs refuse to go into certain rooms because they sense something supersensory. I used to crouch down into the seat and hold my coat in front of my face when I sensed a frightening scene coming, peeking through the buttonhole to find out when it was over. Through the buttonhole Frankenstein's monster glowered; lightning flashed; sweat poured over the bolts that held his face together. On the way home, I ran again, in terror now. Darkness had come, the first show was from seven to nine, by nine even the longest summer day was ending. Each porch along the street seemed to be a tomb crammed with shadows, each shrub seemed to shelter a grasping arm. I ran with a frantic high step, trying to keep my ankles away from the reaching hand. The last and worst terror was our own porch; low brick walls on either side concealed possible cat people. Leaping high, I launched myself at the door and, if no one was in the front of the house, fled through suffocating halls past gaping doorways to the kitchen, where there was always someone working, and a light bulb burning. The ice box. The rickety worn table, oilcloth-covered, where we ate. The windows painted solid black by the interior brightness. But even then I kept my legs away from the furry space beneath the table.

These were Hollywood's comfortable years. The theatre, a shallowly sloped hall too narrow to have a central aisle, was usually crowded. I liked it most on Monday nights, when it was emptiest. It seemed most mine then. I had a favorite seat – rear row, extreme left – and my favorite moment was the instant when the orange side lights, Babylonian in design, were still lit, and the curtain was closed but there was obviously somebody up in the projection room, for the camera had started to whir. In the next instant, I knew, a broad dusty beam of light would fill the air above me, and the titles of the travelogue would appear on the curtains, their projected steadiness undulating as with an unhurried, composed screech the curtains were drawn back, revealing the screen alive with images that then would pass through a few focal adjustments. In that delicate, promissory whir was my favorite moment.

On Saturday afternoons the owner gave us all Hershey bars as we came out of the matinee. On Christmas morning he showed a free hour of cartoons and the superintendent of the Lutheran Sunday school led us in singing carols, gesticulating in front of the high blank screen, no bigger than the shadow of the moth that sometimes landed on the lens. His booming voice would echo curiously on the bare walls, usually so dark and muffling but that on this one morning, containing a loud sea of Christmas children, had a bare, clean, morning quality that echoed. After this special show we all went down to the Town Hall, where the plumpest borough employee, disguised as Santa Claus, gave us each a green box of chocolates. Shillington was small enough to support such traditions.

Concerning the Three Great Secret Things: 1. Sex

In crucial matters, the town was evasive. Sex was an unlikely, though persistent, rumor. My father slapped my mother's bottom and made a throaty noise and I thought it was a petty form of sadism. The major sexual experience of my boyhood was a section of a newsreel showing some women wrestling in a pit of mud. The mud covered their bathing suits so they seemed naked. Thick, interlocking, faceless bodies, they strove and fell. The sight was so disturbingly resonant that afterward, in any movie, two women pulling each other's hair or slapping each other – there was a good deal of this in the movies of the early forties; Ida Lupino was usually one of the women – gave me a tense, watery, drawn-out feeling below the belt. Thenceforth my imaginings about girls moved through mud. In one recurrent scene I staged in

my bed, the girl and I, dressed in our underpants and wrapped around
with ropes, had been plunged from an immense cliff into a secret pond
of mud, by a villain who resembled Peg-Leg Pete. I usually got my hands
free and rescued her; sometimes she rescued me; in any case there
hovered over our spattered, elastic-clad bodies the idea that these were
the last minutes of our lives, and all our shames and reservations were
put behind us. It turned out that she had loved me all along. We climbed
out, into the light. The ropes had hurt our wrists; yet the sweet kernel
of the fantasy lay somehow in the sensations of being tightly bound,
before we rescued each other.

2. Religion

Pragmatically, I have become a Congregationalist, but in the trans-
lucent and tactful church of my adoption my eyes sting, my throat
goes grave, when we sing—what we rarely sang in the Lutheran church
of my childhood—Luther's mighty hymn:

> For still our ancient foe
> Doth seek to work us woe;
> His craft and power are great,
> And arm'd with cruel hate,
> On earth is not his equal.

This immense dirge of praise for the Devil and the world, thunderous,
slow, opaquely proud, nourishes a seed in me I never knew was planted.
How did the patently vapid and drearily businesslike teachings to
which I was lightly exposed succeed in branding me with a Cross?
And a brand so specifically Lutheran, so distinctly Nordic; an obdurate insistence that at the core of the core there is a right-angled
clash to which, of all verbal combinations we can invent, the Apostles'
Creed offers the most adequate correspondence and response.

Of my family, only my father attended the church regularly, returning every Sunday with the Sunday Reading *Eagle* and the com-
plaint that the minister prayed too long. My own relations with the
church were unsuccessful. In Sunday school, I rarely received the perfect attendance pin, though my attendance seemed to me and my parents as perfect as anybody's. Instead, I was given a pencil stamped KINDT'S

FUNERAL HOME. Once, knowing that a lot of racy social activity was going on under its aegis, I tried to join the Luther League; but I had the misfortune to arrive on the night of their Halloween party, and was refused admittance because I was not wearing a costume. And, the worst rebuff, I was once struck by a car on the way to Sunday school. I had the collection nickel in my hand, and held on to it even as I was being dragged fifteen feet on the car's bumper. For this heroic churchmanship I received no palpable credit; the Lutheran church seemed positively to dislike me.

Yet the crustiness, the inhospitality of the container enhanced the oddly lucid thing contained. I do not recall my first doubts; I doubted perhaps abnormally little. And when they came, they never roosted on the branches of the tree, but attacked the roots; if the first article of the Creed stands, the rest follows as water flows downhill. That God, at a remote place and time, took upon Himself the form of a Syrian carpenter and walked the earth willfully healing and abusing and affirming and grieving, appeared to me quite in the character of the Author of the grass. The mystery that more puzzled me as a child was the incarnation of my ego—that omnivorous and somehow pre-existent "I"— in a speck so specifically situated amid the billions of history. Why was I I? The arbitrariness of it astounded me; in comparison, nothing was too marvellous.

Shillington bred a receptivity to the supernatural unrelated to orthodox religion. This is the land of the hex signs, and in the neighboring town of Grille a "witch doctor" hung out a shingle like a qualified M.D. I was struck recently, on reading Frazer's contemptuous list of superstitions in *The Golden Bough*, by how many of them seemed good sense. My grandmother was always muttering little things; she came from a country world of spilled salt and cracked mirrors and new moons and omens. She convinced me, by contagion, that our house was haunted. I punished her by making her stand guard outside the bathroom when I was in it. If I found she had fallen asleep in the shadowy hallway crawling with ghosts, I would leap up on her back and pummel her with a fury that troubles me now.

Imagine my old neighborhood as an African village; under the pointed roofs tom-toms beat, premonitions prowl, and in the darkness naked superstition in all her plausibility blooms:

The Night-blooming Cereus

It was during the war; early in the war, 1942. *Collier's* had printed a cover showing Hirohito, splendidly costumed and fanged, standing malevolently in front of a bedraggled, bewildered Hitler and an even more decrepit and craven Mussolini. Our troops in the Pacific reeled from island to island; the Japanese seemed a race of demons capable of anything. The night-blooming cereus was the property of a family who lived down the street in a stucco house that on the inside was narrow and dark in the way that houses in the middle of the country sometimes are. The parlor was crowded with obscure furniture decked out with antimacassars and porcelain doodads. At Christmas a splendiferous tree appeared in that parlor, hung with pounds of tinsel and strung popcorn and paper chains and pretzels and balls and intricate, figurative ornaments that must have been rescued from the previous century.

The blooming of the cereus was to be an event in the neighborhood; for days we had been waiting. This night—a clear warm night, in August or September—word came, somehow. My mother and grandmother and I rushed down Philadelphia Avenue in the dark. It was late; I should have been in bed. I remembered the night I was refused permission to go to the poorhouse fire. The plant stood at the side of the house, in a narrow space between the stucco wall and the hedge. A knot of neighborhood women had already gathered; heavy shoulders and hair buns were silhouetted in an indeterminate light. On its twisted, unreal stem the flower had opened its unnaturally brilliant petals. But no one was looking at it. For overhead, in the north of a black sky strewn with stars like thrown salt, the wandering fingers of an aurora borealis gestured, now lengthening and brightening so that shades of blue and green could be distinguished, now ebbing until it seemed there was nothing there at all. It was a rare sight this far south. The women muttered, sighed, and, as if involuntarily, out of the friction of their bodies, moaned. Standing among their legs and skirts, I was slapped by a sudden cold wave of fear. "Is it the end of the world?" one of the women asked. There was no answer. And then a plane went over, its red lights blinking, its motors no louder than the drone of a wasp. Japanese. The Japanese were going to bomb Shillington, the center of the nation. I waited for the bomb, and without words prayed, expecting a miracle, for the appearance of angels and Japanese in the sky was restrained by the same impossibility, an impossibility that the swollen waxy brilliant white of the flower by my knees had sucked from the night.

The plane of course passed; it was one of ours; my prayer was answered with the usual appearance of absence. We went home, and the world reconstituted its veneer of reason, but the moans of the women had rubbed something in me permanently bare.

3. Art

Leafing through a scrapbook my mother long ago made of my childhood drawings, I was greeted by one I had titled "Mr. Sun talking to Old Man Winter in his Office." Old Man Winter, a cloud with stick legs, and his host, a radiant ball with similar legs, sit at ease, both smiling, on two chairs that are the only furniture of the solar office. That the source of all light should have, somewhere, an office, suited my conception of an artist, who was someone who lived in a small town like Shillington, and who, equipped with pencils and paper, practiced his solitary trade as methodically as the dentist practiced his. And indeed, that is how it is at present with me.

Goethe—probably among others—says to be wary of our youthful wishes, for in maturity we are apt to get them. I go back, now, to Pennsylvania, and on one of the walls of the house in which my parents now live there hangs a photograph of myself as a boy. I am smiling, and staring with clear eyes at something in the corner of the room. I stand before that photograph, and am disappointed to receive no flicker, not the shadow of a flicker, of approval, of gratitude. The boy continues to smile at the corner of the room, beyond me. That boy is not a ghost to me, he is real to me; it is I who am a ghost to him. I, in my present state, was one of the ghosts that haunted his childhood. Like some phantom conjured by this child from a glue bottle, I have executed his commands; acquired pencils, paper, and an office. Now I wait apprehensively for his next command, or at least a nod of appreciation, and he smiles through me, as if I am already transparent with failure.

He saw art—between drawing and writing he ignorantly made no distinction—as a method of riding a thin pencil line out of Shillington, out of time altogether, into an infinity of unseen and even unborn hearts. He pictured this infinity as radiant. How innocent! But his assumption here, like his assumptions on religion and politics, is one for which I have found no certain substitute. He loved blank paper and obedience to this love led me to a difficult artistic attempt. I reasoned thus: just as the paper is the basis for the marks upon it, might not events be contingent upon a never-expressed (because featureless) ground? Is the true marvel of Sunday skaters the pattern of their pirouettes or the fact that they are silently upheld? Blankness is not emptiness; we may skate upon an intense radiance we do not see because we see nothing else. And in fact there is a color, a quiet but tireless goodness that things at rest, like a brick wall or a small stone, seem to affirm. A wordless reassurance these things are pressing to give. An hallucination? To transcribe middleness with all its grits, bumps, and anonymities, in its fullness of satisfaction and mystery: is it possible or, in view of the suffering that violently colors the periphery and that at all moments threatens to move into the center, worth doing? Possibly not; but the horse-chestnut trees, the telephone poles, the porches, the green hedges recede to a calm point that in my subjective geography is still the center of the world.

End of Boyhood

I was walking down this Philadelphia Avenue one April and was just stepping over the shallow little rain gutter in the pavement that could throw you if you were on roller skates—though it had been years since I had been on roller skates—when from the semidetached house across the street a boy broke and ran. He was the youngest of six sons. All of his brothers were in the armed services, and five blue stars hung in his home's front window. He was several years older than I, and used to annoy my grandparents by walking through our yard, down past the grape arbor, on his way to high school. Long-legged, he was now running diagonally across the high-crowned street. I was the only other person out in the air. "Chonny!" he called. I was flattered to have him, so tall and grown, speak to me. "Did you hear?"

"No. What?"

"On the radio. The President is dead."

That summer the war ended, and that fall, suddenly mobile, we moved away from the big white house. We moved on Halloween night. As the movers were fitting the last pieces of furniture, furniture that had not moved since I was born, into their truck, little figures dressed as ghosts and cats flitted in and out of the shadows of the street. A few rang our bell, and when my mother opened the door they were frightened by the empty rooms they saw behind her, and went away without begging. When the last things had been packed, and the kitchen light turned off, and the doors locked, the three of us—my grandparents were already at the new house—got into the old Buick my father had bought—in Shillington we had never had a car, for we could walk everywhere—and drove up the street, east, toward the poorhouse and beyond. Somewhat self-consciously and cruelly dramatizing my grief, for I was thirteen and beginning to be cunning, I twisted and watched our house recede through the rear window. Moonlight momentarily caught in an upper pane; then the reflection passed, and the brightest thing was the white brick wall itself. Against the broad blank part where I used to bat a tennis ball for hours at a time, the silhouette of the dogwood tree stood confused with the shapes of the other bushes in our side yard, but taller. I turned away before it would have disappeared from sight; and so it is that my shadow has always remained in one place.

MAKEUP

MICHAEL CLARK

"I was born in Chester, Pennsylvania, in a hospital called Crozer Homeopathic Hospital and Home for Incurables. After I graduated from high school, I left the state to go to college nearby, then to the air force for four years, then to a master's program in Ohio, then to the Ph.D. program in English at Wisconsin. It wasn't in my plans to come back to my birthplace, though that is what happened. Now I teach at Widener University, just about a mile from good old Crozer Hospital.

"This has led to a rather odd sense of everyday existence: contemplating from a new perspective the reminders of my early life. I say new perspective because my four years in the military were rather radical in affecting me: four years in starched uniforms boiling under the Texas sun gave me new eyes.

"And, too, I wonder about being included in a volume of Pennsylvania writers. I never really think now (or thought before) of myself as a Pennsylvanian, I suppose because that is a rather large abstraction. But the place where I grew up has always had a special fascination for me. So I guess I see myself as a native of Chester, a place which just happens to be in Pennsylvania. Like most writers, I depend heavily on memory for the things that I write about. Because of the combination of two historical accidents—both my happening to have been born here and my happening to find employment here—my chances of writing about a Pennsylvania locale do not simply double: they rise exponentially. Indeed, that is what I have found. Much of my short fiction deals with my early memories. I am currently beginning a novel set in Chester in the 1950s.

"All of this may sound like public relations stuff for all I know. But things like that are all that I know. I don't know what the state flower is, say, but I do know very vividly a winter noon in 1955: the sense of holding a small chilled bottle of chocolate milk, sitting in the basement of Immaculate Heart of Mary grade school, *eating a peanut butter sandwich, waiting for the end of the school day so that I could walk across Chester, back to my home. The inner state is—and always has been—more real than the outer state."*

*   *   *

This short story by Michael Clark, who also writes essays and poems, originally appeared in a slightly different form in Arizona Quarterly.

H IS HEAD SHONE under the flourescent lights. Seventy-two years old and his hair, slicked down, oily, was still black—mostly, anyway—and his face still had that shadowed look, as if he got that color from using gunblue instead of aftershave.

He had given mother fifteen dollars to have her hair done and to buy another eyebrow liner. He had to buy a tool at the Sears store, he told her. But I think that he really just wanted to go for a walk and have the chance to talk uninterruptedly with me.

We went down the escalator in Gimbels and out into the Granite Run Mall.

I expressed amazement to him about the mall, about its size, its newness, its sleek cleanliness, but inwardly I felt a twinge of regret. It had been an old granite quarry that they had filled in and smoothed over and paved and built upon. When I was young, I and my friends would follow the railroad tracks and hike the seven miles from Chester in order to scale its ragged walls and to play in the undergrowth, which hid decaying machinery. We searched for treasures in the bottom of that pit. The "No Trespassing" signs meant nothing to us.

My father never knew of those and other similar wild excursions of my youth. That added a special twinge to the present nostalgia.

I asked him how he liked their new house.

"Nice," he said simply, but with some emotion. "Just down the road's Media," he said waving his hand in the direction of the county seat. "They keep the crime away."

I didn't know who "they" were. I suppose he meant the judges.

"I don't know what I'm going to do," he said, changing the subject.

These were tough times, I knew. After a tough life—raising seven

children on meager paychecks—now in retirement, times were tougher.
Mom was going bad on him. That much I had learned already. His
pension was running out. Social Security covered the house payments
but wasn't enough to live on.

"I took my gold watch to the jeweler's the other day." I knew what
he was talking about, that gold watch. At the age of thirteen (in 1919)
he started working for Miller's dairy in Chester, Pennsylvania. After
twenty-five years of work, they gave him a gold watch. After thirty-
four years, he quit and took a succession of low-paying (though *better-
paying*) jobs, all in Chester. Several years before, after I had moved
to the Midwest, he had saved enough to move out of the old row-
house. He moved out to the suburbs, to a nice neighborhood where
they might enjoy themselves. It was near the malls, away from the
crime and noise.

Now in retirement, he had to sell the watch.

"Jeweler told me that it wasn't even gold, only gold-filled. Worth
maybe six bucks. Don't even keep time anymore."

I wasn't sure what he wanted from me. He knew that I wasn't in
a position to help him financially, and I knew that he wouldn't ask
for money unless perhaps things were absolutely desperate and even
then I don't think he would ask. But he wanted something. Pity,
perhaps.

"I don't know what I'm going to do," he said.

It was a minute before I came to understand that he wasn't speaking of money at all.

"Mom, she's in bad shape."

I knew that Medicare didn't pay all of the doctor's bills.

"Maybe I can help out some if she really needs to see the docs."

"Doctors can't help her." He had a wistful, helpless look on his
blue face.

I didn't want to bring up the word senility, but I realized that that
was what he was getting at.

"She wakes up in the morning crying. Sometimes in the middle
of the night."

I nodded my head.

"When she gets dressed, she accuses me of stealing her eyebrow
pencil . . . hysterical."

"Ah," I said and felt a sadness stealing over me. I didn't want to hear anymore. Somehow I didn't want to be part of their lives anymore. I felt that I wanted to get away but was chained fast—and him pecking at my heart.

"The other night she cried all night. By three in the morning, I started beating her. I'm ashamed to say it, but I beat her."

There were no tears, but he was sobbing, his fat stomach hitching up and down. Out in the mall, we were seated in plastic chairs underneath some potted trees and shrubs. I felt shame and anger and pity and mostly terror. I wished that I hadn't come to visit.

"She keeps accusing me of stealing her eyebrow pencils."

I had had my own life for a long time, my own problems. I was thirty-five years old. I was busy trying to avoid the errors he had made. I was busy with other errors, no doubt, but one's own problems are a life's work. I was too busy.

We slowly walked back to meet her. We never did get to buy the hammer.

"The priest tells me that people who work at this eight hours and go home can handle it."

I wasn't sure what he was getting at, once again.

". . . but twenty-four hours a day constantly . . . I just can't do it."

He was leading me into new territory. He kept talking, and slowly I came to understand that he was speaking about institutionalizing her. And then I realized what he really wanted from me. Not money, not time, but approval.

"Do it, Dad," I said as we were about to enter Gimbels. It was a hard thing to say, but I meant it.

Before we got back to the beauty salon, we spied her standing at the cosmetics counter. Her cane was lying on the floor next to her, and she was rooting in her purse. The clerk had rung up the price of an eyebrow pencil, skin moisturizers, bubblebath, rouge, and lipstick. She had only a dollar left over from her hairdo. Father paid the $17.76.

I was to stay that night and to leave the next morning. Mother sat on the porch rocking as he showed me around the house. They had sold their other house because they wanted to live in the suburbs in their old age and because the old house was two stories. This one was all on one floor, so mother could get around, not easily, but well enough. He showed me the cellar. "My hideaway," he said. He seemed in a lighter mood. He bantered.

"I go here when I've had too much of the world." But I knew what was unstated; "*I go here to get away from her.*" No, she could never climb those stairs. I noticed a latch on the cellar side of the door. She couldn't even open the door to yell down at him if he wanted to use that latch.

The cellar showed that he was a vigorous seventy-two. An orderly workbench, but signs everywhere of works in progress: an open bag of Sackcrete, a half-made toy still in a vise—for one of the grandchildren, no doubt. *He* hadn't slowed down any.

"I talked with all the others," he said when he turned solemn all of a sudden. "They all agree with you." It was about having her committed. I was the last. Before me the other six had been marshaled home and sounded out, and they said like I did once again, "Do it."

There seemed to be a great struggle going on in him. He looked up at me. "It ain't easy after fifty years together." He had my pity: "You *got* to do it." It meant a lot to him. He had to be free of that which he could not control. But we had to approve, give him a mandate. The sad fact is that some burdens are too great and the duty merely human.

When I woke up the next morning, I heard her crying in her bedroom. Again it made me sorry that I had come home. "You took it," I heard her scream at him.

I had planned to leave early, but Dad asked me to wait till after breakfast, and then he took me aside and asked me to stay with her while he drove up to the drugstore. "Eyebrow pencil," he said, shaking his head.

I didn't say anything but resolved to tell him once again before I left that he should have her committed. She needed better care than he could provide.

He left, and we sat on the porch together, she rocking and I rocking.

As soon as he was out the door, before he got out of the driveway, she was appealing to me for help.

"He steals my eyebrow pencils," she said.

"No, he doesn't," I said savagely, looking up; and for a moment seeing her clear blue eyes that had brought me through life, I wanted to believe—did believe—what she said. We had hardly talked at all during my visit, and now I felt ashamed of myself. I pictured her in a white room alone.

She stared at me a moment. Then, looking away, she brushed her hand in front of her face as if dismissing a fly and then in a note of disgust muttered, "Oh, he *told* you," as if she were used to being disbelieved, in favor of him.

She sat there stoically, as she had acted stoically all of those fifty years; taking his abuse, taking his orders, taking his lovemaking, but not his love. She sat and rocked.

I was angry at her and sorry for her and angry at him and sorry for him too. But mostly I was wishing that I had not come.

"Your license is coming off," she said pointing to my car in the driveway. It was hanging down at an angle. She said it simply, like a child who doesn't know what rancor is.

"I have to get a screwdriver," I said.

I was happy for the opportunity to flee (like my father before me) to the cellar. It was cool and damp. I felt a flood of relief, happiness, even, to get away. I would wait down there until he came back.

Among the tools hanging on the wall, there was no screwdriver. I opened the toolbox that sat on the bench. When I took off its top compartment, I discovered that its interior was filled with only one thing: eyebrow pencils.

GUS ZERNIAL AND ME

JERRY SPINELLI

"Unlike some states, Pennsylvania cannot be characterized as mostly this or that (industrial, agricultural, tourist). Pennsylvania can teach you balance, diversity. Pennsylvania is running the steel girder gauntlet beneath the Market Street El and finding yourself an hour later amid the silos and cornfields of Lancaster County. At one o'clock on an August afternoon, it's passing black bikers lounging in stuffed chairs on the sidewalk before the Wheels of Soul clubhouse, and at two o'clock buying five cantaloupes from a barefooted girl in a long purple dress at a table along Route 340.

"The white suburbanite who dwells between these two extremes is effectively excluded from each. The belief that his color makes him unwelcome in West Philadelphia advises him to punch down the buttons on his car doors, and he moves up Market Street like the rider of a tourist monorail, fascinated by what he sees and somewhat envious that he cannot be part of it. In Lancaster the black garb and beards and buggies of the Amish send a similar signal: We don't particularly want you here gawking at us, but since you are here, you may come close enough to buy a cantaloupe, but no closer.

"And so the white suburban dweller can feel himself an outsider—as if he were in a different state—only a few miles in either direction from his home. It is an alienation to be cherished, for it offers relief from the bland, aluminum-sided monotony of his own landscape."

*   *   *

Jerry Spinelli, who lives in Havertown, has published stories, articles, poems, and young adult novels: Space Station Seventh Grade, Who Put That Hair in My Toothbrush? and Night of the Whale. This short story appeared first in Philadelphia Magazine and was subsequently reprinted in Best Sports Stories 1982.

"LOOK AT YOU. You're dirty again. Your friend is here."
The nun hauled me to the nearest sink and scrubbed my face nearly raw. She took scant care to keep the soap out of my eyes. It was from the soap that I cried. The rough treatment I was used to. I expected it.

I lived in an orphanage. I was therefore known to the kids in town as a "homie." That alone was enough to make me feel different, but even among the homies I seemed to be an outcast.

For one thing I was a wet-the-bed, a status that entitled me to be paddled every night as I emerged dripping wet from the shower. In bed I would stay awake as long as I could, only to be betrayed by sleep. In the morning, with the inevitability of eternal judgment, I would waken to the damp, faint mustiness of my sin.

For another thing, I was smart. I could read in the first grade. My hand was forever waving wildly in the air. Sometimes a whole day seemed to pass with no one volunteering answers but me. Time and again the nun would scan the seats in vain for another hand. She would try to coax answers from slumping heads. Then, with a sigh, she would finally turn to me and, flicking her forefinger, release me from my bondage of silence. Though my answers were invariably correct, the nun never seemed as happy to receive them as I did to give them.

Then one day during recess in the playground, three of the bigger (and dumber) kids in the class came up to me. As usual I was in the dirt near the roots of a huge old tree, playing marbles against myself. One of the big kids said, "Stand up."

I stood up.

"How come you always raise yer hand?" he asked.

I shrugged.

"How come?"

"I know the answers."

"Well don't raise yer hand no more."

I squealed. "What?"

"You deaf?" he snarled. Then he placed my biggest marble on top of my shoe, and with the heel of his shoe he ground the marble into my foot.

I was too upset to appreciate the befuddled look on the nun's face the rest of the day as she kept glancing at my hand which, since recess, had become firmly desk-bound.

Then there was the great three-day mystery. It took place in the classroom. On the first day it started with the nun turning from the blackboard and sniffing into the space above our heads, rabbitlike. Her chalk hand was still pasted on the board, stopped in the middle of a word. Several more times she sniffed that day, and once, while we were doing our spelling, she bent over and ran her pointer along the black, dusty space beneath the radiator.

On the second day she turned from the blackboard, chalk hand and all, and announced, "Alright—out. Out!" We filed outside, the head nun went in, and a half hour later we returned. All windows were open, as was the door.

On the third day she came stalking down the aisles. My eyes were fixed on my spelling, but I could trace her movement by the soft rustle of her skirt. It stopped right behind me. Then came the most horrible shriek: "Eeeeeey ahhhh-HAH!"

It was me. It seems I had an unconscious habit of slipping out of my shoes while sitting in class. And it seems, as I was to learn later, that I was afflicted with a condition in which a perspiring foot, however clean, gives off an overwhelming odor.

Of course, I was thenceforth forbidden to go anywhere unshod outside the shower room. And kids I never knew found it impossible to pass me without pinching their nostrils. "Feet," they would honk.

These things made me feel I was the fly in every pie. Apparently I had been born with a terrible power: I spoiled everything around me.

I had forgotten that a friend would be coming for me on this particular Saturday. ("Friend" was the home's word for anyone who came to visit you or take you out. A friend was usually a perfect stranger, but could also be a relative or even a long-lost parent. Some of the homies had a long string of friends. This was to be my first.) Why a friend would want to visit me, I couldn't imagine.

He was a fat little man, shorter than the nuns. He held a straw hat in front of him with both hands.

He smiled. "How would you like to go to a ball game?"

"Okay," I said.

It turned out to be a baseball game in the city. It might as well have been Rumanian rugby. I had heard of baseball, but I had never played it and knew next to nothing about it. Except for marbles, I was woefully unathletic.

The game was at Shibe Park. A sign said, HOME OF THE PHILADEL-

PHIA A's. Now it began to make sense: the A's were orphans, too. They were playing the Boston Red Sox. The man (Mr. Coleman was his name) took me by the hand, stunned and docile, through dusty, hawking, mustard-sweet catacombs, up endless iron stairways, finally to emerge onto what I was told were the bleachers. We were beyond what was known as left field.

It was the most beautiful sight I had ever seen—a vast, fan-shaped, emerald-green lawn. I had never known the earth could be so immaculate. It was all so ordered, so perfect. Two utterly straight and pure-white lines diverged from a point called home plate and created the borders of this perfection, along with the tall green fence that they intersected. I was vaguely comforted that the white lines did not diverge forever.

Men toting rakes and other implements came out of nowhere and swarmed over the field.

Mr. Coleman saw my puzzlement and chuckled. "That's not baseball. That's the grounds crew. Watch the tractor."

And sure enough a little blue tractor came putting out from under the grandstand, dragging what looked like a large window screen. It headed for the tawny, half-moon-shaped portion of the field where no grass grew. From first base to third base it traveled, tracing exquisite loops, and what the screen passed over, it left in a condition so smooth and flat and unmarked that it could not possibly be called dirt.

Meanwhile the men with rakes were smoothing the field around the bases where the tractor screen could not reach. And other men were smoothing out the pitcher's mound and the home-plate area, or painting home plate itself, or repairing the white lines where someone had stepped.

Then, as if by signal, the men began leaving the field. The rakers trailed their rakes behind, to erase their own footprints.

"Now the water," said Mr. Coleman.

Two men were wheeling a large hose reel to near the pitcher's mound. They pulled out two hoses and began to spray the dirt portion.

"Keeps the dust down," said Mr. Coleman, answering my unspoken question.

Dust or no dust, I did not like the water men. I found myself urging them to pass over the dirt lightly, but they insisted on wetting it down so thoroughly that in a few minutes the infield had turned from yellowish to dark gray.

There was a lilt of expectancy in Mr. Coleman's next announcement, and an almost conspiratorial whisper. "Now—the bases."

What's wrong with the bases, I wondered, looking at the three gray squares on the infield. Then, to my amazement I discovered I had not been looking at the real bases at all. They were just covers which a man was removing one by one. Now the true bases were revealed—spanking snow-white cubes that had never been touched. And I saw now the real reason they had made the infield so dark with water—to dramatically set off the gleaming bases.

The base man left the field. There it was, more beautiful, more perfect than when I had entered. The grounds crew, before our very eyes, had done as much a miracle as man could do.

I leaped to my feet. I clapped and cheered. What a performance!

A few seconds later I was crushed. Men in baggy flannel knickers were springing onto the field, scattering to all points. I felt on my own skin every footprint they left on the immaculate infield.

Until that moment Mr. Coleman had been a man of smiles. Now he was out-and-out laughing, his eyes watering. "These are the players," he said, nodding toward the field. I felt his hand cup my shoulder and pull me a little toward him. "Now the game's ready to start."

Then he drew his face near to mine and whispered, "See him?" He was pointing to a player jogging across the grass toward us. He didn't stop till he was almost to the fence. Then he turned around and faced home plate. He simply stood there. He was almost directly beneath us, so there wasn't much to see except his blue cap and his shoulders and a large blue number on his back. "That's Gus Zernial," Mr. Coleman told me.

"Who's he?" I said.

"The left fielder."

"What's he doing?"

"He's playing left field."

"He's just standing there."

"Well, that's right. He doesn't have much to do out there. But wait'll he gets to bat." Here Mr. Coleman put his lips right to my ear. "Maybe he'll hit a home run."

I turned to him full face. "Is that good?"

Mr. Coleman said nothing. He simply closed his eyes and smiled and nodded profoundly, and I knew that a home run, whatever it was, was a very very good thing.

The game as I recall it was a series of whispered prophecies come true, few of them having to do with the actual action of the game.

Mr. Coleman told me to keep an eye on the third-base coach. And for inning after inning the third-base coach kept me enthralled with his antics and contortions and twitches. He seemed plagued by either poison ivy or a particular insistent mosquito. Even the batters seemed distracted, for they kept turning away from the pitcher to look at the third-base coach.

"He's giving the signs," said Mr. Coleman.

"Oh," I said.

When the hot-dog man came down our aisle, Mr. Coleman raised his arm and shouted, "Two!" Then, as he leaned across me to pass along the money: "Watch the mustard. Watch."

I watched. Like that of the grounds crew it was a virtuoso performance. Two hot-dog rolls in the same hand – up goes the lid of the white carton and into the rising steam with gleaming silver tweezers – a slight hesitation (he's fishing for the best!) – then they're out, two reddish, dripping morsels – deftly laid in their rolls. "Waaatch . . ." came my last warning. Into the giant mustard jar with a tongue depressor and . . . and . . . it was done. Before my eyes could digest the sight, the hot dogs were being passed down the row to us. All I had seen was a lightning flicker of the tongue depressor over the rolls, and yet when they reached us, sure enough, anointing each hot dog was a neat strip of creamy, bright yellow mustard.

Even as I chewed, my eyes never left the lightning-handed hot-dog man until he disappeared into the crowd.

A player slid. Home plate vanished under a layer of dust. Mr. Coleman nudged me. "Watch the umpire." The umpire pulled something from his hip pocket – it was a little whisk broom. With brisk assured ceremony he squatted in the dust and – whish-whish-whish – home plate reappeared. I decided then and there I wanted to be an umpire.

There were many other prophecies. That everyone would boo at such and such a time. That the manager would spit every time he left the dugout. That when the manager and umpire argued they would touch noses. That it would become very hot in the bleachers. That in the seventh inning everyone in the ball park would stand up and stretch.

And they all came true, every one. I relished the predictability of it all. My favorite was the seventh-inning stretch. "Now?" I kept asking. "Now," he finally said. I shot up, determined to be first. I looked around. Slowly they were rising, all around me, by the thousands, rising for the seventh-inning stretch. Not a single soul was left sitting. I honestly did not feel stiff or tired, but I'm sure no one could tell by the great, long stretch that I did.

Inning after inning Gus Zernial trotted back and forth from left field to the dugout.

"Did he hit a home run yet?" I kept pestering.

"Not yet," said Mr. Coleman. The confidential glee was gone from his voice. He sounded a little like a priest. "It's not for sure, now. All he can do is try. Don't get your hopes up too high."

I guess my hopes were up too high, for Mr. Coleman stared worriedly at me for a minute. The smile returned. "But I'll tell you one thing," he whispered, "if he *does* hit a home run, do you know what he'll do?"

"What?"

"He'll tip his cap."

"He will?"

He placed his hand over his heart. "Promise."

It was in the last inning of the ball game when a sudden commotion erupted around me. Everyone in the bleachers seemed to shout in unison and bolt to his feet, including Mr. Coleman. Then I saw it—the baseball—dove-white, like the bases, falling from the sun-squinting sky, angel-white against the murky girdered ceiling, engulfed at last in a mass of frantically straining arms several aisles away.

I didn't have to be told. It was a home run.

"Gus Zernial?" I screamed up at Mr. Coleman. "Gus Zernial?"

The way he hugged me, I knew that it was.

What a wonderful thing is a home run, I thought. The joy that it brought. The ecstasy. I could think of it only as a gift, a kind of salvation. It was a religious thing, a home run, something sacramental. I thought of the priest offering the wafer, and of the Magi bearing gifts, and of the archbishop who came every Christmas and we knew then that we would get ice cream. Now there was the home run, delivered unto the bleachers. Now there was the priest and there were the Magi and there was the archbishop and there was Gus Zernial.

I shaded my eyes so as to see most clearly the man trotting around the bases. I saw him touch every bag. I saw him shake the hand of the third-base coach as he passed by. I saw him step decisively upon home plate and shake the hands of the next batter and the batboy and I saw him received into the welcoming arms of the dugout. But I did not see him tip his cap.

I kept silent, not wanting to show disappointment. All of Mr. Coleman's other prophecies had come true, even the "not for sure" home run. Who was I to quibble over one unfulfilled detail? I—a wiseacre, wet-the-bed, stinky-footed homie.

But inside I couldn't help quibbling. Something was longing for the tipped cap even more than for the home run. Without the tipped cap the home run was incomplete, tradition was left dangling. I couldn't help wondering: *Is it me? Does Gus Zernial know I'm in the bleachers?* I tightened my shoelaces.

The answer came a few minutes later. Gus Zernial was trotting out to take his place in left field, and again the bleachers erupted. They flailed their arms. They screamed and whistled. "Gus! Gus! Gus!" they chanted.

But Gus Zernial did not seem to hear. He merely stood there facing the infield, while just behind and above him 5,000 people were going mad.

I dared not join the crowd. Oh, I wanted to. I wanted to chant his name, wave my arms and cheer him. I wanted to go mad, too. But I was afraid he might see me.

Suddenly the cheering shot to a deafening pitch. Down below Gus Zernial was turning—not all the way, just his head and shoulders, so that the brim of the blue cap was now facing the bleachers and you could see the the fancy white "A" on it, and now his head was tilting upward and there was the face of the great Gus Zernial and he was looking right up into the bleachers—*he was looking right at me*—and with a delicacy I would never expect, he took the blue brim between his thumb and forefinger and briefly, briefly and forever, tipped his cap.

Solid Walls

Karen Rile

"My father's ancestors landed near Philadelphia in the seventeenth century. My mother's hung back in the British Isles for a few hundred more years, but southeastern Pennsylvania is where they've all stayed, all except me. I had to move to St. Louis, Missouri, in 1983 because my husband was scheduled to continue his postgraduate medical training here, but when I say the word 'home', I think of Philadelphia: City Hall, the huge, rusty clothespin, soft pretzels with brown mustard, the Wissahickon Creek. And though the weather here by the Mississippi is strikingly similar to home—humid in summer and freezing in winter—and though the traffic flows freer at 5:00 P.M. here than at midnight on the Schuykill Expressway, and though prices are low here and liquor may be purchased in supermarkets, I am constantly looking over my shoulder back to the Delaware, the Schuykill, the Wissahickon, back home. I want to watch the scullers from the East River Drive at dusk, to sit behind a plaster column in the amphitheater of the Academy and listen to the orchestra, to trot along the Fairmont Park bridle path beside the horses, all the way to Valley Green, to mingle with the one-legged pigeons on the Chestnut Hill Local platform at Thirtieth Street Station. Why would anyone ever leave?"

*   *   *

Karen Rile's first novel, Winter Music (1983), was published when she was only twenty-five years old. She lists as hobbies: distance running, swimming, writing in notebooks, cooking, animal husbandry, listening to music, driving on Highway 70 from Pennsylvania to Missouri and back. This short story has never before been published.

I GREW UP in a house in Philadelphia with bars on the basement windows. The bars were the same rusty red-brown color as the roof tiles and all the exterior wood and metal work. They must have been as old as the house itself, built in the nineteen-twenties. Perhaps the bars had been installed to catch the drifting leaves that swirled to meet the window glass. Those dead leaves stuck in bunches and we had to clean them out with our fingers at the end of every autumn. I think that the bars were really intended as a half-hearted deterrent against crime: all of the houses on Upsal Street had them, but we also had big old-fashioned flat cellar doors with no locks, and no burglar would have had trouble breaking in.

All the houses in West Mount Airy, our neighborhood, seemed to get burglarized, some more than once, and one of our neighbors actually surprised some thieves and chased them out of her house, down the street. They were teenaged boys: we saw them; we were out raking leaves when they ran by.

Our house was invariably spared, for all the years we lived there. We guessed it was because we had a junky old Ford Falcon and so many kids, and anyone glancing at the mess of toys and tricycles littering the front porch would know our parents couldn't have much of value inside. Our grandfather, who lived on the Main Line, took advantage of this by storing his trunk of silver coins in a remote closet on our third floor. My sisters and I would go up there now and then and open it, gazing at the rolls and rolls of ancient dimes and quarters, a regular treasure chest, safe and sound.

All day long we ran inside and out of the house, slamming the screen door behind us, never bothering to lock it because we were too lazy to wear keys on a string around our necks. We left our bicycles leaning against the back porch and nobody touched them. We thought of our property line as a magic circle that no one would violate—perhaps because we believed this, it was true.

There were seven houses on our side of the street and twelve on the opposite, because some of those were twins. There were four other white families beside us, though by the time our parents moved away, in the late seventies, three elderly black couples had retired and sold their houses to young whites. It was a precious neighborhood, even to the children, and we spoke of it with a reverence. Even the youngest of us knew that we were special: living in a perfect integrated community encased by a city which was seething with hostile segregation.

Our neighbors who weren't lawyers or doctors were the principals of public schools. This was almost without exception. There was one concert pianist, then our father, with his small advertising agency and our mother who managed the careers of a dozen classical musicians from two rooms on our third floor. None of the children on our street went to the public school four blocks away, where the kids were dangerous, rough, bussed-in from the inner city. Likewise, no one went to the parochial school around the corner. This was also an all black school and the kids, most of whom were not Catholic, came from a dangerous zone, blocks away, on the other side of Germantown Avenue.

Everybody went to private schools. My sisters and I went to a Catholic convent school about two miles away, but most of the other kids, like Walter and Wimple and Charles went to the various Quaker schools all over the city. These were expensive, progressive places with names like "Germantown Friends," "Greene Street Friends," and "Friends Select." The Society of Friends are pacifists, so these kids had to go to school on Memorial Day, although none of them were really Quaker. In fact, hardly anyone who went to these schools was a Quaker, since there are few Quakers left. This filled us with pride, since that half of our heritage which is not Catholic is mostly Quaker. Those were Quaker dimes and quarters hidden on our third floor.

At the top of our street, in the first house past the train station, lived Walter and Wimple, two brothers. Wimple was a few years older than me and Walter was younger than my sister Kathryn. Behind their backs we called them Palter and Pimple. Wimple's name was short for Winifred, and for years before I learned the correct pronunciation, I thought it was the same as the name for the light slotted ball we used with our plastic baseball bat. Walter and Wimple were black and they were both fat, but Wimple was very tall. He had a peculiar circle of orange hair, the size of a quarter, on his scalp. Our mother told us not to ask him about it because it might be worms. The thought of Wimple having worms in his head bothered us, so we avoided him. Walter was the plumper of the two and he always shouted. Our mother said maybe he was hard-of-hearing, so we took to yelling back at him, just in case. Walter and Wimple went to a Quaker school near ours, but theirs was more expensive, as they liked to point out. They bragged

that their school had a football field and they got out of class to go
to meeting, which meant sitting around doing nothing. We didn't like
to play football and we got to skip Monday morning classes once a
month for Mass, where we sang nice guitar folk hymns. We asked them
if they liked Quaker school so much, how come they didn't turn Quaker.
This made them mad, since their family was Methodist.

Walter and Wimple were the only boys in our lives for years until
one day in the Acme we ran into the mother of a boy I used to play
with before we bought our house, when we used to live in an apartment over on Pelham Road, three blocks away, when Kathryn was
only a baby. Charles, his mother and father, lived in a house on that
street, and until I was six I used to walk down to his house to play.
After that we moved and I didn't see him for a long, long time, which
was fine with me.

Charles' mother had a way of talking with her eyes closed. Her eyelids were bulgy and she would open them only when she got to the
end of her sentence. She called Charles "Charles," never Chuck or
Charlie. She talked about nothing but Charles and she talked a lot.
I could tell our mother was trying to get away from her because she
was hopping from foot to foot. Sometimes she got terrible foot cramps
from the supermarket floor, which was cold and hard, and hopping
helped prevent them. Our baby sister, Clarissa, who was sitting in the
little seat at the front of the grocery cart, started to throw up on our
mother's sleeve. Our mother said she really had to be going, but maybe
Charles would come over and play tomorrow. I was furious. We walked
away, leaving Charles's mother to squeeze the avocados.

The next morning Kathryn and I were sitting on the steps playing
Concentration and listening to Clarissa, who was wailing about something inside. We looked up and saw Charles up by the train station,
coming in our direction. I hadn't seen him in years, but I knew his
round face and curly blonde hair. I ran inside, past the babysitter who
was bouncing the grouchy Clarissa on her lap, upstairs to the third
floor, past our mother's secretary, and hid in the closet with the silver
coins and our mother's office stationery. Our mother knocked on the
closet door and asked me what was wrong. I told her to go away, but
downstairs Charles was already ringing the doorbell. Through the stairwell we could hear my sister Kathryn telling him that I was home and

then her calling my name. Our mother made me go down, though I glared at her. I was embarrassed to be seen with a new boy.

I showed Charles the backyard, the side yard, the tree house and the violet patch. We came inside and drank Hi-C. Charles asked if we didn't have any Coke and I told him we didn't like it. Really we did, but it was expensive and we weren't allowed to open a bottle without permission. Our family had rules about food, like: never eat more than half a banana at a time; no more than a small glass of orange juice at breakfast. Only my sister Kathryn was permitted to drink the store-bought milk because she was too thin. The rest of us drank powdered instant, which was supposed to be good for our hearts.

Charles said Hi-C was gross, but finished his anyway. He went outside and I told him I'd show him the special place where I got samples for my rock collection.

The rock bed was part of the train station. It was really a path that rush hour people walked on as a shortcut up the grassy hill. They must have been tromping over that path for as long as the trains had been running, because it cut more than a foot deep into the clay soil, so rocks, stones, and pebbles jutted out everywhere. Kathryn and I went there almost every day in search of mica and quartz. In the evenings the commuters would have to step over us, but no one seemed to care. We considered it our private rock mine.

On the way we passed Walter and Wimple's house. Walter was on the lawn playing with a model airplane, which was attached to a wire, and which flew in circles around him. He always had extravagant mechanical toys like this or Rock'em-Sock'em Robots. He asked us did we want to come in and play with the toy cigarettes his mother gave him. I was about to say didn't he know smoking was bad for your lungs when Charles said in a loud voice,

"Boy is he fat!" He said it just as though Walter wasn't standing right there. Walter didn't say anything, just kept the airplane going in circles.

"He's a fat Ne-grow," said Charles. This was 1969, the year that everyone had begun to use the word "black." Even Walter Cronkite was saying "black" now and our mother had told us that it was considered an insult to use the word "negro." It was like calling someone a "caucasian" or a "mongoloid."

I wanted to kick Charles, but I didn't know him well enough to do that. I wanted to make him shut up. Most of all I wanted Walter to know that Charles was not really my friend. I didn't know what to do, so without looking back at either of them, I turned around to go home. As I was stomping away thinking maybe Walter was hard-of-hearing enough that he hadn't noticed what Charles said, I heard footsteps behind me: Charles. He wanted to know where I was going. He didn't understand.

I told him he just couldn't do that. He couldn't go around calling black people Negroes and saying people were fat right to their faces. I told him I was mad and now I wouldn't show him my rock collection.

Charles told me he had a new tire swing in his backyard, and offered to let me try it. I was tempted, not having a tire swing of my own, so I went with him to his house, and Kathryn came too.

The tire was dirty and there was a pool of smelly water collected on the inside. It was too big for my sister and we had to lift her on to it. When it was my turn, Charles pushed me harder and harder and the tire zoomed up so close to the garage that I screamed for fear I would smash. It was wonderful. On my third time I looked down from the twirling tire and saw two red-haired boys running into the yard. One had a bat, the other a ball and glove. They wanted Charles to come with them to a ball game in their yard. The tire was moving fast and I was afraid to jump off till it stopped. I thought Charles would ask us to come, too, but he just waved to us and left.

My sister wanted another turn on the tire, but I told her no, she couldn't do that with the owner out of the yard. Charles's mother came out, and with her eyes closed asked if we wanted sodas. She looked around for Charles and I told her he had gone off with some boys. She didn't seem surprised that he had left us, just said those would be the McNeill boys. My sister said that she would like a soda, so I kicked her gently and announced that we had to be going home for lunch. As we marched down the block, back to our own neighborhood, I was seething with frustration that Charles had left us for those McNeills, Charles, whom I didn't even like. I kicked at every stone I saw. Years later, it was Dover McNeill who became the object of my first, secret, earnest, mournful high school love. Even then he was only a glimpse, someone who kept leaving the room or the yard as I entered.

If Walter was bothered by what Charles said, he never let on. I suspect that he hadn't actually heard. After all, Charles hadn't been addressing him directly, and the motor of Walter's airplane had been buzzing the whole time. Walter played with me and Kathryn on and off till his family moved up to a fancier neighborhood in the suburbs and sold their house to two lady doctors from New Zealand.

I didn't see Charles again for years, except occasionally at the Acme, where we would both hide in back of our mothers and ignore each other. Then one day when I was thirteen he turned up at the door.

It had been an awful month for me. I had the ignominy of my first period, which I was certain everybody around me knew about and was being either patronizing or disgusted. And I had recently discovered my feelings for the marvelous Dover McNeill. I spent a large amount of my spare time quietly writing his name over and over on scraps of paper and tearing them into a thousand pieces. When I grew bolder I would write my name under his, and encircle both with a little heart pierced through with feathery arrows. These I also ripped into unrecognizably small shreds. It was at the end of this month that Charles chose to appear at the door. Our mother answered, and he told her he was selling hoagies to help raise money for his school's baseball team, the Friends Selections. Our mother ordered six, which he said he'd bring the following Saturday, and the two of them chatted about his mother and father. All the while he kept looking past her, peering into the hallway, looking for me.

I know this because I'd been on my way upstairs with a basket of clean laundry when I saw him through the screen door coming up the porch steps. I'd dropped the basket right there and ducked straight into the hall closet with the stuffy winter coats. Our mother knew I was in there, but she was kind enough and didn't make me come out and say hello.

The next week I stayed up in my room most of Saturday morning till I heard him arrive with the hoagies. I crept out to the stairwell and listened to him talk with our mother about the Acme.

"What a bozo!" I whispered to Kathryn, who was crouched beside me. She muffled a giggle, glad to be part of any intrigue. Charles finally cleared his throat and told our mother that he had tickets to

a Who concert next Friday and he would like to invite me. His father
would drive, he added quickly. My heart pounded. I had never been
asked out on a date.

I heard our mother telling him that she was sure I would love to
go, but she knew I had arranged to babysit already. I sighed, to show
Kathryn I was relieved, and made a face. When he left, the whole family gathered around the dining room table and ate the hoagies, which
were soggy with oil. Our mother didn't mention Charles's invitation,
not even to me, since she knew I'd been at the top of the steps listening. That Friday night when I really did babysit, I lay on the carpet
wondering what would have happened if it were Dover McNeill who'd
come by asking me to the concert. I was going through my snobbish
phase, when I only listened to classical music, so I turned up the stereo
and sang along with Brahms' Requiem, and thought, "Take that,
Charles! Charles and The Who!"

I was twenty-two years old when I next heard from him. By then
my parents had moved from our beloved house on Upsal Street to
a big flat one in the suburbs. I was living there, having finished college
and, being a writer, having no money for an apartment of my own.

One night our mother came back from the Acme, the newer, better Acme in the suburbs, and she asked me to guess whom she'd run
into there. I came up with a dozen names before she stopped me and
told me it was Charles. Charles of West Mount Airy, and his mother.

"They haven't changed!" said our mother, putting away the egg-
plants. She said Charles had asked her for our phone number, pre-
sumably to call me. Had she given it to him? How could she not? She
defended herself with a smile and handed me some radishes to wash.
I was old enough to take care of myself.

A week later the phone rang during dinner. In our house the phone
always rang at least three times during any meal, usually a business
call for our mother or one of somebody's many friends. Clarissa
answered it on the first ring, and then, with visible disappointment,
handed it to me. My mouth was full. I wanted to know who it was,
maybe my boyfriend who was in medical school in Grenada and who
called me at strange hours, whenever he could make a free call at a
broken pay phone. Of course it was Charles.

He wanted me to come contra-dancing with him on Friday. I wasn't sure what that was, but it sounded awful. I said I'd love to, but I already had plans. He invited me to a Peter, Paul, and Mary concert the next week. I closed my eyes. I could forsee endless phone calls and invitations from him unless I did something to stop it. All right, I said, I'll go.

My family wanted to know who was on the phone and when I told them it was Charles they found it hilarious. All week long they reminded me of my date, lest it slip my mind.

On the evening of the concert Charles arrived while we were still in the middle of dinner. I did not invite him into the kitchen where my family was eating, but my parents went out to say hello anyway. Charles was wearing enormous green and yellow duck boots. He had gone to college in Maine, and I supposed they were popular there. On his head was a baseball cap, just like the one Sluggo wore in the Nancy comic. He was curly-haired and thick-set, like he'd been fed a steady diet of beefsteak and whole milk—my family was in the vegetarian stage then and we all looked down, temporarily, on meat-eaters. I considered nicknaming him "Sluggo" behind his back.

He owned a gray Pinto, which he said was silver and which he drove as though it were a Corvette, thrusting the stickshift from gear to gear, revving the engine. He told me that he'd just been transferred back to Philadelphia by the insurance company he worked for, and he was living with his parents until he could find his own place. During the ride to the theater he told me all about himself: he named every course he'd taken in college; he described his trip to the Caribbean where he'd studied seaturtles for two weeks; he told me what he did at work, where he worked, what he ate for lunch most days, where he'd bought his car and how much he'd paid for it. He told me all about his girlfriends in college and about the nurse he was dating here. Every once in a while I would interrupt to say, "My boyfriend this" or "My boyfriend that." My boyfriend had gone to Friends Central, which was the football rival of Friends Select, and though Charles said he didn't remember him, I kept bringing the subject up. I wanted Charles to know I had somebody, even though he was in Grenada, and that I was technically not available, not at all.

When we got to the concert I was suddenly seized with dread. I didn't like Peter, Paul, and Mary enough to pay for tickets. The only song of theirs I could remember was "Puff, the Magic Dragon." But what if somebody I knew was here tonight? I would be seen with this bozo in the Sluggo hat. I slouched down as we walked to our seats. I didn't know the songs, but Charles sang along and clapped his hands. Not everyone in the audience was doing this, and I was wilting with embarrassment. When they sang "Puff," Charles joined in extra loud. I'd expected this song to bring back nostalgic feelings for my kindergarten days, but instead I was cringing.

Back outside I slipped into the car as fast as I could. While he tried to start it I made the mistake of asking how, as a child, he'd gotten from his house all the way out to Friends Select, which was on the other side of the city. Really, I didn't care; it was just for conversation that I'd asked, but he took this question as seriously as any.

"Well, in kindergarten Mom drove me because we had half days," he began. "After that I got a ride home with Mr. Peekins, who was our Social Studies teacher and lived on the block. He was good for a ride to and from until fifth grade, and that's when after-school sports started." He paused to snap his fingers for emphasis.

"So, in fifth grade my mother had to come all the way down and pick me up after practice. Then in sixth grade the football coach moved to our neighborhood, so he was good for a ride in football season, and—"

"Charles," I said, "Why didn't you just go to a closer school?" Charles looked hurt, I don't know whether from being interrupted or because of my question.

"It was the *best* school," he said, and finished reciting his catalogue.

Didn't he want to know anything about me? I'd never spent so much time with someone who didn't ask me a single question. Not that I cared what he thought, no, but the conversation had been awfully one-sided.

"I'm a writer," I said, breaking in between sentences. He didn't say anything. Maybe he was used to being interrupted like this. Maybe this was the only way anyone could talk to him.

"I'm working on a novel," I said. "I'm living at home with my folks to save money and I'm writing a book." Charles said nothing, which was odd because most people immediately asked me what the book was about. Most people were impressed when I told them that I was a writer.

Charles didn't say a word. Maybe he was waiting for me to continue. Well, if writing a novel didn't interest him, sports probably would.

He seemed to be very concerned about sports, with all that practice in grammar school.

"I'm a distance runner," I said. "I'm training for a marathon in April." I felt silly volunteering this information about myself, but I'd found that people like to hear all about these things, usually.

"I tried to jog once, but I'm too heavy and it messed up my knees," said Charles. Then he started to tell me about his bicycle, where he rode it, how far and how fast.

I leaned back against the vinyl car seat and waited for the ride to be over. I did not invite him inside for coffee.

"Maybe we could go contra-dancing sometime," he said.

"My sister loves contra-dancing," I replied evilly.

Charles left messages for my sister and for me several times over the next two years. Fortunately we never answered the phone these times, and whoever did knew to say we weren't home. I begged Kathryn to go out with him, though, since now that she was in art school she had dyed strips of her blonde hair purple. I wanted to see how he would react, but she refused.

One day I picked up the phone when he called. I was caught off-guard: I admitted I was myself before I realized it was Charles.

That was a busy time for me, for all of us. I had broken up with my boyfriend in Grenada and in two months I was going to marry someone else, right there, in my parents' backyard. We were all busy painting and gardening and getting the house ready. I had no time to be annoyed by Charles.

"Look," I told him, "I can't go contra-dancing. I'm busy. I'm getting married in June."

He didn't say congratulations, just, "Oh."

"It's nothing personal," I said, staring at the ring which sparkled on my left hand. Suddenly I felt very safe. I nearly said, I don't like you anyway, but I just smiled into the receiver.

"Well, then can I talk to your sister?"

"Kathryn's not home," I said, and pretended to write down a message.

I don't drive through my old neighborhood anymore, not because I don't want to run into Charles, who may still live there with his parents, and not because it's not safe there these days, though it's not, but because I loved it so much and I know I'd be filled with that gooey, lump-in-the-throat yearning that I abhor. I couldn't bear to see the graffiti that must be spread across the train station—there was a murder there last spring—or to see our old house, which our parents sold to a woman who wanted to turn it into a loft, knock out all the walls and the second floor ceiling. She said she was an artist. Our mother had laughed out loud and said she must be a trapeze artist, but they sold it anyway because they needed to. Don't worry, she told us kids, she can't do it. Those walls are a foot thick. Those walls are solid.

WINDFALL: GROWING UP IN THE ALLEGHENIES

DAVID MCKAIN

"I left the mountains nearly thirty years ago to go to college in Connecticut, and since, I have lived in Big Sur, New York, San Francisco, Greece, Mexico, and maybe fifty other places; but all these strange and temporary shelters hardly seem to matter when I try to understand who I am. During my various relocations, I have come to understand that a sense of self is intimately connected to a sense of place, and that the most telling bond has been between myself and western Pennsylvania."

*　　*　　*

David McKain's second collection of poems, The Common Life, *was published in 1982; he is on leave from the University of Connecticut where he teaches, and is currently poet-in-residence at Andover Academy in Massachusetts.*

THERE IS A spell in the forest which includes decay; a blowdown stays where it falls and rots. The Lenape Algonquins called the rotten wood of the blowdown "punk," and they called the small biting flies that hummed over it "punkies."

Punxsutawney. I was born there. Syllable by syllable, my mother translated the name of the town with mock contempt. "Punxsutawney," she would laugh, "the Indians named it that—where the punkies live. The home of the gnat." An expressive woman, she snorted when she talked about the place; my father's last church had been in nearby Valier. He had been a minister for seven years: in Riceville, Parkers Landing, Forestville, and Valier. Now they had to find another way to earn a living. He tried to sell tropical fish in Punxsy for awhile, but he never made enough to put food on the table.

Shortly after I was born, while we were still living in Punxsutawney, my father baptized me in the kitchen sink. He was wearing a green velvet smoking jacket and parted his thick black hair in the middle. I have a black-and-white snapshot of him taken on the same day he baptized me. He was standing under a clothesline in the backyard cradling my sister Joanne in his arms, squinting into the sun. As always, his black hair seemed wet, his face a ghostly white. My mother said the rusty sink was the least of our problems. The faucet leaked, we had silverfish and mice, and the pipes in the house froze in the winter. My mother told me his smoking jacket was green; "a God-awful green," the words hollow in the front of her mouth, as though the color made her sick.

We moved to Clarion to live with Grandma Crawford while my mother looked for work and took courses at the State Teacher's College. Disgruntled, my father moved alone down the road to Elmo to sell parakeets and canaries to anyone happening along Route 854. "Elmo," according to a recent history of Clarion County, "was named by someone with a sense of humor. . . . Saint Elmo was the patron saint of the sailors on the Mediterranean to save them from the storm." I learned to count to ten by keeping track of the number of cars floating by on a busy summer day. The front porch of the house leaned toward the road, a sign of decay my father took advantage of by displaying the birds so they could be seen at an angle from the road. Our landlords, the McIntyrres, lived next door, and because we had no electricity, the rent was cheap. We primed the pump on the back porch when we needed water. My mother refused, she said, "to put one foot inside the front door of the disgraceful place." When I visited him, we slept on mattresses on the living room floor because in the back of the house, the morning sun would wake us. He brought the birds in off the porch at night, and they flicked out seed that ticked onto the linoleum floor like a clock gone haywire. Words were play-ful: there was the ticking that came from the birds and the ticking that covered the mattress. With pride, my father called himself jack-of-all-trades: subsistence farmer, prize-fighter, Methodist minister, and, as the hand-lettered sign in the yard proclaimed, owner of "McKain's Pet Shop." In addition to the lovebirds and a few small turtles, we had a dog named King—a chow chow he chained to the outhouse as a watchdog.

By contrast with the house in Elmo, the house in Clarion com-manded respect. It stood in the center of a perfect acre set back far enough from the wide slate sidewalk to be something of a showpiece. Grandma made sure the lawn was trimmed, the hedges clipped, and the earth around the border flowers black and rich with coffee grounds. The massive square house in the middle of this plot had fourteen rooms with French windows in the front which ran from floor to ceiling. My grandfather had the house built to his specifications from investments he had made in Coca-Cola, Warner Brothers, and Florida real estate. Coal miner, baritone, and preacher, he had saved all his life. He wanted the house to please his wife and to help them both forget the poverty from which they had sprung. Now that he was "gone" (Grandma's word), it was her house, and her vegetables grew all the way to the alley that ran alongside the tracks of the Clarion and Franklin Railroad. The railroad line ended right there in our backyard. I played at the depot nearly everyday, climbing in and out of the boxcars and sitting inside the caboose with the men when it rained. If the sun melted the ice in a layover refrigerator car, the yardman loaded me down with full-sized watermelons; one day I made three trips home before my mother stopped me at the back door with a lecture on greed. At night, by lifting myself up on one elbow and looking out my bedroom window, I learned to read the names of the railroads on the sides of the freight cars. "The Great Northern" had a white circle with a battering ram inside. My lucky car, which I saw only twice, was the "Sante Fe." It was painted the color of the sun: gold, my favorite color.

The names of faraway places on the rolling stock in the yard soon became familiar. In Clarion, my entire world was familiar; family was everywhere. I had relatives in four out of the five houses on the block where we lived, most of them, like my grandfather, immigrants from

Scotland. Uncle Jim Harvey lived next door in a red brick house with fancy dadoes and scrollwork in the green trim along the rake of the roof and around the windows. He was the first in the family to build on East Main Street. Uncle Jim Harvey (all three of his names were run together when we spoke of him) had been a coal miner. He had yellowish white hair and sat by the window inside his house most of the day. I saw him wave when I gathered the good apples that dropped from his trees across the hedge into our yard.

The Sedaris family lived on the other side of Grandma's house, and their daughter taught me to count to a hundred. She tried to teach me the Jew's harp too, but when I stuck the metal frame in my mouth to pluck, it set my bad teeth on edge. The Sedarises owned the restaurant across the street from the Clarion County Courthouse called "The College Grill." My father said it was the best restaurant in town, but we didn't eat there because liquor was served. Aunt Mills lived next door to the Sedarises, and next to her, the Borrowmans, my Uncle Tom and Gertrude. I did not understand much of what they said for they spoke in broad Scots. "Never call it a brogue," my mother warned, "and it's not exactly a burr either. But when he gets 'is engine goin, ken ye ketch a wee bit a whirr in it?"

My mother's pride in being a first generation half-Scot had begun to rub off on me. My grandfather was born in Cumbernauld, and at the age of fourteen, sailed steerage alone for America to find work. At Ellis Island, he asked directions to the coal mines, setting off on foot for Pennsylvania. He stayed for a time in Snow Shoe, then wound up around Stump Creek where he was later joined by ten brothers and sisters. Together with three or four of his brothers, he opened up a coal mine in the backyard and worked it with a mule.

I don't know how long he might have stayed a miner if it were not for a circuit rider on horseback who saw spiritual promise in the young man. Without my grandfather's knowledge, the itinerant preacher raised enough money among his five congregations to send him to college. He graduated from Bucknell in 1895 at the age of twenty-seven, and shortly thereafter, he was ordained into the Baptist Church. He died several years before I was born, but his obituary in *The Clarion Democrat* said, "Reverend Crawford was a thorough Biblical scholar. . . . His sermons were of a clear expository character . . . revealing God's beneficent purposes for man. He was also very clear and forceful in the delivery of the Gospel. . . . It has been remarked . . . that the sermon he delivered on a baccalaureate occasion was one of the ablest, and best, and most inspiring ever delivered on such an occasion in town." I knew only that he had been a rich baritone, was kind, and had favored my mother with boundless love. His photograph hung in an oval frame over the mantel in the music room – a life-sized picture my grandmother had touched up with peach watercolors and wash.

Grandma altered the lives of the living as well as the dead. According to the *History of the Pennsylvania Woman's Christian Temperance Union*, she hung the picture of Frances E. Willard (WCTU World Leader) in every public and private school in Clarion County, installed two water fountains in Clarion High School and, in New Bethlehem, placed an especially large fountain with a plaque which read: "For Man, For Horse, For Dog." At East Brady, along the banks of the Allegheny River, Grandma and her friends sponsored a dramatic presentation on the evils of alcohol called "Tell the World About Ethyl." As an acknowledgment of the importance of her work, Grandma's photograph appears in the front matter of the *History*. She is wearing a dark blue tulle dress and rimless glasses, looking every bit as formidable as I remember her when she spoke from the pulpit against those who misused the Holy Sabbath. The *History* also states she led a successful campaign to close down the only movie house in Clarion on Sunday.

She interpreted the Ten Commandments beyond the letter, and her rule at home was absolute. "Thou Shalt Not Kill" meant that I could not have a cap gun – not even the pearl handled one John Paul Chandler had traded me for my seasoned cherry slingshot. Although I had hidden the gun carefully behind a jar of canned beets in the pantry, the next morning the gun was gone. Not a word was spoken. "Don't complain," my mother warned, "we're lucky to have a roof over our heads." Nothing my parents were able to do seemed to support our lives until my mother, without her diploma, landed a teaching job in Bradford, a distant city three hours to the north. My father was happy about the move. I heard him say that Bradford was five times the size of Elmo and Clarion combined; and business would boom. But he tried for seven years to sell small birds and tropical fish and couldn't make a go of it. Twice flooded out by the Tuna Creek, he finally crossed the border into Olean, New York. I went with him on the bus to help him carry his supplies. The parakeets and canaries flicked seed into the aisle of the last four rows of the near-empty Greyhound, and the water sloshed out of the quart-sized coleslaw containers that held the tropical fish.

I guess the excesses of a place give a town its character. In Bradford there were characters everywhere—or so it seemed to me as a child when even a pair of mismatched blue and purple socks would make me cringe. In second grade, I used to watch a woman dig a ditch in front of the railroad station on Main Street. She carried Luckies in her T-shirt pocket and had a blue snake with red eyes that crawled up her arm as she swung her pick. Two blocks from our house there was a family in a tarpaper shack who stood a bathtub on one end in the yard to shelter the Virgin Mary. One winter evening they saw a miracle of light take the shape of the cross on their living room wall, and all of Hilton Street was cordoned off. Two priests worked their way through the crowd touching the foreheads of the children, Protestant and Catholic alike. After school, a homosexual named Duane waved and rang the bell on his bike as he passed, delivering messages for Western Union. Downtown after supper, in front of the Carnegie Public Library, we could count on finding the tall thin man who stopped in the street and howled. First he would give a little head fake, as though he would drive to the basket, then he faked all over, his body shaking until he howled. We called him "The Wolf Man" and howled after him as the poor man crossed the street. Later, we found out he was slightly touched, the black-sheep son of a prominent area family who had given up hope.

But I found it a relief to single out the odd ones in town, for each eccentric proved my father was not the only one. The town accepted people with differences, and this was its strength. Marvin Lowenthal, the editor of *The Autobiography of Montaigne*, also grew up in Bradford, and he wrote, "People from all over the world, including Jews, came there, many of them in the spirit of adventure, all with a lot of gambling blood in their veins. That type isn't given to hating overmuch." The behavioral norm was a guideline, not an absolute. The town accepted my father's epilepsy, making it that much easier for me to accept it as well.

My father was a big man—a half-foot taller than other men, and he weighed two hundred pounds. Wearing his Dobbs hat, he looked a whole foot taller, and he always carried himself, he said, "as straight and tall as a Prussian soldier." I knew one of his spells could come at anytime, and he would fall backward, indifferent to soft earth or concrete. When one day he fell at noon right on Main Street, I hardly noticed. I had turned for a moment to look in a store window when I heard the muffled thud. He was lying between two parked cars, having fallen sidewise off the curb, his face the ghostly color of the overexposed snapshot from Punxsutawney. Already, his eyes had rolled back and his tongue was working to return inside his mouth where it belonged. I watched his hat roll and wobble to a dead stop as a woman put her hand to her mouth. A policeman appeared and knelt down beside him, touching him reassuringly on the shoulder. "You okay, Reverend?" he asked calmly. "Well, you don't want to sleep out here on Main Street all day, do you?" My father didn't answer, and a stranger stopped to help the policeman gather him up out of the gutter and drag him up against the wall of Widdman and Teah Drugstore, the spot where the man without legs sat on Veteran's Day, his hat full of yellow pencils. That evening, just before supper, a stranger brought him back from the hospital with a turban-style bandage around his head, a tulip of gauze. Whether intentionally or not, the town absorbed many of our problems and much of our pain.

On balance, I feel lucky to have grown up in Bradford. The demands on my parent's lives to pay the rent gave me independence. As a result, they turned me over to the mountains and the town—the most wonderfully lax set of parents a boy could know. The strongest rebuke I ever received came from Miss Pike, my teacher in third grade. On the back of one of my report cards she wrote, "David wanders about the room and leaves at will." I was, I suppose, intensely haphazard: one of those kids with the vacant look that comes from having their hair cut off for ringworm.

One morning in fifth grade, Mrs. Grove, the principal, called me out of class with George McCune before we read the Bible. She took us into a narrow stockroom at the end of the hall where she boiled a can of stewed tomatoes on a hotplate in the corner. George and I sat on wooden crates while she broke bread into each bowl, then poured in the steaming tomatoes. Scrawny kids, George and I both wore a nylon cap for ringworm.

The next year, in sixth grade, I was sent to see Dr. Black, a dentist. After ten minutes with his little pick and tiny mirror, he recommended false teeth. My own were buck, snaggled and green: decayed beyond hope or repair. No doubt my kind of freedom had its price, but I think now I would always choose bad teeth and an occasional, well-meaning bowl of stewed tomatoes if I could grow up wandering in and out of school, down by the Tuna Creek and along the tracks all the way out of town to Hedgehog.

Wandering seems to run in the family. In more recent years, my mother began to wander, too. She would put on three layers of clothes in July and wander four miles from home to the new mall on the other side of town. There, she would rest by the fountain inside until a neighbor or friend would sit down on the wet stone beside her, strike up an easy conversation, then drive her back home as though they had set out together. Later, when she began to lose control in the classroom, the District Superintendent of Schools, Fred Shuey, appointed her to an administrative post. In Bradford, recently, I stopped by the school office to thank Mr. Shuey for covering for her until she reached retirement. "Oh," he said smiling, "we don't think of it that way." He didn't say how he did think of it, and he didn't have to. A neighbor across the street from my mother, Clyde Cleveland, stopped in from time to time, and toward the end, saw to it that she had a gas range with an electric pilot light so she could not turn on the gas and forget it. Strut Bauer came every day. He shoveled snow, walked her downtown to appointments, picked up prescriptions, shopped for her, and every day at five o'clock, came to prepare her supper. "Make sure," he put it, "she'll have one balanced meal a day."

Today, in the Mystic Manor Convalescent Home in Mystic, Connecticut, only her diet is balanced; she is not. My earliest days are filed away in the snarled circuitry of her brain, deep in the base of the nucleus in what doctors call "the neurofibrillary tangle." We can no longer converse, at least not in words. In Alzheimer's disease, the cerebral cortex sinks, creating on X-ray a kind of saddleback. I call the declivity the "valley" of her life because I think she might like that, an image which puts her up high on a ridge in the Alleghenies surveying the endless mountains. When I visit her now before work, sometimes an aide touches her arm and shouts, "Ida! Ida! David is here. David! Isn't that nice?" They shout as though she were hard of hearing, pronouncing each syllable as though she spoke a foreign tongue. But she brightens when she sees me; she smiles, and a distant light flickers in her eyes. Usually I squat down beside her chair and take her hand. I tell her about the slightest change in the weather and praise her hair. On good days, she nods, battling through the aphasia to say, "Good . . . we, we, we . . . yayaya . . . oh." Just last week, she said, "Oh dead dead dat," then, "no." Her face clouded over from a misfiring "known only to God Almighty," as she would have put it once.

I no longer have blood ties in Bradford, but I have family everywhere. I go back each year to be in the presence of this family, however invisible they might seem to some. It surprises me, but I feel at home in a motel on the outskirts of town. I walk around, up and down Main Street and across the bridge at Mechanic. There, I peer over the silver railing into the lazy brown waters of the Tuna Creek. Flood Control has dredged the bottom and replaced it with poured concrete; without rocks and shadows, there is no place for the crayfish to hide. No more floods either. I head out South Avenue and up Cliff Street to get lost on Quintuple, or I hike out to Shaw Hollow and climb the firetower on Hedgehog. Up there, commanding a lookout from the tower on the highest point around town, it is easy to understand why the Indians called the Alleghenies "The Endless Mountains." When I come back into town and sit at the counter at "Jane's" for a cup of coffee and a piece of homemade pie, I feel at home with myself. It is like the way I have felt standing on top of one of the hillfarms outside Port Allegany, a few miles to the east. Looking west, you can see over Two Mile Creek, Open Brook and thousands of acres of state game lands across the Allegheny River Valley. From the hillfarm you can see Prospect Peak, the highest point of land in a straight line all the way from the Atlantic Ocean to the Rockies. Up that high and with that long a view, at first the mountains look like the ocean. But then one ridge begins to resemble the next ridge, sharing features and contours common to the entire range. The mountains become familiar again, almost familial: family. Then, finally, the mountains are mountains once more.

WAITING FOR HER TRAIN

AUDREY LEE

Audrey Lee's fiction and poetry have appeared in Playgirl, Essence, Black World *and* The Saturday Evening Post. *Two novels have been published,* The Clarion People *(1968) and* The Workers *(1969). This short story first appeared in an anthology called* What We Must See: Young Black Storytellers.

S HE SITS IN Thirtieth Street Station watching the newsman over the three-screen television. She is waiting for her train to come in. The station vibrates with arrival and departure of trains. Hers does not arrive. But she has time. Other people are waiting, too. Expectant. Anxious. They have schedules to meet. Destinations. They have purchased tickets—round trip or one-way. She has not purchased her ticket yet. A ticket represents a destination. She has not decided upon her destination. But who is to know. . . .

She recognizes the old woman wearing two dresses and two sweaters and carrying the shopping bag full of her possessions. She will not be as obvious as the old lady. There will never be a vagrant look about her. She has locked her possessions in one of the station lockers. Her presence in the station is temporary—just until her train comes in. And for all anyone knows, her baggage is being shipped ahead of her. She is waiting for her train no matter *what* anyone might think.

The railroad workers for the day shift are coming into the station. They are looking at her as usual. They think they know but they don't. Those tolerant looks that express knowing—as if she were a distant relative in their house. A poor distant relative who has had a bad stroke of luck. What of it? She has had a taste of the finer things. She has been to the Art Museum, stood among the Picassos and the Powells—and oh too many paintings to be mentioned. The fact remains that she has been. She knows something about fashion, too. About designing. About labels—labels tell so much about quality. And they lend respectability to clothing. She has no proof that she knows, except the dress she is wearing. Her creditors have reclaimed all the others, along with the shoes. They were right, of course. But they couldn't deny she had discriminating taste. But that is behind her. She must look to the future.

At eight o'clock the Horn and Hardart Restaurant will open. She will go there as usual. And afterwards—well, she would see.

"North Philadelphia. Trenton. Princeton. Newark. New York. Now loading on platform number three."

Not her train. She is waiting for something more exotic. A tropic island with palm trees. There are so many people going places. And so many people returning. She likes this time of morning. Her train would come in the morning. It would pull into the station on velvet springs. And it would purr, not screech. Her man would be waiting with her bags. And she would be clothed in quiet elegance, the labels of the day's fashion turned in, reassuring against her skin, the quality turned out for everyone to see. That would teach the know-alls. The railroad workers who passed her bench, throwing their tolerant glances. That would prove that she had been waiting for her train after all. That she was going somewhere.

Horn and Hardart opens. She gets up from the bench, brushes the wrinkles that resist her pressure. When she bought the dress it was wrinkle-resistant. She puts on her soiled gloves and respectable walk, feeling the kinks loosen in her knees, giving them a jerk or two when no one is looking. She picks up a newspaper from a bench. Someone is always leaving a newspaper. Then she checks the return coin slots of the telephones. No forgotten dimes. She will not have coffee this morning.

Inside Horn and Hardart, she is reading the specials posted on the menu. Later on breakfast will cost more. She is giving the menu a respectable glance, demonstrating her discriminating taste with proper deliberation. Then with the same deliberating eye, she looks at the long line of people waiting to take advantage of the early morning special breakfasts. A glass of water will do until the line is shorter. That is her reasoning. She tugs decisively at her glove and fills her glass with cool water from the fountain and sits down to a table near the window to read the newspaper. But first she will make the table ready for breakfast. She lays knife, fork and spoon, the napkin. There.

The newspaper. She will choose a supermarket to visit from those advertised. She wonders how many different supermarkets she has shopped in over the past.

Nine o'clock. She is entering the supermarket. She fills her cart with steaks, chops, parsley, fruit. She will eat an orange while she shops. Cheese — she would taste a piece of cheese, too. Not the same brand she had yesterday at the other market. This cheese is sharper. Raisin bread. She will eat a slice or two.

She opens a jar of herring. Herring for breakfast — oh, well, one eats what one finds convenient. Besides, fish is a necessary part of the diet, too. The manager is smiling and handing her glove to her.

"Looks like you're having your breakfast. . . ."

Kidding her, of course. People are always chewing on something when they go to market. "Yes. You have good herring." The compliment pleases him. "Very good herring," she is saying for emphasis. He is smiling and walking away.

Bananas — bananas are filling. She needs something that will fill her. Meanwhile, she must appear in earnest. She must fill her cart with household articles. A mop handle and mop. That would look impressive jutting from the cart. There — now another bite of banana. Paper napkins from the shelf. Table salt. Black pepper. Paprika. . . .

She swallows the last of the banana. Then she puts on her gloves, pushes the cartful of groceries to the front of the store, places it in a respectful position just to one side of the checkout counter, out of the path of shoppers waiting in line for the cashier. And in a respectable voice:

"Cashier — I forgot my purse — I wonder if you would be kind enough to let my cart stay here until I return. . . ."

"Certainly, madam."

"I appreciate it. Thanks so much." She burps. Bananas take a while to digest. But she has time. She hurries from the market. She does not want the manager to see her leaving. He might suggest sending the groceries to her—sweet of him, of course—but how could she explain—what could she say—that she was waiting for a train? Well, she had escaped now. Explanations are not necessary.

In D-D's Department Store she stands before the cosmetics counter, trying on a sample lipstick. She doesn't like it well enough to buy it. She tries the expensive face powder which the saleslady mixes for her. A spoonful of white powder. A spoonful of pinkish powder, mint-colored powder. Then blending them with a spatula.

"You look absolutely gorgeous—this is wonderful and it's good for your skin. Put this on and wipe it dry—work that in—truly pink would be equal to your natural—"

"I was looking for something quick and easy. I don't have time to do much in the morning. . . ."

"Try this," dipping the spoon into the powder. Wiping the spoon and dipping it into another powder. "This has orange in it. You have to use it sparingly—you need some color—it's a sample portion. Try it out at home—try them both—and see how you like them."

"Thank you very much. Maybe I can come back tomorrow—if I decide I like the way it looks on me. These lights—if I were only at home. . . ."

"You'll like it."

One mirror is seldom true. One has to consider the majority of mirrors. She smiles at the woman. Then she walks toward the perfumes. Aura of Emotion—Charles of the Ritz—Desert Flower—Desert Flower is too incongruous a name to be considered by a bench sitter. Still she must try something new. Yesterday it was Heaven Scent. Today—well—it would depend—Chantilly—she felt like *Chantilly*— but first. . . . She looked at the bottles of perfume and toilet water, picked them up, read their labels. She is a discriminating shopper. All the bottles scrutinized. She picks up the spray bottle of Chantilly. Poof—savors the scent with a sensitive and discriminating nose. That is what she wants. She sprays her ears, wrists, clothing. All very quickly and tastefully. Subtly. She wants to be sure of catching the scent.

"It smells good. May I show you something, madam? We have the talcum, too. It will make a nice set. . . ."

She is very discriminating, so she will not answer right away. She has not made up her mind—not really—Chanel No. 5. Intimate.

"Excuse me a minute, madam. I'll wait on this customer—I know you want to take your time—when you decide. . . ."

Poof. Chantilly behind her ears once more. Subtly. Discriminatingly. The saleslady is busy. Several customers are waiting. She pulls her gloves securely over her hands, resumes her respectable posture and walks out of the store. The scent does indeed smell good on. Now she will return to the station and wash her gloves. She will lay them on the bench to dry. If only she had a portable hair dryer, she could wash her hair. But portable hair dryers are made for people of means— not for people of predicament.

Back at the station powder room. She washes her gloves, touches her hair, and checks her makeup. The powder goes well with her complexion. And so does the lipstick. She checks her purse, making certain she still has the samples in her purse, touches her hair again, approves. Still she would like to get her hair washed and styled. She will think of a way. But having the new makeup and the perfume makes her feel somewhat refreshed. She will settle down on a bench to watch the pictures, plan the dinner menu, decided upon the evening's entertainment.

And of course, she will watch the evening flow of men and women in and out of the station. But before that, she will check the coin return slots of the telephones. Nothing yet. She will have to wait for her coffee a little longer. The best time to check the slots is just after the rush hour. She might even be able to afford two cups of coffee. And who is there to deny that her train might have arrived by then.

WHY I DID IT

WILLIAM D. EHRHART

"I've never thought much about 'being a Pennsylvanian.' I've never been either proud or ashamed of it; it's just been a fact of life, more or less. In fact, since graduating from high school and leaving home, I've spent more time elsewhere than in Pennsylvania. Somehow, though, I keep finding myself back here every so often—and several years ago, as usual quite by chance to all appearances, I returned again.

"I'm married now—to a North Carolinian I met while I was living in Maryland—and my wife and I own a home in Doylestown. It's just down the road from Perkasie, where I grew up. I get to see my parents often, which is nice, and I travel the same roads I used to pedal on my bicycle and drive in the family car back in those heady days after I'd first gotten my license. I have no idea how long I'll stay this time, but Anne and I are happy here, and we're in no particular hurry to leave. For me, it's—well—familiar, comfortable, like a well-worn easy chair or an old friend.

"And maybe there's a reason I keep coming back. My roots grow deeper than I know. I've never really thought about it much. But I guess this is home."

*   *   *

William D. Ehrhart is a writer and editor, whose fiction, nonfiction, and poetry have been published in many prestigious magazines and anthologies. This essay originally appeared in The Virginia Quarterly Review.

I ENLISTED IN the United States Marine Corps in 1966. I was seventeen years old. Under what was called a delayed enlistment program, I actually signed the enlistment contract two months before I finished high school, though I didn't leave for boot camp (basic training at Parris Island, South Carolina) until I graduated. I knew I would go to Vietnam—I wanted to go—and my recruiter, a Staff Sergeant Robert Bookheimer, assured me that I would. (Whatever else you or I might have to say about Bookheimer, he was an honest man; he told me nothing during our long discussions that did not turn out to be true. As I have gathered from friends, acquaintances, and a great deal of reading since, he was a rarity among military recruiters.) And I did indeed go to Vietnam, where nothing I had anticipated happened, and everything I never dreamed of came true. *But that's another story.*

Most people who learn that I've been to Vietnam, but who haven't yet been told the details, invariably assume that I was drafted. Not an unreasonable assumption. After all, relatively few bright, "college material types" willingly enlisted in the military—certainly not in the mid-sixties, when student deferments from the draft were readily available—though many did accept their draft notices if and when they got them rather than choosing the alternatives of prison or exile. Enlistment was the choice of only juvenile delinquents, blue-collar kids, and dimwits.

Thus when I correct the erroneous assumption, the reaction is equally invariably an astonished, "Why?!" The response that, "Well, it seemed like the thing to do at the time," is both accurate and expedient, especially when accompanied by a shrug of the shoulders indicating an intense desire not to pursue the matter further. But it doesn't answer the question at all, and I suspect more than one person faced with that response has concluded that I must fall into the category of dimwit. Which may be true, but that doesn't answer the question either.

Well, why indeed? Though I was born in western Pennsylvania and lived for a few years thereafter in the central part of the state, I really grew up in Perkasie, a town of five thousand in upper Bucks County between Philadelphia and Allentown. In recent years, Perkasie has begun to show unmistakable signs of having contracted terminal suburban sprawl; but while I was growing up, it was a quiet little country town. (Between 1960 and 1970, for instance, census figures show the population remaining almost constant, varying by something like ten souls.) People left their houses unlocked at night, and neighbors called to each other from large front porches on warm summer evenings, and kids went sledding on Third Street hill when it snowed in the winter. There were no traffic lights in town; there was no need for them. The whole countryside around was dotted with small family farms, and you could get on your bicycle and in ten minutes be coasting between corn fields, or go down to Lake Lenape (which was really a branch of the Perkiomen Creek that ran right through town; I never have figured out why it's called a lake) and catch painted turtles and water snakes. Carolers strolled from house to house on Christmas Eve, and Jimmy the shoe repair man knew the shoe size of everyone in town.

There were no blacks in Perkasie (we called them Negroes in those days), and only two or three black families in the entire Pennridge area (the school district that encompassed Perkasie, three other small boroughs, and four rural townships). There were few if any truly wealthy people, and I don't recall anything resembling real poverty. Most Perkasians worked hard and honestly for what they had, and most were comfortable. And the belief that life in America (which for most people in Perkasie meant life in Perkasie) was as it should be, and was the direct result of the bounty and blessing of God, the wisdom of our revolutionary fathers, and the sacrifices of succeeding generations was not a notion to be scoffed at.

It would not be difficult to make Perkasie appear contemptible and silly. The response to suggesting the removal of a tree from the grounds of the public swimming pool would likely be a bewildered, "But it's *always* been there." The almost nonexistent crime rate was extremely fortuitous, since the few cops (most of which were part-time) were mainly useful in chasing small dogs and serving as chauffeurs for the favorite target of adolescent snowballs and water balloons (i.e., Perkasie's one police car). The reigning quarterback of the high school football team was a celebrity on a par with movie stars and statesmen, and coach Wayne Helman was a folk hero. Our high school guidance counsellors actively discouraged students from considering such schools as UCLA—in fact, couldn't understand why anyone would want to go to school so far away—considering it a solemn duty to shepherd as many kids as possible into the likes of Millersville, Shippensburg, Kutztown, and West Chester. Going to New York City, ninety miles to the northeast, was an exotic and rather dangerous venture to be planned months in advance and talked about for years after—I don't think many people in Perkasie ever went to New York City; those that did were considered adventurous and perhaps a little eccentric. Year in and year out, generations advanced as the generations that had preceded them, and nothing much out of the ordinary ever happened except an occasional shotgun wedding. Rotary Club meetings and church were well attended.

But to paint Perkasie merely as a laughable little hick town, to dismiss its complacence and neighborliness and the vicious blindness of its provinciality as grand farce would seriously mislead you. For, in spite of the ridicule I heaped upon Perkasie in my rebellious teen years (a redundancy, I suppose) and my active desire to get out of town as fast as I could, the values and standards by which Perkasie measured the world became my own. I might drink beer and skip church and give my parents and teachers the fits, but I never questioned the meaning of Duty, Honor, and Country. (And beneath the anger and bitterness growing out of the colossal rip-off of the Vietnam War and my part in it, I know that no one who taught me those values and standards deliberately tried to deceive me. Perhaps that is the saddest thing of all. As people inevitably do, they merely showed me the world as they saw it themselves. It excuses neither them nor me, but it is important to understand.)

So I grew up on a steady diet of America as the greatest and noblest nation on earth—a nation flawed only in minor and correctable ways—in an environment that offered no visible contradiction to those beliefs. In elementary school, I read books about John Paul Jones and Pecos Bill, and at Halloween, I collected money for UNICEF to help the children in countries less fortunate than our own. Leaving food on a plate brought a stern admonishment to remember the starving millions in Red China. Ike, the good soldier and fatherly statesman, was the president. Each school day began with the Lord's Prayer and the Pledge of Allegiance, in that order; and we learned about peasants in Bolivia and William Penn and wampum belts, and sometimes had atomic bomb drills where we would all have to sit in rows in the halls, facing the wall and curling up with our heads between our knees and our hands clasped behind our necks. As far back as I can remember, every Memorial Day I decorated my bicycle with red, white, and blue crepe paper and rode in the town parade; and every year I could hardly wait for the awesome and thrilling twenty-one gun salute fired by the uniformed members of the Hartzell-Crouthamel American Legion Post, and the playing of taps at the end of the salute that sent chills through my body and left everyone reverently silent for a moment like the end of a church service. I knew the twenty-third Psalm and the Gettysburg Address by heart and earned enough money selling newspapers to buy a subscription to a magazine called *Our Navy*. Elvis Presley was a sensation, and the Russian Sputnik was a very bad thing indeed.

2

I was in the tenth grade when John F. Kennedy was assassinated. Together with my oldest brother, John, and his girlfriend, I stood in line from ten at night until six the next morning to see the casket lying beneath the great Capitol dome; and when I saw it, I cried. On the cover of my school notebook for that year, I wrote, "Ask not what your country can do for you; ask what you can do for your country." Beneath that, I added, "*Ich bin ein Berliner.*" The Cuban Missile Crisis was still recent history, and I can still see clearly the photograph in *Life* magazine of U.S. Army helicopters suspended in the air over the green rice fields of Laos, and Vietnam was beginning to appear in the news more frequently; and over it all loomed the sinister figure of Nikita Khrushchev, pounding with his shoe and shouting, "We will bury you!"

In November of 1964, I rode around Perkasie one evening on the back of a flatbed truck singing Barry Goldwater campaign songs. I was impatient with Lyndon Johnson and his dovish approach to Vietnam. I was sixteen then. In an English class that year, I wrote the only piece of fiction I have ever done: a story about a teenaged boy behind the Iron Curtain who tries to flee across the border. He is killed by border guards just as he reaches the wire, and the last sentence reads: "He doubled over and slipped to the ground, his mouth twisting into a smile." In history class, we discussed that guy, Miller I think his name was, who publicly burned his draft card at Yale, uniformly concluding that he was a Commie creep and a coward. (That same year, I wrote a poem called "Friendship," which went something like this:

Two hands reach out to each other
across the gap between them.
One hand is white;
the other is black.
Why can't it be this way?)

In December of 1965, soon after the battle of the Ia Drang Valley, which first confirmed the presence of North Vietnamese regular army troops in South Vietnam, I began thinking about enlisting in the service. America, the beacon and hope of the Free World, had bestowed upon me the blessings of freedom, and it is no joke to say that I felt very deeply that burden. In a journalism class the following spring, I wrote an editorial which, sincerely patriotic, said: "The casualty rates in the war in Vietnam are rapidly rising. More American boys have been killed in the first four months of this year than were killed in all of 1965. Just this past week, more United States soldiers were killed than South Vietnamese.

"These are staggering realizations. But even more staggering are the anti-American demonstrations that are rocking every major city in South Vietnam. It appears that we are not welcome there. We are fighting a war to liberate a people who do not wish to be liberated. American boys are dying for no good cause.

"Yet is this true? We don't believe it is. The people of South Vietnam live in constant fear. No, perhaps not the city-dwellers, those who are doing most of the demonstrating. They have the security of the city to protect them. But the people who farm the thousands of rice fields, the people who live in the fishing villages, the mountain tribesmen, these people truly live in fear. Vietcong guerrillas roam the country controlling the fields, jungles, rivers, villages, roads and everything except the few small strongholds of United States Special Forces and Marines. The people are forced to hide VC from pursuers. Vietcong strongmen tax villagers heavily for food—food which they use to feed their guerrilla bands. Vietcong 'recruiters' take men and boys and forcibly impress them into the rebel army. All of this is done under threats of destruction of crops and villages, torture and death—and the VC have proven that they do not bluff.

"There is no freedom in South Vietnam. To have freedom, there must be free elections. Yet how can there be free elections in South

Vietnam with such strong influences as the VC have on the vast majority of the people? And without free elections, how can there be freedom?

"As long as the Vietcong or any other subversive influences exist, there can never be a free country of South Vietnam. This, then, is the cause for which so many Americans have lost their lives.

"To those of you who feel that these boys are dying for no reason, we say this: What more noble a cause can a man die for, than to die in defense of freedom?"

I had other reasons for enlisting in the Marines, which I will shortly come to; but underlying them and making it possible to act on them as I did was a fundamental belief in the essential rightness of America and all that the American government did in the world. I had been taught that I owed something to my country (and in those days if you were male, of age, and healthy, what you owed was military service, end of discussion), and I had been taught why. And as the war in Vietnam grew hot, and the draft cranked up in defense of freedom, America needed me now. The day I took the Oath of Allegiance at a Marine Reserve substation in Bethlehem, Pennsylvania, I felt more than anything else virtuous and noble. I knew, I really *knew* that George Washington and Abraham Lincoln and John Kennedy were proud of me.

Still, the upbringing I'd had was not substantially different from that of the rest of my peers in the college-preparatory sections of the class of '66, yet I was the only one who chose not to go to college. Thus, those other reasons I had are important, too.

To begin with, though I'd been accepted at four universities by the middle of my senior year, I was quite undecided about what I wanted to study or what I wanted to be. It seemed reasonable that a few years in the service might help to make those decisions easier, give me some time to think things over. I knew I would also then be eligible for federal financial aid under the G.I. Bill, with which I could pay for my college education. And since I did owe something to my country (which meant only one thing), and since college deferred one from the draft but did not exempt one entirely, I felt it would be better to get it over with before I went to college rather than after, when I would just be getting ready to start a career.

(None of these deductions turned out to be true. If anything, I was even more confused about what I wanted for my life by the time I was discharged three years later. And the G.I. Bill allotment was a ridiculous pittance—in 1969, it was $135 a month, period, as opposed to tuition, books, and $75 a month cash for my father's generation. And by 1970, when I would have graduated from college, the lottery system of selection was in effect, and I would have ended up with a number too high for me to be drafted. Life's little ironies. Nevertheless, at the time, these seemed like plausible reasons for enlisting when I did.)

I had also at the time a rather unrealistic perception of what it meant to be in the service and fight a war. Is it even necessary to say that? I'd grown up on John Wayne, Audie Murphy, and William Holden. I knew all about Nathan Hale, and Alvin York and Eddie Rickenbacker. As a kid, I'd spent hundreds of hours building plastic models of bombers and fighter planes and battleships, carefully painting them and displaying them all over the house, and I could tell you all about each one. Along with cowboys and Indians, war was a favorite pastime, and my two most memorable childhood Christmas presents were a lifesize plastic .30 caliber machine-gun, and a .45 caliber automatic cap pistol in a leather holster with USMC embossed on the military-style cover flap. (I was so proud of that pistol that I ran up the street first chance I got to show it off to Margie Strawser.) I'd seen many times the old newsreels of the troops coming home at the end of World War II and was in awe of the fathers of my friends whom I knew had been heroes in that war (as far as we were concerned, anybody who had been in the service during wartime was a hero). Parades and medals and girls kissing you in the streets—I'd been through it all countless thousands of times in seventeen years, and now I could really make those fantasies come true—Aladdin's magic lamp.

I had also, by my senior year of high school, developed a fondness for the attention and notoriety one receives by doing the daring and the unexpected. The summer before, Pete Kosiak and I had gone to California without bothering to tell our parents in advance; it was a great adventure, and we'd returned at the end of the summer to accolades of wonder and admiration from our peers. That winter, I took the family Volkswagen and, again without notice, drove alone to Amarillo, Texas, and back in four days. I always had other reasons for doing those kinds of things, but I certainly relished the attendant attention they produced. And joining the Marines—oh, wow, that would *really* leave 'em gasping.

3

Of course, the decision to join the Marines was made simultaneously with the decision to enlist at all. For, once I began thinking of enlisting, it was obvious which service I had to join. The Marines had the most glorious reputation and tradition. Marines were heroes by virtue solely of being Marines. (Our high school had an Armed Forces Day all-school assembly every spring during which representatives of all four branches of the military would address the students. The Marine, in his dazzling dress blue uniform with red trouser stripes and gold piping, was easily the most impressive.)

And although I was a good student, graduating in the top ten in a class of 276, and no discipline problem in school, I was pretty wild on my own time. I drank and partied a lot and made little secret of my contempt for the social mores of Perkasie and Pennridge High. Many of the town parents suspected I was seducing their daughters, and while it wasn't true—I didn't really have the slightest idea how to go about it, and was far too scared of VD and pregnancy, considering bare breast and perhaps a little feel between the legs an immensely successful night at the drive-in—I did little, well actually nothing, to discourage the suspicion. More than one adult, teacher-types mostly, had suggested to me that I wasn't capable of conforming to "society's standards." (On the first day of our three-day senior class trip to Washington, D.C., I was caught smoking cigarettes in the men's room of Scholl's Cafeteria—a violation of trip rules, the only disciplinary violation I was ever nailed for at PHS. When the trip chaperones magnanimously suggested that they wouldn't send me home if I apologized to the entire class and henceforth never left the tour buses except in the company of a teacher, I said, "Where's the bus station?" It was that kind of recalcitrance that rankled them, I think. They sent me home, threw me off the track team, tried unsuccessfully to expel me from student council and the National Honor Society, and wouldn't talk to me pleasantly for weeks.) So at the time I enlisted in the Marines, I was thinking, "I've got to prove something to myself." Which I now realize meant, "I'll show them."

In addition, the Marines offered me the chance to exorcise the devil
himself. All my life, I'd avoided physical confrontation passionately;
I was a devout coward. I still remember vividly and painfully a winter
day on frozen Lake Lenape. I was about nine or ten at the time, when
Jerry Doughty punched me in the face over and over again, taunting
me to fight, and I didn't know how and was too frightened even to
try to defend myself, and so I just stood there crying and let him beat
me bloody while Les Kappell and the other boys stood around us
laughing at me. And the time in the boys' room on the second floor
of the junior high school when Lloyd Detweiler, a boy half my size,
though I was only just over five feet at the time, started pushing me
around, and I was saved only by the appearance of my tough pal, Larry
Rush, and Larry and I went off to lunch with me telling him what
I had been about to do to Lloyd and knowing it was all lies and still
shaking inside. And the time, only a year before I enlisted, when Jimmy
Whiteneck spit in my face at a party and said he was going to kill me
for "messing with his girl," and I left by the back door in utter humiliation, and after that "his girl" never treated me the same again.

But the Marine Corps could change all that ("Ask a Marine"; "Tell
it to the Marines"), erase all those degradations, and transform me
into a Man To Be Feared, a man no one would dare to mess with.
I liked that thought at least as much as the idea of being a hero.

Finally, there was another reason at least as important and com-
pelling as any of the others, though I didn't understand it until years
later (there were a lot of things I didn't understand until years later).
I have two older brothers. My father is a Protestant minister in a town
where ministers are notable and noticeable figures. Everybody knew
the Ehrhart boys. And no matter what I did—good grades in school,
varsity letters in sports, you name it—my brothers had already done
it before me. And everybody knew it. And reminded me of it often.
"You're almost as good a student as your brother was," was Mr. Smith's
highest praise for me in history class, and he meant it sincerely as a
compliment. On the night Bob graduated, winning the outstanding
history and Spanish awards—I was finishing ninth grade then—the
school superintendent, Mr. Rosenkrance, jovially said to me, "Bob really
cleaned up tonight. Do you think you can do as well?" Though neither
my parents nor my brothers ever laid that rap on me, the rest of Perkasie sure as hell did. And I think now, as much as anything, I en-

listed in the Marines because it was something neither John nor Bob had done (both were in college then). Let them follow me for a change. (They did, Bob receiving a commission in the Air Force in 1967, John in the Marines in 1968. My younger brother, Tom, recently joined the Peace Corps and is now in Thailand. I'm dubious about the efficacy of a person who has never planted more than a row of carrots teaching agriculture to people who have been farming for ten thousand years or so; but it's certainly better than killing them. And besides, *he's* doing something none of *his* brothers have done.)

So there you have it. Ball all of those reasons up together so that they get all mixed in with each other and overlapping and superimposed and nearly indistinguishable from each other, and you get some idea of what was going on in my head when I decided to enlist in the Marine Corps in the spring of 1966. You see now, perhaps, why I usually just say, "Well, it seemed like the thing to do at the time," and let it go at that.

My parents, of course, were not exactly thrilled with the idea. Because I was only seventeen, they had to sign the enlistment contract, too—and they were reluctant to do so. They're just folks, really, and who wants a son to join the Marines when he could go to college? But we talked about it for some time, and finally they agreed. I don't remember this part of the conversation, but my mother says that what changed her mind was when I asked, "Is this how you raised me, to let somebody else's kid fight the wars?" Well, Mom and Dad "believed in America," too—after all, a lot of what I believed, I'd learned from them—and they couldn't conceive of a government that would lie to its people or send its sons off to fight a war where God wasn't on our side; and given that, there wasn't much more they could say.

A few people tried, in their own ways, to get me to see things differently. Though my journalism teacher, Mrs. Geosits, gave me an A for the editorial quoted above, she also wrote at the end of it: "I hope your feelings are strengthened along these lines—but not to the point where you no longer see the whole picture." And after a feature story assignment in which I described how, after twelve weeks of boot camp, I'd be a "full-fledged Marine," she wrote: "To your satisfaction? To the satisfaction of the USMC? Be careful of the twelve-week package; there's no guarantee." And John Diehl, my senior English teacher, himself a former marine and a very broad-minded man, who would bring in full-page ads from the *New York Times* protesting the war (I suspect now that he was far more radical than he was safely permitted to let on in the narrow atmosphere of Perkasie and Pennridge High School), sat me down one night at his place and tried to talk me out of enlisting.

But I was young and full of juice, and you couldn't tell me a damned thing. And surprised as people were, the general response was one of approval and admiration. No doubt, the older set thought it would make a man of me, settle me down and discipline the wild, rebellious streak. Mr. Kern, the teacher who had busted me in Washington, shook my hand and wished me luck. I got my picture in the local weekly, the Perkasie *News-Herald*, standing with Sergeant Bookheimer in front of the high school—and in the neighboring Quakertown *Free Press* as well. My high school sweetheart, Ginny, began wearing a Marine Corps eagle, globe, and anchor pin on her blouse.

And thus, willfully and voluntarily, I went to war in Vietnam, where I learned that it takes no courage to kill, and that acting under fire is mostly a function of training and the instinct for survival, and that most folks in Perkasie didn't have the foggiest perception of what was going on in Vietnam or anywhere else in the world. And where, though it took years for me to comprehend fully what had happened, the belief in Duty, Honor, and Country as I had come to know it fell beneath the boots of armed men acting on the orders of the United States government and in the name of the American people and died under the terrified and hate-filled gaze of human beings who wanted little else but for me to stop killing them and go away.

GOING HOME

LINDA LESHINSKI

Linda Leshinski has worked as an editor and journalist, and since 1978 has served as coordinator of the writing program at the University of Pittsburgh at Bradford. "Going Home" is an excerpt from Dancing Without Music: Stories of Italian Families in America, *an oral history which explores the lives of first generation Italian-Americans who settled in Pittsburgh, and the second and third generations who succeeded them.*

Gina

GINA LOOKS HAPPILY out the window of her Chevrolet as she drives, nodding and pointing at the changed and the unchanged.

"This used to be a nice neighborhood in those days," she says.

"This building here used to be our candy store—now it's a bar. We would go there to buy our penny candy. There was a bakery where that deli is now—it was called Mueller's. There were a lot of German people in this area, and Slovaks, too. I remember the Kavechick family, and the Soloki family—they lived across the street from us.

"Now, I have to get my bearings—let's see—oh, there's the funeral home, it's still here. And here, this was the Italian Club—maybe it still is—no, there are no Italians in this neighborhood anymore."

The yellow brick building is half-hidden by weeds and vines, "White Power" and a peace sign scrawled in blue spray paint on the wall reminders of the brief struggle over this property before the whites moved up the hill.

"That's Lincoln school—that's where I learned my American history. That monument with the cannons—it's for veterans, I think—yes, World War I. See the names on the plaque?

"It's not the same. I don't remember the streets being so narrow. Oh! This is where we used to roller skate! It was the only street that had no cobblestones. Roller skating was my one big passion."

Just as we turn the corner, a black kid in jogging shorts and a Pittsburgh Steelers T-shirt skates by, his feet flashing silver. Gina laughs.

"I guess some things haven't changed," she says.

We turn onto a street of small, neat houses boasting neither poverty nor extravagance, houses musing quietly over the neighborhood like the residents who doze here and there on their porches.

Flanking the dormer-style homes of red, yellow, and plum-colored brick are tiny, fenced-in yards. Petunias, marigolds, zinnias and morning glories glow in the dusty afternoon light, beans, tomatoes, and grapevines climbing slatted fences. Green and orange striped awnings shade cement porches, and crew-cut hedges define the boundaries between home and sidewalk.

Here and there is a larger home—"castles," Gina calls them—mosaics of stone and mortar, emblazoned with iron letters: "M" for Mascaro, "N" for Navarro, the Italian construction dons. We circle the "M" castle, passing a wrought-iron gate scrolled with "M," and find a yard full of junked cars, some on blocks, some pulled into the high grass on flat tires. "M" doesn't live here anymore.

Back on the street, we drive a few blocks in silence. Then Gina spots another memory. "There's the Sebastian Service Station—it's still there! Daddy got his trucks fixed there. That building that's boarded up, that used to be Mangione's grocery store. And that was the swimming pool—it's all torn up now. And up on that hill there was a big old house where "La Signora" lived. She was this dark, ominous figure. We were forbidden to go up there."

We turn another corner, and Gina is looking at house numbers expectantly.

"Here! This is it!"

She pulls the car up to the sidewalk in front of a small, dormer-style house much like the others except for its yard. Tiny like the rest, this one also has a sloping three feet of terrace spread with wood chips and enclosed by a sturdy looking chain-link fence. Gina turns off the ignition and sits back with a sigh.

"They've kept it up nice—look how nice it is."

She points to an upstairs window. "There, that was my room. This is our house, this is where I grew up. And Mommy and Daddy slept in the front room downstairs—there. I wonder who lives in this house, now?"

A tall young black man in regulation blue shorts comes striding down the street toward us, and Gina rolls down the window of the car while I try to make myself invisible by sinking into my seat. "Hello!" She smiles her brightest, prettiest Gina smile. No one can resist it. The mailman stops, smiling hesitantly back at her.

"Excuse me, sir—do you know who lives here? You see, this is the house I grew up in as a little girl, and I just wondered who lives here now."

The mailman looks down at the letters he carries in his hand, and then up at the number of the house before us. "Simon," he says.

"Simon," Gina repeats, as if tasting the word. Then she sits back and sighs with satisfaction. By some mysterious process, the name has met with her approval.

The mailman undoes the catch on the chain-link fence, and goes up the steps to the front door. From the shadows within, a woman's hand pushes open the screen and takes the mail.

"It's still a nice house," Gina says, gazing out the car window as the mailman continues on his appointed rounds. The woman at the door stands in the shadows, watching us parked at the curb, but Gina doesn't notice her. "We always had a swing on the porch, there, and my father had a rock garden instead of those wood chips, and he had a big stone urn planted with flowers, right there." She points.

"Like every other Italian family, we had a grape arbor, and a fig tree in the back yard. My father brought that fig tree from Italy, some-how. He took such good care of it, you know, in the autumn he cov-ered it with dead leaves and wrapped it all up in a tarpaulin to keep it from freezing. He pampered that tree like it was a baby. And you know, when it bore its fruit every year, those figs were so good—I have never tasted figs so sweet.

"And in this little alley here he would wheel up his load of coal and dump it into that cellar window. He brought loads of coal for the whole neighborhood. My uncle would come down that alley almost every night after dinner. They were so close—they helped each other out, lent each other money when times were bad, traded tools and made wine together for the entire family. At night, they'd drink their wine, and tell their stories about the war. They were always the same stories. Sometimes, one would fall asleep while the other one was talking. My uncle would poke Daddy and say, 'Hey, Salvie, wake up!' And then Daddy would wake up and resume the story where he'd left off.

"I wish you could have known those men, their personalities. They were strong, in a gentle sort of way."

She looks out the window, and nods, and nods again.

"Our fathers worked real hard. My father, Salvatore, had his own business, and what he made was his own profit. He and his brothers worked hard all day, from sun-up in the summertime, and in winter even in the dead of night shoveling snow. When they came home, they were always tired. But after dinner in the summer they'd go up to the farm and plant tomatoes—they worked more, until it got dark.

"During the Depression, they did anything—no job was too small. Daddy rented out his truck to the WPA, hauling loads of stone, cement, topsoil, anything—and he was paid for driving the truck, too. People nowadays talk about the WPA as if it were a handout—welfare, they call it. But it wasn't welfare, it was a job. I wonder how many of the walls, sidewalks, and bridges in Pittsburgh were built by the WPA? I'd love to go up to Point Breeze, where my father had so many of those wealthy families for clients, if I knew where the walls that he built could be seen.

"And when he hauled dirt and stone for them to build foundations, he watched them do that. He started building the foundations himself, and then later on he and my brother were building houses. And you know what? The walls and the steps that my father built around our house have never cracked. Why is that? They stand firm.

"In winter when there was no garden work my father and his brothers shoveled snow. I remember them getting up before dawn when the snow had just stopped, to put chains on the truck and go out to clear the clients' driveways for morning. No job was too small. I remember writing out bills for one dollar. My father used to have a paisan who was a bank teller, an educated man—I think his name was Vincent— and he would come over on a Sunday afternoon and do our accounting. But I had good handwriting, and my father thought I was smart because I wrote so well, and got good grades in school, so when I was just nine years old, he said, 'You can do what Vincenzo does.' So then he told Vinnie he didn't have to come back anymore, and I would do his monthly bills and write his checks and keep track of his jobs.

"Daddy would come home every night and go over what he had done that day, and I had the book there, and I would write the customer's name at the top of the page, and write down what he did and put down the date, and how much it cost. Once a month, we would write out bills for all the customers. There were a lot of addresses in Point Breeze, and in Shadyside, too.

"One Christmas, Mrs. MacMillan sent her chauffeur. She was one of Daddy's customers. Oh, he was so impressive—he had this big, long black car, and he was all dressed up in his chauffeur's livery and cap, and he brought us kids this huge snowball made out of cotton. Inside were all kinds of candies and goodies to eat. We were so happy, we gorged ourselves on the candy for days. What a nice woman she must have been, to think of us, the gardener's kids, at Christmastime.

"The hardest part of it was that for them in the landscaping business, they would work all summer long, and then whatever they made would have to carry them through the spring. Most of the time they didn't make it. Always in the spring when my father had to order his grass seed, he had to get that on time. They would take his order, and he would have to pay it in two months, when he had some money. Sometimes he would even have to borrow money from a paisan, and that was a humiliation, I think.

"The thing I hated most about winter was beans. We always ate well, but sometimes we ate very simply. We would have beans three or four times a week. Beans and greens—*minestra e faggioli*, and beans and pasta—*pasta e faggioli*. It was probably very nutritious, but whenever we'd all sit down to dinner and out would come those beans again, I would be there gagging. My father would say, 'Whoever doesn't want to eat go and get the strap.' He had this big strap that he hung in the bathroom to sharpen his razor. But he never used it. You may think beans are very charming, but I'll always hate them."

In the doorway of the Simon residence, the woman who has been observing us shuts the door now and goes inside, as if she knows we are talking only about beans. But Gina is in no hurry to leave.

"We had little meat, really. My mother would make a chicken on the weekends. And in spaghetti sauce there was sometimes *bracciole*. For *bracciole*, you take a round steak, and you pound it thin, and you put a kind of stuffing in it, with eggs and bread crumbs, and then you roll it up and tie it with string. My mother would put it in the sauce then, instead of meatballs. I don't ever remember having meatballs. When the sauce was served, you would take out the *bracciole* and slice it down, and get a piece that looked like a pinwheel.

"And in the fall, my father would go out with my uncle and pick wild mushrooms, and they would come home with a big basket full. You have to be very careful with wild mushrooms, but they knew which ones to pick. My mother would boil them, and as an extra precaution, she would put a fifty cent piece in the water. If the fifty cent piece turned dark, the mushrooms were poisonous.

"In the fall, my mother would do a lot of canning, and she'd put up tomatoes three or four ways—as puree, as sauce for pizza. And she'd put up peppers. She made frittatas for lunch with eggs, onions, and tomatoes and peppers. I'll never forget our teacher at school, Miss Miller. We Italian kids would come back to school after lunch and we must have smelled of onions, peppers, and garlic. Miss Miller would go to the windows and throw them open. 'My goodness,' she'd say, 'let's get some air in here! The smell!'

"Maybe it was the cod liver oil. My mother had a big bottle of it she kept on the shelf, and she gave us each a spoonful every day. What was it for? I don't remember. It smelled awful, like spoiled fish. And every Saturday, we'd each get a spoonful of Milk of Magnesia, whether we needed it or not, as we all lined up for our bath. One bath per week—we probably did smell.

"Miss Miller was so beautiful. She was tall, and she had straight blond hair that she wore pulled back in a sleek bun. And she wore beautiful clothes—fresh white blouses and black skirts and high, high heels.

"But she was such a snob.

"I did love my mother's pizza. She used to make it thick like bread, and then put oil on the dough before she spread it with sauce. We had pizza every Friday because you weren't allowed to eat meat on

Fridays. So every Friday morning my mother would get dough from the bread man who came around. He kept track of our purchases in a little book. Then every so many months my mother would pay him, and when she did, he would give her empty flour sacks, and she would use the flour sacks for different things—dish cloths, aprons. I guess people today think recycling is something new. We didn't waste anything in those days."

A young mother walks by, pushing a child sleeping in a stroller. The baby is shielded from the hot sun by a little fringed awning that sways and makes fringed shadows on the child's face as the stroller sways on the uneven pavement.

"We were never alone, here. The neighbors were very close on this street. I remember Mrs. Lisetti, and Mrs. Armandi, and our Capelli cousins—these people would always help each other out if someone was sick or out of work. I remember when my mother took care of Mrs. Armandi's kids while she was in the hospital. One of them had the whooping cough, and we all got it. I was so sick—I couldn't stop coughing. It was serious business—little kids died of whooping cough in those days. But you didn't think of what trouble it might bring you to help someone else—you considered it your duty. Now, people hide from each other. I don't even know my neighbors to say hello to. No one wants to get involved. It's sad.

"When we kids were ill, we had meatless, plain spaghetti. We called it 'white spaghetti'—just boiled, with butter on it. The theory was that tomatoes weren't good for you when you were sick, because they were acid.

"When we had colds, we always got smeared with Vicks salve, and a hot piece of flannel applied to our chest. If we had a sore throat, my mother would take a white cotton stocking and fill it up with salt that she'd heat on the stove. It would make a kind of roll, and she would tie that around your throat. You know, it really was soothing. I guess it was the heat.

"We weren't sick very often.

"But once a year in the wintertime when he wasn't working, my father would be down with the flu. Then my mother would get a big red brick from the garage. She'd heat it on the stove, wrap it in flannel, and put it on my father's chest.

"There was one remedy I liked very much. When I had a cold, my mother would boil blackberry wine and put sugar in it for me to drink. Oh, that was good! I loved the sweet, hot taste of the wine going down my throat.

"If the doctor had to be called, what a production! My mother would get out her best bed linens, with the cut-work and the embroidery.

"I wonder what my mother thought when she first came to this country? It must have seemed strange, to be plunked down in America, with none of your family, and nothing—she had some beautiful linens she brought from Italy, and some gold, but I remember she sold her jewelry to a man who came door to door. I guess we needed the money.

"Life used to revolve around the neighborhood. You spent less time away from home than you do now. We always walked down this street from school for lunch. And the hucksters sold everything door to door—you didn't go out shopping so much. I remember the man who sold rags, he would come down the street singing, *Rag-o, rag-o, rag-o. . . .*

"There was the fish man, the bread man, the fruit man, and the ice man. If you wanted ice, you would put a card in your window and he would stop and bring in a block of ice for your icebox. There was the man who sold Old Honesty soap—blue flakes that come in twenty-five pound boxes. A lady came door to door with clothing and dish towels she made to sell you. One man came by to sharpen scissors, and another to fix umbrellas—he walked from door to door with this machine on his back, for fixing umbrellas. Another man came by to sell vacuum cleaners.

"The men used to play bocce in the alley," she says, pointing, "they had a court set up there. And we would all sit around the radio every night and listen to Amos 'n Andy. And the fights. Oh, the Italians were so proud when Primo Carnerra won the championship one year. He was this huge man who just could not be beaten down.

"I remember in the summertime how we kids would run to see the parades when we heard the brass band coming down the street to announce the beginning of a festa. Our big festa was always on the fifteenth of August, the feast of the Assumption. The men carried the statue of the Virgin through the streets all the way from the church down to the bridge and back again—several miles, and the brass band accompanied them. One man carried a silver tray to collect money for the church.

"And then in the evening, everyone went to Larmar Field to see and be seen, and there were booths where you could get food, and the bands played again. I remember how the fat ladies would get up and dance the tarantella. It was really a very sexual kind of dance, and it was the only time these women were permitted to act that way.

"We kids were sent home at dusk, and as we walked back to the house, we could see the fireworks go off.

"Oh, those were good times. And you know, it never seemed to rain that night on the feast of the Assumption.

"In the summertime, Carnegie Library would bring a supply of books to our school, and my cousin Palma and I would go there every Monday morning and get books. I loved to read, anything I could get my hands on. My favorites were Victorian novels, and historical romances. I remember reading *Ann of Green Gables*, and *Jane Eyre*. I don't know how many times I read *Jane Eyre*. I couldn't wait for school to start again in the fall.

"You know, that's what amazes me about my father and mother — they had maybe two years of learning to read and write, and they did so much. Many of the people who came over from Italy were illiterates. We didn't exactly prosper, but we got along. The Capellis got together and pooled their money to buy that farm, that piece of land where they grew their vegetables. Land cost practically nothing in those days. Daddy was smart enough to buy up a lot of land. I admired him for that — as soon as he got a little money together, he didn't stick it in the bank, he did something with it.

"He never had too much money in the bank, and he didn't speculate. Before the bottom fell out of the stock market, people were buying stock on margin. They ruined the economy, and they caused the crash, all of those people buying on margin. But my parents weren't smart enough to know about buying stock on margin.

"They just bought up land.

"After the war, Daddy sold our old house in the city and bought ten acres of land in the suburbs. Each time he sold and bought, he had a little more. Slowly, he accumulated, and he also built on the land.

"The whole family seemed to have that instinctive feeling for enterprise.

"I remember that Tony Capelli, for instance. His wife was very thrifty — she would save every penny for him. She was such a thrifty person. She used to can peaches. She had no children—she would spend days and days canning, every time there was a crop of something. Then when company came, she wouldn't have to go out to buy anything special. She would just get out a jar of something—usually peaches. Or if she had to give someone a gift, she would just take you down to this basement lined with shelves and shelves of canned fruit and vegetables. Maybe it seems boring to you to always get peaches as a gift, but they were good peaches.

"She cowered when her husband spoke. And she saved all his money for him so that he became wealthy. And then she had a terrible death. It must have been cancer. Her name was Assunta—Sue would be the American version. Assunta . . . there were a lot of Assuntas in those days. I always hated my name—Gina—because it sounded so Italian. I went by 'Jean' whenever I could get away with it. When we talk about discrimination today, it's always in regard to blacks and women. But in our younger days, being first generation Americans, bigotry was a fact of life. Having an ethnic name seemed to be an invitation to make snide remarks or subtle innuendos.

"During World War II, I was working as a secretary with a firm in Pittsburgh. I worked as hard as I could, and my letters and files were always perfect—so no one could say anything against me. For a while, they tried to make things hard for me. There was a guy in the office who was prejudiced against foreigners. He himself was German, but I guess his family had been in this country for awhile, so he considered himself qualified.

"Anyway, he never said anything loud enough for anyone to hear. He just used to pass my desk every so often and he would lean over and whisper in my ear, 'The trouble with this country is that there are too goddamn many foreigners.' I was seventeen, and I was scared to say anything to anybody.

"In my heart I was very proud of them, my mother and father. My father had come to this country with five dollars in his pocket and he started his own business. In a very small way, he was enacting the American dream.

"But when our parents came to school, for whatever reason, and spoke their broken English, I always cringed a little. I remember I was only four years old when I went to school, and in the second grade when the teacher asked us what year we were born in, I said 1923.

She got mad and said that couldn't be right, but I insisted that it was, not realizing that I was giving away my mother having sent me early. You see, she wanted me to learn English, and she thought I was ready. I was embarrassed when my mother had to come to school to explain, and she had to bring a neighbor with her to translate, because she couldn't speak English.

"I didn't want to sound Italian, or look Italian. I wanted to be American."

The hot afternoon sun beats down on the windshield of the Chevrolet. "We've been sitting here long enough, I guess." She takes a last look at the quiet street, perhaps hearing some other voices from another time. Then she starts the car and pulls slowly away from the curb. The alley is lined with newly painted industrial gray garbage bins. "Those are new," she says, "of course." We turn the corner with the funeral parlor and the school, and then we are on our way out of the old neighborhood again. There is one more landmark.

"That's St. Francis Church, my husband and I were married at St. Francis, but not here." She turns her head, looks, and points. "There."

I look in the direction she is pointing and see a dusty vacant lot. "There's nothing there."

"I know. The old church was torn down a few years ago." Gina taps her fingers on the steering wheel and gives the car a little gas, pumping the accelerator with a hesitant foot, as if she is reluctant now to go back up the hill into the suburbs. We pause at the last redlight.

"And here, at Hartman Road, was the way to our farm. We'd all pile into Daddy's truck and go up there with him. We felt so important, going to our farm. The girls weren't allowed to do anything, though."

We wait at the corner for the light to change, and a city bus stops to let off a few passengers. One is a woman with orange hair. She is wearing a white halter top and a short, black skirt. She teeters a few steps in high-heeled sandals. Motioning silently to the man in shirt sleeves who falls into step beside her, she stops, leans on his shoulder, and adjusts the strap of her shoe. The bus pulls away and they walk off together in the haze of heat and diesel fumes.

Gina presses her foot to the accelerator and urges the Chevy back up the hill.

"This used to be a nice neighborhood," she says.

You Taught Us Good

Claude Koch

"The setting of most of my fiction is the Germantown and Chestnut Hill sections of Philadelphia, which I named 'Wallingford'—not realizing that there actually is a Wallingford in Pennsylvania. It is too late to do anything about that."

*   *   *

Claude Koch is a professor of English at La Salle University in Philadelphia, a novelist, playwright, and poet, as well as a respected and widely published short story writer, whose most recent work has appeared in Prize Stories 1985 and The O. Henry Awards. Koch has lived in Philadelphia most of his life. This story was originally published in Four Quarters.

MONSIGNOR STEPHEN DENT, Superintendent of Schools of the Archdiocese of Mt. Pleasant, had begun his labor that afternoon over accounts that a blind man could see would never balance. A tall, tired, aristocratic man, with a long back and a long neck and a short temper that simmered with a smokeless burning behind a facade of ice, he stiffened at his coffee break when the special delivery letter came from the Catholic Teachers' Association requesting a conference on contracts.

"There is no Catholic Teachers' Association," Monsignor Dent said. He flipped the letter across the desk to his assistant, Father Fly, and gave no more thought to the matter. A week later, Father Fly corrected him: he nicely rearranged the lace curtains of the Chancery window, scrumbled in his throat, padded heavily across the room to the coffee urn, and as he drank said, "They're here, Monsignor."

"*Who's* here?"

Paul Fly wiggled a finger away from the handle of his cup toward the window, and rolled his eyes.

In charity it must be said that the Monsignor had stood the elephantine indirectness of his assistant for three years, and had even developed some degree of indifference to it. It was Fly's innocence—or foolishness—not his manner, that the Monsignor relied upon. He was that rare administrator who believed in checks and balances. He swallowed a sigh, arose, and swept aside the window curtain. His face filled momentarily with blood, but his expression did not change.

Outside the monumental window, directly below him, paraded pickets to the number of five or six. It was cold, and scarves flapped in the wind. Signs tilted as their bearers struggled to support them and still keep their hands in the warmth of their coat pockets and their chins under wraps. The signs spoke rhetorically:

Does the Archdiocese Believe
in "Rerum Novarum"?

"4500 A Year"—
A Living Wage?

Three Kids—Three Jobs

Father Fly came to his side and jostled the Monsignor behind the curtains. The big fellow could hardly desist from throwing his weight around—age, if scarcely wisdom, had removed it from his control. "Sorry, Monsignor," he said. "Sorry. Why, that's Walter Noonan! I remember him as a kid in the C.Y.O. What a nice boy he was!"

Monsignor Dent turned upon his assistant the same detached glance he had directed toward the marchers. "This was *your* C.Y.O.?" he asked. His voice, for one sensitive to it, was honed to a knife's precision. His smile was as economically thin as a sliver of ice. But Father Fly was immune: "Yes," he said. "And what a fine backcourt man he was! That was the year we took the Eastern Coast Tournament for St. Aggie's."

"And what do you think he'll expect to take this year?" Monsignor Dent asked.

"Take?" Father Fly sucked his upper lip. It was a sign he was in deep water. "He's teaching at Archbishop Cêrnek. Why should he take anything?"

"Exactly. Now, Father, you trot down there please and get me the names of those promenaders." The Diocesan Superintendent of Schools returned to his coffee. "Cold," he said with disgust.

"Take their names? You mean ask them their names, Monsignor? How can I do that?"

"Well, ask your friend Noonan. You'll find a way." Stephen Dent placed his palms flat on the table and leaned forward like the Archbishop himself. "His Eminence will be in from the Bahamas tomorrow. I won't have him run into *that* . . ." One more alert to such things than Father Fly could have completed the sentence: *this* is trouble enough. The Superintendent's eyes shifted ever so slightly to the last sad ledger of school accounts.

"He'll never tell me," Fly said mournfully.

"Catholic Teachers Association!" Monsignor Dent lifted his chin toward the window. "They'll be unionizing priests next!"

Father Fly had some gossip on that, but he had also a last-ditch instinct for self-preservation; so he kept it to himself. He had always been a timid man.

"Hello, Walter," Father Fly blew into the roll of his fist. "Now what are you doing out here?"

That fine backcourt man of yesteryear leaned his sign against the iron fretwork of the Chancery railing and, in chill and embarrassment, blew also into *his* fist. "You ought to be out here with me," he said. "What are *you* doing over there?"

Father Fly was genuinely shocked: "Walter! I'm not *over* anywhere. I'm just about my job. In fact," he spoke without guile, "I'm here to get some information for the Monsignor."

Noonan pulled back the sleeve of his overcoat. He caught his gloved finger in a lining thread and muttered. "I'll buy you some coffee," he said. "My hour is up."

"You're as bad as the Monsignor, always sloshing coffee." The priest slipped an arm through Noonan's. "But I'll go with you, for old time's sake, even if you are a commie."

"And you? Are you still the old man's footstool?"

"Walter, Walter, you don't understand him. He's a good man. And there's great change has come over *you*. What do Sally and the kids think of your parading around like a sandwich man?" Father Fly shook his head at the world. "It's not like the old days at all."

"You can say that again. Let's try H & H's." They threaded the tail end of the picket line, and crossed by the fountain of St. Joan in the Cathedral Square. Ice, formed on the point of her lance, thrust a jewel toward the cathedral dome, and her visage, normally serene, goggled shockingly out at them through a slurred visor of ice. From across the square, where they paused and lighted cigarettes, the pickets were small and discouraged under the vast renaissance portals of the Chancery, each huddled and displaced and frosting the air with his breath.

"Now look at that," Father Fly said. "They'll all be sick by tomorrow. They look like panhandlers back in twenty-nine."

"A very apt description," Walter said. "Come along, or your natural charity will overcome you."

Father Fly had never understood why he should have been chosen as the Monsignor's secretary. It was times like this that bowed his head to the yoke. His success had been with boys—as parish moderator of C.Y.O., and then as Archdiocesan Director of all Catholic Youth Organizations. He wasn't even a good buffer for the Monsignor. But he had a wonderful memory for his boys.

"Do you ever see Pete and Michael Stacey?" he asked. They had been Walter's great boyhood chums.

Noonan tugged at his arm: "Do you want to be killed?" The Volkswagen rounding the curb at Sixteenth Street lurched and roared away. "They're both at Republic Can, packers or something."

"It was a great team we had that year."

Noonan softened. "Yes. I think of it sometimes. I saw Wally Jansen last week. He's back from Vietnam—a sergeant, no less."

"I must call his mother and get to see him."

The cold was so persistent that five yards inside the revolving door at Horn and Hardart's the tables were empty. "We'll try the corner," Walter said. "You go sit down and I'll get the coffee. Buns?"

"No, thank you." Father Fly felt better as he hung his coat. He sat mightily and propped his chin in his hands. A passing diner bobbed his head: "Good afternoon, Father."

"Well, a fine good afternoon to you," Father Fly said. He meant it now. What a grand boy Walt had been! Watching him as he popped nickels into the automatic coffee dispenser, the priest saw what no one else whose absent gaze might fall upon that nondescript back could possibly see: the long, frail arms of adolescence, accomplished as a maestro's, moving easily with the ball down the backcourt at St. Agatha's. That was twenty years ago and Walt Noonan was sixteen. Fly sighed. He himself had been in his early forties then, and it had been a great feeling to have the boys needing him, hanging on his words as Coach—greater than all the parish work put together, greater than anything that had happened since. He had been happy.

Noonan turned, the two cups out before him. It wasn't so easy now to see the boy: not so much the natural fleshing and hardening of age—Fly was accustomed to that—but the grace, the openhanded ease . . . ? Ah, well, perhaps he imagined it—it must be there, under the coat a bit too wide at the shoulders, a bit too short in the arms. . . .

"I remembered you take cream," Noonan said. He hung his coat beside the priest's.

"Tell me about the children, Walt. I've not seen you in a dog's age."

"Paul's in the eighth grade at St. Aggie's." Noonan looked over his cup, and Father Fly blushed at his own name. Walter Noonan spoke gruffly: "He's quite a ballplayer, you know."

"How could he be else with such a father?"

"The twins are in seventh. Doing well. There may be a scholarship next year for Sal. God knows I don't want her over at that factory where I teach if I can help it."

"Now, now." Paul Fly patted Noonan's arm. "It's not as bad as all that. There are a number of fine young teachers like yourself . . ."

Walter Noonan smothered a growl in a gulp of coffee. "And the baby," he said grimly, "is in the fifth grade already."

"Time . . ." Father Fly shook his head. "Who would have thought twenty years ago . . . ? By gosh, I can still see you down there at the play-offs in Maryland with that big colored boy looming over you. . . ."

"Yes," Noonan smiled faintly. "I must say I took his measure that day."

"Thirty points from the outside!" Father Fly remembered with admiration. "A great day!"

"You remember Charlie Waters."

"Indeed I do. He caused quite some trouble in the semi-finals with Saint Joe's."

"He's over there in the line." Noonan waved his cup toward the Cathedral. "He's teaching math at Bishop York. Has two kids playing with Joe's this year."

"Imagine! I guess he was so bundled up I didn't recognize him."

"Hank Wittaker will be coming on at four. He has three girls, remember?"

"Good old Hank, best center in C.Y.O. ball that year."

"Yes. Quite a few of them are in the Catholic system now. And," he set his cup down firmly, "you can be sure they're in the Association. Bowers, Jenkins, Baldy—all of them. They'll all be outside your digs. Wave to them now and then."

"You know I will," Paul Fly said. *Digs*, of all things! Walt was literate, and even as a boy there had been that slight, delightful affectation, that half-mocking tone. He had been, in many ways, a delicate boy, with gentle, almost feminine tastes. "But what are you doing out there? You know the Archbishop won't tolerate this. What good will it do?"

"Do you remember," Walter's voice had a shocking, unpleasant note to it, "do you remember that I wasn't the only one 'loomed over' in Maryland? Sometimes the big boys get their measure taken." He stood. "We'll have a team now—trained in the C.Y.O., as it were. You might say that you helped train us, Father."

"But your loyalty . . ."

"It's *your* loyalty I'm worried about." He held the priest's coat. "I've another hour to go. You know," he said over Father Fly's shoulder, "you can't blame us for believing what you taught us. . . ."

"I . . . ?"

"All of you," Walter Noonan said bitterly. He threw his scarf around his neck. "We believed all of you."

They walked back in silence which, on Father Fly's part, was contrived of bewilderment and sorrow. He understood the quixotic temperament of boys—but there was no malice in that. He would have to get out of this office where even the familiar faces appeared shadowed. They walked apart. At Sixteenth Street he was very careful of traffic. Before the fountain Father Fly tugged at Walter Noonan's arm and pointed—it was the sort of thing the boy Walter would have liked: underfoot in a great mirror of ice the bronze dome of the Cathedral swelled into a chalk-blue sky. Pigeons rose like dark *ave's* flung from a broken rosary. But *their* faces, leaned over the lip of the frozen water, were cracked and strange. Walter stooped, and a rock broke the Cathedral tower. Father Fly gasped. The water beneath was dark; and through the virgin wool of his new coat, the priest felt the chill.

"I wonder," Walter Noonan said, "if the Archbishop knows we've the unions with us?"

"My dear boy, what possible difference could it make?"

"It's the end of school construction, and deliveries. *They* won't cross the line. . . ."

The sign was where he had left it. Father Fly shook hands with Charlie Waters. Hank Wittaker arrived, stringy and droll as ever. It was quite a reunion, even if the snow did start in the middle of it.

Monsignor Dent made notes on his desk pad. "I guess you saw a few friends out there," he said.

"Yes." Father Fly was nostalgic. "There's many of the old C.Y.O. crowd. It's been years since I've seen some of them: Charlie Waters, Hank Wittaker, Baldy, Jenkins, Bowers . . . what teams we had in the city then. . . ."

The Monsignor wrote carefully. "Well, perhaps you'll see some more of the old crowd tomorrow. . . ."

"Perhaps," he went into the adjoining room. There was the noise of washing. He came back, drying his hands. "Will the Archbishop meet any of their demands?" he asked.

"The Archbishop won't see them." Monsignor Dent placed his pen meticulously in its holder, annoyed that the splashing of water lingered in his ears. "And they'll get short shrift from me. In fact, they'll get support from no one."

Father Fly sucked his upper lip. He could have corrected the Monsignor then, but he decided, with his last-ditch instinct for self-preservation, to wait until the morrow to mention the unions. And perhaps even his own misgivings. . . . Instead, he went to the window.

"Why, there's even Obie Peters," he said.

Monsignor Dent listened to the dripping of water and the ticking of the clock, sitting erect and composed behind the desk with the chill dignity that was so appropriate to his state. At the window, Father Fly blocked what little natural light there was left, his huge shoulders ruffling the drapes, an ungainly and foolish and grotesque figure for that renaissance frame. The Monsignor sighed that darkness should come so early, and with so much still to be done. He straightened from the desk and walked quietly up to his subordinate. He tapped him on the shoulder. As Father Fly stepped deferentially aside with the sad clumsiness of a shy big man, the Monsignor saw the buildings beyond the square lodged against a leaden sky, and the snow powdering the pickets and their signs. Against the element that flurried and obscured, they flapped their arms and scarves; and passers-by bent to the storm. Who would notice them now? The storm had risen quickly indeed.

Monsignor Dent looked at Fly. The priest's eyes met his, a harmless beatific smile on his face and memories of an uncomplicated past in his eyes. How could he recognize out there Obie Peters or Charlie Waters or Hank Wittaker or Baldy or Jenkins or Bowers—or Joan of Arc, for that matter: a sparse, discomforted rout indeed to clutter the chancery portal.

"They were wonderful boys," Father Fly said "and I wasn't much of a coach. I could never understand how we won." The shy smile embraced Father Dent, and excluded and defined the austere and lonely places beyond him in that room.

The Monsignor sighed again. He went back to the desk, turned on the light, and crumpled up his notes. Let the Archbishop come home on the morrow—there were some accounts that a blind man could see had to be kept open on the books. For who could balance them, who render justice? At the same time, his temper smoldered. He knew he had been had, and he was not quite sure how it had come about.

THE LAST MIRACLE SHOW

EVAN PATTAK

Native Pittsburgher Evan Pattak is a freelance writer and a contributing editor of
Pittsburgh Magazine, *where this profile of Kathryn Kuhlman first appeared.*

A T TEN O'CLOCK the night before people are already waiting on the steps of the First Presbyterian Church. By Midnight there is a crowd, spilling over the steps into the medieval court-
yard and out onto the sidewalk. At seven o'clock in the morning they
are an army, Death's irregulars, crutches poised, shivering in the chill
winter air.

A fanciful observer, noticing how they press across Sixth Avenue
so close to Gimbels and the Duquesne Club, might imagine that they
are an army, massing against the forces of health and privilege. At
some silent signal from their unseen commander they will shatter the
showroom windows, spearing the chic mannequins and steering their
wheelchairs into the shimmering displays and cases. They will push
past the doorman of the Duquesne Club, taking their cases to the
paunchy millionaires who have pulled up their towels in astonish-
ment. Having no answers, the rich men too are gored and trampled,
laid waste by the Crippled Crusade.

But the people here have little interest in cause or blame. They seek only relief. Like the long night's wind, suffering has numbed them to all but the most basic thoughts and feelings. Because they must, they visit the doctors, clinics and specialists, try patent medicines, foolish nostrums, mysterious exercises, Eastern incantations and propitiations. Always at the end, they come here, or wherever she is. Hoping for everything, expecting nothing, they come to see Kathryn.

About half of them will get into the church, and about half of these will be able to see Kathryn full view. Others will see her back, the top of her head, perhaps only a shoulder or hand. For the rest, the ones closed out of the church proper, there is still the possibility of squeezing into the church basement or remaining outside on the steps, where loudspeakers will carry Kathryn's voice. At most miracle services Kathryn cures someone who is not in the building, so you dare not go away after coming this far.

It is quiet in the crowd, almost unnaturally quiet. Absent are the usual sounds of people conversing, coughing, the reassuring hum of small talk. Occasionally someone up front sings, but the song dies out before it reaches the sidewalk.

Ambulances pick their way through, depositing stretcher cases sent by doctors who have done what they could and, despite their skepticism, figure that no further harm can be done. A woman faints but is kept from falling by the crush of bodies. She is placed in one of the ambulances after the patient inside is borne out.

In the middle of the hump on Sixth Street, incongruously, a slender woman sits in a brown folding chair. Next to her is a woman from Rochester, N.Y., with her mother, husband, and Frankie, whose hand she is holding. Frankie is approaching middle age, but he has the wide-eyed, gossamer stare of a child. His hair has been combed in an old-fashioned, wavy upsweep. He has been dressed cleanly but hastily. His shirt collar flaps against his chin. Frankie clutches the woman from Rochester's hand and smiles, a little afraid, a little flirting.

The woman from Rochester has a broad, determined face, piled graying hair stiff and brittle from spraying. She is wearing a printed blouse that hangs over her too-tight red stretch pants. She cranes her neck, trying to get a glimpse of the door.

"We were here at 12:30. We were right up there, close to the door. We waited until 5:30. Then we just couldn't take it any more, the cold. We had to go warm up, get something warm to drink."

A man close to the door turns and shouts. The cry echoes through the crowd. Let women with babies through. Let people in wheelchairs through.

"This is the second time I've tried to see her. I went when she was in Buffalo, but I couldn't get in. They had three thousand people inside and six thousand people outside. Christ, they have buses from Connecticut, from Canada."

There is a creaking of doors. The crowd begins to move. Suddenly your feet leave the ground. You are being carried along, as if by a jet-stream. You aren't walking but are supported by the backs and shoulders of the people around you and there is nothing you can do if the stream carries you away from the door. The woman from Rochester, clinging to Frankie, is separated from her mother and husband. Her eyes glass over. She begins to whimper.

"Frankie, Frankie. C'mon Frankie." This, although Frankie's hand has never been out of hers.

Her mother and husband appear at the top of the steps near the door. The husband cups his hand around his mouth.

"Don't get panicky! Don't get panicky!"

But she can't help it. She is frightened and can't get her feet on the ground and she has been there since 12:30 and now there is a good chance that she won't get in again.

"Frankie, Frankie, where are you Frankie?"

The stream leaves her at the steps. She runs up, still dragging Frankie, and rejoins her mother and husband. They are stopped at the door by a smiling usher.

"Plenty of seats. Plenty of seats. Just hold on a minute there. Plenty of seats."

He lowers his arms and lets them pass. There are several corridors leading off the entrance, and each is guarded by rows of ushers, looking bored already, who steer you to your seats. When she is safely seated, in a row of folding chairs behind the platform, the woman from Rochester pats Frankie's hand. She smiles at her husband, embarrassed, but she can smile at it now, for they are inside. And though of course you don't ask for miracles, have no right to expect one, you certainly have a better chance of one inside, where Kathryn can at least see you, than you do huddled around a loudspeaker on the steps.

The woman from Rochester and her family will be able to see the upper part of Kathryn's back. Most of the nearby seats are taken by a group from Lancaster, Pa., whose members wear printed nametags around their necks. One of them, Helen Devereaux, the name tag says, is sound asleep.

But for a blinding spotlight tilted toward the elevated platform, the church is dim. An organist high up on one of the layers plays softly, building to a crescendo. When nothing happens he tapers off and plays quietly again. The ushers, guarding the pews like sentries, pass out paper and envelopes. These are to be used for prayer requests to be presented to Kathryn. She won't get to all of them today, but she will read some of them on her daily radio show, carried by more than fifty stations, and others on her weekly television program, broadcast by more than sixty stations. People who have never seen Kathryn claim to have been healed after such a reading. The woman from Rochester's mother has been sending in her prayer request for nearly three years, though she has never heard it read.

Without warning she appears. Waving from the platform as if pulled up through a trap door. There is a belated standing ovation. She is a tiny, distant figure in a white chiffon dress with billowy sleeves. Her cheeks are pinched with rouge, her strawberry hair teased into little doll curls. She might be a doll, a walking, talking doll, but for her hands. They are enormous. Oversize without being grotesque, somehow appropriate. She points elegant, expressive fingers, witch's fingers.

"While you're standing see if you can squeeze in as far as you can go. All seats are open. We reserve no seats. We're full inside and outside. Maggie, there's two here. Are you the people, the uh, uh, we can't wait. Two more here, Maggie. Bring those two here. Move over a little tighter. That's right. Over here. One behind them. They can fit tighter. That's right. How about the balcony?

"It's not by might, not by power, but by my spirit, sayeth the Lord. Not one person seeks Kathryn Kuhlman. We each seek JEEsus. Will the ushers please remove the woman who is making the noise? She doesn't know we have no manifestations of the flesh here. This is serious.

"I'm so excited, because of this cancer cure. As I tell you, I'm often the last to hear about these things. Come up here. Where are you from?"

A woman named Val is led to the platform. She carries a newspaper clipping that says she had a tumor the size of a football on her hip and had never been told it was cancer. She had twenty-five cobalt treatments and her doctors had given her up as lost. She was cured by Kathryn at a miracle service.

"Where are you from?"

"Ontario, Canada."

"The first thing she said this morning was that now she can tell people 'JEEsus healed me.'"

"My doctor put it in the paper."

Kathryn grabs the clipping and waves it.

"Her doctor put it in the paper!"

"They didn't believe me, they didn't examine me. Finally they examined me. When they couldn't find the tumor, well, they were bewildered. They ran out of the room and got other doctors. They didn't believe it. But I got a paper. My doctor said, 'I have so many hopeless patients they have to go to God. They have nothing. They have to go to God.'"

"This is really something. And you're from where, Honey?"

"Ontario."

"And how large was the tumor?"

"Football. They told me like a football. All along I thought it was a hernia. Then they said to me, 'But you had cancer.' 'So what,' I said, 'I left it in Pittsburgh.' I was sitting in the third row right where that woman in the white sweater is. You said, 'There is a woman here with a tumor who has cancer and doesn't know it. Stand up. You are healed.' Every hair on my body shook."

"And you knew nothing about the power of God?"

"No."

"God love ya. Were you frightened?"

"No. I was happy."

"And here it is." She waves the clipping again. "The doctor has verified everything. He wants it known to the whole world that his patient was healed."

"My doctor sent prayer requests for him and his family."

"Dear JEEsus. I beg of you. It's not by might. It's not by power. It's by my spirit, sayeth the Lord. We stand here amazed at what we have heard. It's so simple, yet we can't believe it. There's no mystery about it. All we can say is thanks, a million thanks.

"It's so simple. It's so simple. Thanks is all that I can say to you. It's so simple. I rebuke that lung cancer in the name of JEEsus. Oh, you're going to find one of the greatest healings of cancer we've ever had. Wouldn't it be wonderful if everyone here who had cancer was cured? There's somebody with a brace on. You've been healed. Take it off. This is the lung cancer?"

The ushers have brought a man to the platform. She places witch's fingers on his head and closes her eyes. He swoons into the waiting arms of an usher.

"There's an asthma. I rebuke it in the name of JEEsus. The power of God flow through that body. What is it? It's another asthma. I rebuke it in the name of JEEsus. Somebody's arm has loosened. What happened? Where are you?"

Half a dozen hands wave.

"You may never have expected it. What happened? Is there no pain there? For you have been healed and can't believe it. You can feel it come back to you. Which arm was it? There's another cancer. I rebuke the cancer. There's another cancer completely cured. There's another arm, a side and arm. Don't come up here until after you've been healed."

The ushers bring two women to the platform. Kathryn's fingers reach out for the arm of one, clamping it like a vise.

"Just move it. Just move it. Just move it. She's scared to death. Bring the wheelchair, if you please."

Two different women are on the platform, the younger one in tears.

"She's my mother. She didn't know it."

"Where are you from?"

"Miami."

"Miami? Did you fly in?"

"Yes, but we had trouble getting the money."

"Where do you go to church? What is it? Baptist? Pick up your legs now. Just pick 'em up. What nationality are ya? Cuban? Well God love ya. Oh, dear JEEsus. Bless this woman. Bless this daughter."

The daughter, touched by the fingers, falls into an usher's arms.

There is something confusing, maddening about the crazy-quilt roster of healings and testimonials. It is sprawling, hectic, healings raffled off like bogus antiques at an auction. Cosmic diseases are linked with those merely comic. Cancers and carbuncles. Blood clots and bunions. Welts and warts. There are no patterns, no pauses. You would expect the congregation to be delirious with joy because in that crazy hub-bub just maybe, who knows, just maybe it could happen, *it could happen!* But if anything, the despair deepens. Nobody knows where to look next or who has been cured of which disease. Like kids at the circus, they are torn between the elephants, clowns and tumblers in the three rings, caught in a frustrating dilemma of riches.

Only on the platform is there order, and there it is consummate. Everything about Kathryn is studied, professional, from the buffer of ushers between her and the cranks and zealots, to her dramatic pro-nunciation of the word "JEEsus," over-accenting the first syllable each time. She is neither frantically possessed nor the shy woman trans-formed into a stuttering Sibyl by the touch of God. Her voice is that of a game show host, glib, confident, drawing the expected answers from the rattled players. In all that wild curing, sobbing and praising, she coolly works in a plug for a local restaurant.

Her movements are exaggerated, aimed at the top rows of the skinny tiers, and one senses in her mind the picture of a stern drama teacher reproving, reminding, pro-ject, prooooooo-jeeeeeeeeeeeect. She steps backward in amazement, clutches the railing in wonder, clenches her teeth in reverence. The spotlight shimmers off her lipstick, giv-ing the illusion that her lips are in constant motion, anticipating what the healed will say or even mouthing their words for them. That is the dominant image. The ventriloquist.

"There's an ear opening up!"

Helen Devereaux from Lancaster awakens. She raises her hand. An usher comes to her.

"Can you hear me now?"

"Yes."

"Which ear gave you trouble?"

"The right one."

"And you can hear now?"

"I can hear, Kathryn."

The usher leads her to the platform. Another woman cured of deaf-ness has got there first, already has her head locked in the witch's fingers.

"Can you hear me now?"

"Yes."

"Can you hear me now?"

"Yes."

"Say, I am happy."

"I am happy."

"Say, I am very happy."

"I am very happy."

"Say, I love JEEsus."

"I love JEEsus."

"Can you believe it?"

"I wished for it and I believed."

"Where are you from?"

"Canada."

"Well, take off that hearing aid. You don't need it."

Helen Devereaux waits against the wall while Kathryn talks to more of the cured, a man who had nine operations on his back, several people paralyzed by pinched nerves. Finally the usher leads Helen Devereaux back to her seat. She smiles and goes back to sleep. The woman from Rochester watches her, near tears. Frankie looks sullen, turns accusing eyes on his family.

"People, I have to tell you something, the funniest thing. I know God has a sense of humor. Show them the potatoes. Hold them up. He says he heard that potatoes are good for gout and arthritis. He says it just left him. His gout is gone and his hip is gone. And he says, 'I don't know what did it, the potatoes or God.' Isn't that something? There he goes. He left the potatoes.

"We're gonna pause now to praise Him. This is another way of expressing gratitude. This is another way of expressing appreciation. That's all I'm gonna say about it. It's an expression of what you feel inside. Give nothing less than your best at this moment. Give us your best at this moment. The best is what you give. Whatever you give, pray over your own gifts. Use your own words."

The ushers pass through the aisles, circulating pouches of maroon velvet. In moments the pouches are distended with bills. The woman from Rochester's husband puts in a five.

Why? They drove all the way from Rochester, waited nearly nine hours in the cold, listened for four more hours while others were cured.

"It was wonderful," the woman from Rochester says, "just wonderful. No, no cure for our family. But it's all right. It's all right."

She will watch Kathryn's television show while she irons, listen to Kathryn's radio show while she fixes Frankie's lunch. And the next time Kathryn Kuhlman is within driving distance, the woman from Rochester will come see her again.

"One week ago Sunday, I think it was one of the greatest thrills in my life. We were in Jerusalem. We held a miracle service there. Four thousand people packed in the auditorium and the overflow in others. You'll never know what a thrill it was.

"There were thirty-six to thirty-eight nations represented in Jerusalem. It was the greatest miracle service we ever had. They had booths, and in these booths were translators. There were more than three hundred people from Finland alone. Over three hundred! Three of the newspapers sent their best reporters. How many wish they'd been there? Put up a hand. I don't know where we'd have put ya. There was a large delegation from Germany. From Ghana. From South Africa. It was a thrill.

"The newspapers said there were over two hundred definite healings in that one service alone. From all nations. That's what it said in the Jerusalem Post. Thirty-six or thirty-eight nations! How many think it's marvelous? You should've been there."

DISTANCES

W. S. MERWIN

W. S. Merwin is a recipient of the Bollingen Prize, the Pulitzer Prize, and the fellowship of the Academy of American Poets. He has spent most of his life traveling and living in far places: Spain, Portugal, France, Southern Mexico, but in this essay, originally entitled "Tomatoes" and published in Grand Street, *Merwin returns to the scenes of his childhood in western Pennsylvania and to the people that helped shape his life. I call this excerpt "Distances" because of Merwin's observation that his parents' attitudes toward the regular journeys between those western Pennsylvania river towns of his father's roots, and Union City, New Jersey, where they were then living, "seemed to me to be expressions of a single course, two sightings of the same destination. But the returns to Pennsylvania may have revealed, more than anything else, distances. And added to them."*

M Y FATHER'S DRIVING — he spoke of it as though it were something he could point to — was a treasure he cherished all his life. From the start it was a proof, to him, of his own exceptional ability and what it could achieve, a sign that he had made good and not disappointed his Mumma's hopes, or his own. My grandfather could not drive a car. He could drive a team, and was said to have had a river pilot's license — but what did those matter in the world that my father had entered in college and the clergy? Very possibly his brothers did not drive at that time either, though they were older than he was. So it set him apart, and permitted a freedom of movement which, in his case, could be deployed in such a way as to suggest special responsibilities. Even after driving had become all that is most ordinary he remained proud of his own as something distinctive, and was prompt to refer to the number of years he had driven, how early he had obtained his license, and—until he was in his sixties—to the fact that he had never had even a minor accident. "Not a scratch," he said, though it was not literally true. Yet he never learned to shift into second without grinding the gears, although he winced, clucked his tongue, shook his head, if he heard someone else do it. Sometimes his gear-crashing was blamed, by an elliptical process, on the Ford, or the car he had learned on, and the peculiarities of their gear systems. As far as I can remember from early allusions, his first car had been a hand-me-down, passed on because neither the car nor the former owner had much to lose by the transfer, and because the machine would be suitable for a novice to practice with. And then, I think, came The Ford, the first real car. In my mind it is green, with a rumble seat, but I never saw it, and it is possible that the car acquired that color in my mind from nothing except the fact that my father bought it from a doctor friend in Greenville, who warned him that it was no car for a preacher because it ran half on gas and half on cuss. It started reluctantly, by all accounts, in response to a handcrank in front. The fuel line worked by gravity, so the only way for it to climb a hill was in reverse. It stalled in the rain, or in long puddles, and had to be cranked again in cloudbursts until it shook itself. It served my father and mother, in this way, for a couple of years, on the rutted roads of western Pennsylvania.

Then and later, all through my childhood, whatever car they had or we had was indisputably my father's. At some time in their first years together he had started to teach my mother to drive. It must have been early in their courtship, or their marriage—an exceptional, romantic gesture. And he must have felt some ambivalence about it even when it was suggested. My mother maintained (it was a word she used often) that he had shown no patience at all, and perhaps in an attempt to ease the situation by generalizing it, she came to express the opinion that no husband or wife should try to teach the other to drive. The lessons came to grief quickly. I do not know what car they were driving—a borrowed one, or the Ford soon after they got it. But my mother had failed to change gears correctly on a hill, and then had not used the brakes promptly enough, nor steered accurately enough, and the automobile, which fortunately was not going very fast, had bumped the entrance to a narrow iron bridge, and injured a front fender. The curriculum ended at that spot. My mother refused to drive further, and she stuck to the decision, to which she had been brought, she said, by my father's behavior on that occasion: his annoyance at the accident and the harm done to the car. The issue became a fixation in their lives, one that they used to air the multiplying disappointments and resentments that arose between them. In the thirties my father made fun of women drivers, and my mother would remind him that he had been taught to drive by a woman—a round which neither pursued. My mother arrived at other refusals, and compared them to her refusal to drive. "It would be just like the car," she said. "If anything happened, I would never hear the last of it." She said it again when, twenty years after the accident, in Scranton, at the time when my father bought the new Olds (from a man named Burnie) he urged her to take driving lessons and get a license. And she did, finally. First Burnie himself came, a rotund man wearing his garage coveralls, and fetched her away for driving instruction—out of sight of the house. And after Burnie, a professional instructor, in a brown hat and a gabardine. And she took her test and got her license, and still would not drive the car. The license was allowed to expire. My father cited the story as proof of his own desire to remove the problem, and of her clinging, instead, to her grievance. She insisted that she would have no peace if she drove that car. Every little thing would be her fault. He went away on a trip and left her the keys and the tank of the car full of gas, in the garage, and she never took it out once while he was gone. She said he left her the keys only because he knew she would not use them, and that he never really wanted her to drive. No doubt they were both right. It was not until another whole decade had gone by, and they were in their fifties, and my mother had a job of her own in the Kittanning court house, that she renewed her license—and bought a car of her own, which she was very particular not to let him drive, citing his way of changing gears as one of her reasons. By then, if he ever spoke of women drivers, it was with a certain amusement at the joke itself, a touch of nostalgia at being reminded of a rather silly period piece. And she could give up—partly because she seldom rode in his car, with him driving—her sharp intakes of breath when he crashed his gears or braked too suddenly or turned without signalling. She could adopt an attitude of resignation, expressed with raised eyebrows, toward his driving as a whole, to which he no longer drew attention.

But back at the end of their twenties, in the months when my mother was pregnant with me, the First Presbyterian Church of Union City, New Jersey, extended the call—as it was phrased—to my father, and he was happy to accept. They moved. A new place, within sight of Manhattan. In a new state, where people pronounced their words differently. A new church, a city church, and in comparison with the former ones, a rather large one. A new house, new to them at any rate, considerably bigger than any they had lived in. A child on the way, as part of their new life. The pregnancy dated from the beginning of the year. In keeping with the turn of the moment, The Ford was replaced with a new car, The Buick. It represented distance already traversed. And a boast of arrival.

My father remained proud of The Buick for several years, its make, model, everything about it. It is true that I do not remember ever seeing another one just like it. Neither a sedan nor a coupe; a two-door, with a deep back seat, a large hump of luggage compartment on the rear, and the spare tire bolted on a rack behind that. The middle section stood up like a deck house or a top hat, and was covered with a textured black patent leather. A broad visor extending from the front of it shaded the windshield. The body of the car, from the windowsills down, was a lustrous blue, a twilit sky color. It looked as though you could see far into it, as into water, and my father, and a series of men from the church ritually, indeed reverently, washed and Simonized it. My father pronounced the word Simonize as though it were a spell. When new license plates arrived he called me into his study for the ceremony of removing them from their waxed paper and holding them up with a little "Hm" of pleasure. The rear plate was fastened behind the spare tire, under a small black oval box from which the glass corneas of three lights protruded, one white, one green, and one amber. Each glass was fluted on the inside, like the reverse of an orange squeezer, so that looking at them one saw what appeared to be the undersides of three flowers with precise narrow petals. Only the white light worked, by the time I was old enough to be interested, but I considered all three of them, and the red tail lights—particularly when seen in the dark, with the smoke of the exhaust swirling past them—to be objects of urgent but inexplicable beauty.

Besides, there were the wooden spoke wheels, the spokes enamelled the same lucent blue as the body, with fine black lines along their centers. And running boards on which I yearned to ride. I was never completely content with the plain, almost flat radiator cap with indentations around it for grasping it, once I had seen caps adorned with thermometers standing in metal rings. It made no difference to me that my father shook his head and pursed his lips at the thermometers, and said they worked only for a short time and then were no use. I was not interested in what they were supposed to do.

The Buick's importance extended to its housing. It had to itself the whole ground floor of a real (small) barn that walled off half of the back yard: a two story structure with hay-loft door upstairs above the main ones. The building must have been the same age as the manse. Both of them harked back to the 1870s or '80s at least, the time of horses and carriages. It was obvious that the barn had had other lives that had been concealed but were there in it still. For a while, I learned—I no longer remember from whom—it had been used as a warehouse for hides, which had been hoisted from wagons in bales, by means of the pulley that was still there, up under the peak outside the hayloft doors. For us—for me, and later for my sister—the whole building was absolutely forbidden ground, and only once did I ever see what was on the upper floor. My father, one day, in an expansive mood, allowed me in beside the car, where the walls were hung with rakes and shovels and chains and there were shelves sagging with paint cans. On the far side a ladder went straight up to a hole in the ceiling. He held me up, with my head above the level of the upper floor, so that I could peer around in the cardboard light. There was nothing there but bulges. When he lifted me down he told me that I must never go up there, for any reason. In time that upper story was populated with wasps, and with assorted people and creatures of my invention, many of whom did not even suspect each other's existence. When my father was about to take the car out, the barn was called the garage. He would open its doors, and then open the gates of the fence along New York Avenue and back the car out onto the white-pebbled driveway, and whoever was going with him would get in there.

For those trips "back home"—which was another of my father's

ways of referring to the periodic journeys across New Jersey and Pennsylvania to New Kensington, where my grandmother had moved after
he left for college, and where he had never lived—he believed in getting an early start. By one route the distance, according to the Buick's
odometer, was 444 miles. He had made it more than once in a single
day, which he and his listeners considered a wonderful achievement.
It allowed him, at any rate, to declare that he *could* do it in a day,
though it meant leaving early and arriving late at night. Most of the
trips on which he managed to do it were ones that he took by himself; usually, when the family was along, we broke the journey somewhere on the way. But whatever the plan, or absence of plan, he—
who ordinarily did not like early rising—wanted to be on the road,
if possible, by four o'clock in the morning. You made your best time,
he repeated, during the hours before daylight. So we got up in the
hollow dark, my mother cooperating with the arrangements, but bus-
tling and clucking her tongue at the proceedings as she went, because
getting up so early violated the children's sleep. Her pursed lips and
her impatience with the last minute packings and closings expressed
a deepening reluctance concerning those trips altogether, but I did not
understand that, at the beginning. My father assumed full authority
for the expeditions, and ignored, or pretended to ignore, her lack of
enthusiasm. "The darkest hour," he would say to me, eyebrows and
finger raised, "is just before the dawn." As we got ready, and floated
out of room after room—bedrooms, bathroom, dining room ("the children have to have their breakfast if they're going to be up that long")—
the light in the house looked sallow and unlikely, and the smell of
wallpaper followed us and then abruptly was gone, replaced by the
startling yet elusive scent of what my mother called the night air, which
had its dangers. There were no cars at all, at that hour, and the silent
darkness was freighted with that odor speaking of the earth. Our footsteps echoed on the gravel walk. The hinges of the back area-way door
squeaked behind us. The street car wires hummed above the avenue.
The garage doors grated open. The Buick started up, waking huge
echoes, and the tail lights moved toward us with the smoke rising around
them. My mother spoke to us, and we answered, in whispers, and we
climbed in onto the stiff velvet upholstery with its own dusty night
smell. In the light of the street lamp its inky blue looked black.

Now for years the trips have run together into a few scarcely distinguishable variations. As a child I could not see that they were steps in a progression, and that their quest for continuity betrayed change. I supposed that the decision leading to each of those early starts — never quite as early as my father had hoped they would be — arose from a clear and identically formed impulse, as definite and indisputable as a day on a calendar. Even my parents' different, and diverging, attitudes toward those journeys and visits seemed to me to be expressions of a single course, two sightings of the same destination. But the returns to Pennsylvania may have revealed, more than anything else, distances. And added to them.

From the beginning of her acquaintance with my father's family, my mother had felt that its women — my grandmother and my aunts who had remained her satellites — had been unwelcoming to her, had received her as an outsider, and preferred to keep things that way. She was probably right, and it would not have made much difference to her to consider that their behavior was only in a limited sense personal; no doubt they would have done as little to make anyone my father married feel at home. As I could see later, they were not remarkably open or flexible or thoughtful, and my mother's tastes and admirations, and most of her interests, were alien to theirs. They were habitually suspicious of anything or anybody from outside. And for her part, coming into a closed family circle made her particularly conscious of having no parents, herself, and no close relatives except her brother Morris, who died soon after she was married. Her own lack of kin must have made their minute ingrown sanctum, with my grandmother at its center, seem particularly exclusive. If she was withdrawn they found her snooty. And in their eyes, of course, my father remained their possession — and they too were right. He was the youngest son, and his achievements and distinctions, real or imagined, were adjuncts to their own carefully hedged self-esteem. Their adulation, dependable and uncritical, helped to nourish and restore a view of himself which my father clung to. Before he and my mother had moved east to Union City, and so before I was born, it was possible for him to drop in on them, surprising them; but once he and my mother lived in New Jersey, a visit was an occasion. He came alone less often, and if things were different, they knew why.

The atmosphere of those visits apparently improved for a while soon after I was born. There was a baby for them all to attend to, and my mother was in charge. She was meticulous and protective, and very sure of what was needed; but they, for their part, were zealously strict in their notions of what was proper, and they respected her suddenly revealed unhesitating authority. Besides, my grandmother was doubtless beyond caring much about the details of child care. She was old, and had reared seven children of her own. The process appeared to have used up most of her interest in the subject. Unless children made noise or otherwise violated her strait views of what was good conduct she appeared to take only a remote and vague interest in them. Her relation with them—with us—was largely indirect: she spoke to someone else about them. The role of the matriarch had grown up, had been built up, around her, gradually replacing some earlier insulation, and she accepted it absolutely. My two aunts, Alma and Edna, had no children of their own. I was a toy. During my first two years, before my sister was born, we stayed longer, on some of those visits to New Kensington, than I remember us ever doing later—a matter of weeks, sometimes. I was taken along, swathed in baby things, to the houses of my parents' old friends in that region. Occasionally my mother consented to entrust me to Aunt Edna's care for a few minutes at a time. When I was almost two my father's health was not good; my mother was pregnant again; there were other demands upon my parents that called them away. By then I could be left with Eddie and her husband, Port, for slightly longer periods, and when I was alone with them they tended to spoil me. I have an impression—formed mostly of details long forgotten or subsumed in others—of the intervals with Eddie and Port as a halcyon age, and my fondness for the smells and sounds of that drab, smoky, grating town comes from those days.

My grandmother lived at 1154 Stanton Avenue, New Kensington, in what I now realize was a small house, the ground floor yellow brick, the upper story white-painted frame. Her daughter, my Aunt Eddie, and Uncle Port, lived next door at 1152, in a house that was virtually its twin, except that Eddie's front porch was enclosed in windows, and my Grandma's was open, with a big dark green porch swing at the end. The swing was not to be sat on, unless a grown-up came first and dusted it off; otherwise the soot got on one's clothes and hands and legs. My Grandma's house, inside, was the darker of the two, and it felt quieter. A black marble and ormulu clock ticked before a mirror, on the mantelpiece. Both houses faced west onto tiny patches of grass set between clipped privet hedges. At the end the grass fell away abruptly on a steep bank. Each house had a cement walk out in front, and a flight of cement steps down to the sidewalk. Beyond that there was another small bank, and at intervals a few more cement steps led down to the street—a detail that pleased me, invited me: it conveyed a remote suggestion of living in castles, with ramps and battlements. The street was not paved in those years, as I recall, but was oiled and strewn with small pebbles, and there were deep cracks and holes. It was just wide enough for two cars, but there were seldom two at once moving along it. They appeared rarely, picking their way slowly along, and they almost never parked on the street. On the far side the bank fell away again, a real drop, half as high as the house, to the railroad tracks. There was a whole broad current of them, running past the front doors of the houses, glinting and ringing. It seemed to me that the sound of them was present all the time, at those two houses. The roar and shriek of trains rose out of it and faded back into it again, echoing, as did the puffing and chugging, clanging, thumping, bell ringing and hissing of the short engines from the switching yard that fanned out, a half block to the north. When the wheels had gone the sound was still there, a clear impersonal note travelling from the springs and concerns of the outermost world, neither menacing nor address-ing nor pausing, completely free of the injunctions and opinions of the family, and always there. Other sounds spoke of the actual houses. The cement walks between them echoed like slapped inner tubes, when someone's footsteps passed through. The nails of the rat terriers kept in both cellars clicked and rattled like rice on the wood and linoleum of the cellar stairs and on the cement around the furnaces. But the sound of the tracks and the thunder of trains were the ones that stamped the place and claimed it continuously, and in coming to know them close at hand I was hearing a note that led back through my grandparents' lives to the beginning, and before.

My grandmother came from farther north, along those tracks. As long as she was alive I never knew where she had been born and brought up, nor anything about her parents. I did not at any point feel inti-mate enough with her to ask her anything about herself and—at least by the time I knew her—she tended, as a matter of habit, to turn aside questions that were put to her, and to suspect the motives of anyone who questioned her. Whether that trait was inborn and inherent, or a commonplace of her background, I can only guess—and I imagine it was both. Some of it she, and the life they shared, passed on to her children. When I asked my father about her parents and where she had grown up, he seemed not to know, or to have forgotten; his manner offered little hope that he would remember. My grandmother's maiden name was Anderson, "from up around Clarion there." The Andersons had family reunions every so often, my father told me once as we passed such a gathering—men in white shirts, women in summer dresses, standing around trestle tables under big trees, outside an unpainted farmhouse—and he had been invited but had gone only once or so, and had not found much of interest there.

He did tell me that his mother's father, whom they had called Grandpap Anderson, had had a donkey he used when he worked on the roads, hauling and setting out crushed stone and gravel, to pay his taxes, and keeping track of the hours worked in a tattered notebook. My father showed me the notebook, held it up rather as a magician holds up a pack of cards. In time the notebook itself passed into my hands and a closer inspection evoked a different image, less bucolic but more likely, perhaps representing a later stage in Grandpap Anderson's—and the region's—life. The man with his donkey, tapping stones into the loosened surface of the road, has become, by 1897, the date on the cover, "E. Anderson, Sup.,"—I suppose the "Sup," is short for "Superintendent." S. Anderson by then must have been around seventy. On the cover darkened like wallpaper in an old house it says, "Always Bring This Book." Inside, in fine copper-plate penmanship, are accounts for the householders of an unnamed community which must be Templeton, totalling, for that year ("Less a/c for J. D. Paul") $206.99. The tax was 6 Mills. Registration was in May. Among the accounts on page ten are two in the name of Zellafrow—one N.R.'s to the amount of $4.25, and beneath, that of John, for the amount of $.45. Thirty five years after the murder, and the birth of the rumors. On the last page of the book, in another hand, unsteady, uneducated, in pencil:

> "For 1904 W Sumers Grane
> 24 October Reedy Mill
> Sumer 8   5 Bushels Wheat
>   10 Bushels Buckewheat
> _____
>   to mill
> 25th   10 Bushels Buckwheat
> 25th   8 for Anderson"

Someone else was keeping the records by then. Under the last entry
there is a child's drawing of a man in a hat, and a house with a smoking chimney. Three years later, in mid-summer, Samuel Anderson
died. He had been born in Templeton. If my own father ever knew
him—which he almost certainly did, since at the time of his grandfather's death he was eight years old and living only a few miles away—he
seemed to retain, and certainly he conveyed, no clear image of the
man. And as for his mother's remoter forebears and where they came
from, I know nothing at all.

My father told me one legend of my grandmother's. Some antece-
dent of hers supposedly had been eaten by wolves, in a hunting lodge
in the woods, in a blizzard, somewhere out in Ohio (pronounced
"Ahýa"). The details were vague or missing—who it was, when it happened, just where. But years ago it was thought to be a good story
and was repeated occasionally. I have not believed it for a long time.
To me it seems interesting only as an isolated index of the fantasies
and self-justifications of the unknown minds that produced it, accepted
it, and passed it on.

It was only after my father himself was dead that I found my grandmother's dilapidated thistle-blue autograph book from the time of her
youth in the 1870s and '80s. "My love for you shall never fail As long
as pussy has a tail By Maggie E. Bechtel," in purple crayon. Inspira-
tional poems, "I know God's in His heaven," "Thoughtlessness," "The
Marines' Hymn," sent by my Uncle Sam during the first World War.
In pencil, in a margin, "Sam gave me this long a goe." A dried pansy
between the pages. And obituary notices, in no discernible order—
some of the crumbling bits of newspaper pasted on top of the pencilled dates, eclipsing them. "There was a band of angels that wasn't
quite complete, so God took Mother Gifford, to fill the vacant seat."
Many of those born in the river settlements had moved into Kittanning and Ford City, and died in town. And from the book I learned
a few of the dessicated facts that make their way into such places. My
grandmother's mother had been born in Templeton, date unspecified.
Apparently her name before her marriage had been Elizabeth Bechtel.
One of the pencilled notices in the autograph book reads:

> "Arvill
>   In the days of Solm reflections
>   in the Hours of Social glee

> *Keep me in thy Recollections*
> *for I often think of thee*
> *—Your Aunt*
> *(illegible) M. E. Bechtel"*

I suppose the name was originally German.

There is no obituary notice for Samuel Anderson, and there are several for his wife Elizabeth, whatever that may indicate. She died on July 22, 1904, ten months to the day after her husband's death. They had baptised my grandmother, born at Maple Furnace, Pa., August 8, 1854, Arvilla. When she was alive I was never certain whether she had brothers or sisters, though my father referred absently to relatives with unfamiliar surnames. In fact, Arvilla had been one of five children, all the rest of whom, at different times, had moved out to California.

Templeton is a hamlet strung out along the railroad tracks on the east bank of the Allegheny River, some sixty miles northeast of Pittsburgh. It may have been larger in the 1850s, when my grandparents were born, and around the time of the Civil War, when they were children, than it is now. Most of the settlements on that winding stretch of the Allegheny—Wattersonville, Redbank Furnace, Cosmus, Rimer, Hooks, Gray's Eddy, Mahoning, Mosgrove, Gosford—have probably shrunk in the past hundred years and more. The river, in the middle of the nineteenth century, was the main artery of transportation and the central earthly presence in the minds of those who lived near it. I imagine that those river hamlets, up until the first World War, still bore a general resemblance to Mark Twain's Hannibal. The broad river dominated the mental geography of the region's inhabitants even after the advent of the Ford. Among many of those who had been born there in the nineteenth century and had not moved away nor learned to drive, it continued to do so after the Army Engineers had thrown their dams across its current, and the days of river traffic were effectively over. Not only my grandmother, but my Aunt Mary in the following generation assumed that one envisaged any place in the region in relation to the river.

At the time when my grandparents were born, the railroads were new-fangled. It was a number of years before the rails came down the river valleys, around the time of the Civil War. The various lines through the region – the Buffalo, Rochester, and Pittsburgh Railroad along Little Buffalo Run, Patterson Creek, and Long Run; the few miles of the Winfield Railroad, from West Winfield to the Allegheny, along Rough Run and Buffalo Creek; the Low Grade Division of the Pennsylvania Railroad, along Redbank Creek; and the main line, the Buffalo and Allegheny Valley Division of the Pennsylvania Railroad, along the east bank of the river – all followed the river and its tributaries. The river settlements through that section are on the east side of the water, which may have had to do, in the first place, with currents and boat landings. The talk of the coming of the trains, the requisitioning of land for them, the cutting of the woods, the grading of the slopes and building of the roadbeds, the laying of the tracks, were a long progression in the valley, impetus and form of irreversible changes, but it was still the river valley, enduring the general eager theft and defacement that characterized the building of the American railroads. The conflict between the older water transport and the new rail companies had begun with the inception of the railroads themselves, and it figured in the daily talk of the era. It must have been a matter of common knowledge when the railroads bought up, one by one, the dams that maintained the levels of the doomed canal system, and let them fall into ruin. On one page of my grandmother's commonplace book is the date of the Johnstown Flood, caused by the collapse of one of those dams. It was one of the spectacular catastrophes of her lifetime, a date that she was unlikely to forget as long as it meant anything to her, and she may have written the bare cipher on that page less as a simple reminder than as a somewhat incredulous mark of her own presence, like initials on the bark of a tree. The flood happened when my grandmother was thirty-five, a mother of three children. Rumors reached her of people seeing bodies floating in the river far below Johnstown. Some said they had seen them passing under the bridges at Pittsburgh, and down the Ohio. There were people who went to Pittsburgh just to look. As an old woman my Grandma spoke of the bodies as though she had seen them herself, floating down the Allegheny past Rimerton.

The right-of-way there and in Templeton runs close to the river, and many of the houses, which must have been built at about the time when the rails were laid, are set between the edge of the bank that drops steeply to the water, and the tracks. They face the railroad

line: long, low front porches, a few board steps up from the ground.
I do not know what Samuel Anderson did for a living in Templeton;
he may have been a tax overseer for years before the notebook that
ends with a child's drawing, but the book itself does not look like the
record of a full-time public official. As for my grandfather's father, Old
Jacob's hotel was probably no larger than most of the other frame houses
lined up along the slope, with their chicken coops and vegetable gardens and outhouses in back of them. Everyone in the place knew everyone else pretty well. Arvilla was two years older than my grandfather,
and had known him since he was a baby. She was eight when his father
was murdered.

Some time not long after that, Old Jake's widow, Hannah, decided
that she could not manage to bring up the three boys herself, and she
farmed out Jim, aged seven, with the Heinz family at Widnoon. John,
my grandfather, went to the Rimer family, up at Rimer or Rimerton.
One of the obituary notices pasted across its date in my grandmother's
commonplace book is that of Annie A. Rimer, who may have been
John's foster mother. Neither the hamlet of Rimer, as my Aunt Mary
referred to it, or Rimerton, as my father, who was born there, called
it, nor Widnoon up on the hill, where some of them went to school
and are buried, was more than five or six miles from Templeton. It
was all in the neighborhood. And when Mr. Heinz began delivering
his wife's locally celebrated chili sauce from door to door in his wheel-
barrow—as the legend goes, at any rate—it was only a year or two before he had to take a wagon and go farther afield, or get somebody
else to go for him. All the way to Templeton, before long. Jim left
the Heinzes in 1871, when he was sixteen, to go to work in a furnace,
perhaps at Mahoning, for a dollar a day. In his early thirties he moved,
with the beginning of the exodus from the river settlements to the
industrial towns. He went down-river to Kittanning, where he ran a
barber shop, and in later years worked as a night watchman. Young
Jacob, whom Hannah, it appears, kept with her and brought up at
home, later had something to do, my father told me, with the barge
traffic on the river, and for a while was a policeman.

But of John, my grandfather, and the Rimers, at that time, I know
nothing at all. I have heard from several members of the family that
John had a river pilot's license, but no details about when and how
he acquired it or used it. He seems to have worked in various capaci-

ties, up and down the river, and to have known the waterway at least as far as Pittsburgh. My father's family legend about the Heinzes has it that as they grew more successful in selling an increasing assortment of bottled vegetables, their sons set up an office in Pittsburgh and distributed the produce from there. Eventually they began to urge their parents to move the whole enterprise to the city. The elders were reluctant to leave, suspicious of the Babylon down-river, and they held out, preferring the world they knew. At some point they said they would go only if they could take their own house, the actual building up on the hill, six hundred and fifty feet above the river, along with them. They may have supposed that putting such a condition upon their moving would rule out the idea once and for all. But arrangements were made for uprooting the farmhouse from the site on which it had been reared, and the shade of its trees, and its garden, and edging it on rollers down the narrow, rutted, steep road, several miles to Gray's Eddy, or more probably to Rimerton, and sliding it onto a barge. The operation would have been complicated by the final grade down to the river. By the time I first saw Rimerton, the boat landings had gone from that part of the shore, but my father told me of seeing a team of beautiful horses, when he was a child, come down the road to cross the water on a flatboat, and on the way down the brake of the wagon failed, and the wagon rushed ahead, out of control, pushing the horses ahead of it onto the landing and the wharf, and off the end into the river, where they drowned before they could be cut loose from the harness. He remembered them being dragged out by other teams, and how he cried, and he showed me the spot where they had been buried—at least he thought it was the place. It is one of the handful of clear images of that time that he conveyed to me, something that had continued to impress him. And they had brought a house down that road, on rollers? So the story goes, and my father said that his uncle, young Jake, had something to do with providing the barge, and with the loading, and that my grandfather piloted the house down to Pittsburgh, where I was told it still sat unassimilated among the red brick mill buildings of the latter-day Heinz plant. If it happened like that at all, I imagine it was in the 1880s, in the decade after my grandparent's marriage. I know nothing else of that period of their lives except the dates when their first children were born.

They lived in Rimerton, perhaps from the time they were married, and I assume they called it that, since their children did. They ran a store in the house, and my grandmother took in sewing and did millinery work. I have heard that my grandfather actually owned a house in the village at one time—whether bequeathed to him by the Rimers or bought with earnings, or indeed whether he owned one at all, I am not sure. Nor do I know anything of his habits, his appearance, how much of the time he was away working on the river. And of my grandmother there are no pictures from that far back. In the oldest one I have seen she is already a woman in her sixties, heavy set, heavy jawed, heavy lidded—the heavy eyelids she passed on to several of her children—with gray hair; but still, in that picture, she looks startlingly young to me, since I never saw her until some years later.

No doubt her religion, which was to become the principal concern and focus of her life, was important to her from early childhood in Maple Furnace and Templeton, during the years of the Civil War. It is not easy to see, through the features of a woman past seventy, the child far behind them, but I find it hard to imagine her except as a very serious little girl, and the form of her religion—what my father referred to as "her church," "her Bible," emphasizing the pronoun— must have set early and changed little over the decades except to grow more obdurate. But she was born into it, or into something very like it. An unquestioning and vehement fundamentalism, a literal insistence upon the letter of the Word of God—taking the King James version for the original. A fierce self-righteousness and a view of the world in the light of an imminent Last Judgment—they were all around her as she was growing up. They were thundered from the pulpit in voices emulating the already legendary travelling evangelists of the days of her parents' youth. And they served her, as they served all of the faithful, in making a day-by-day sorting without appeal of the sheep from the goats, the saints from the dwellers in outer darkness in Templeton. But even among neighbors who had grown up to the beat of that same relentless piety and had accepted it as their own special salvation she was remarkable, and admired for the unbending force of her conviction and the rigor of its application to decisions and events and people. She was a Methodist, as it happened, no doubt following the affiliation of her parents, and the sect that was represented most pertinently—it may have boasted the only church—in Templeton. And the Methodists in particular, among the denominations in the river settlements, harked back directly to the itinerant Wesleyan preachers who had whipped up the Fear of the Lord there within the memory of the middle-aged. The fire of the earlier years had subsided—by comparison, at least—to a scripture-quoting pietism, a pursing of lips and a willing suspicion, a straight and narrow Grundyism. It had soured. In that faith she had brought up her children. Before my father could read, she taught him:

> It is a sin
> To steal a pin
> And how much greater
> To steal a tater.

She made "Be sure your sins will find you out" into a household motto—"sins" meaning, above all, lies or theft. During my father's childhood the family was poor much of the time; sometimes the children had no shoes, and there was not enough to eat. One summer day when he was four or five my father picked a few ears of corn from a field along the lane, up the river, and brought them home in his wagon, and his mother asked where they came from and how he had come by them, and when he told her she scolded him severely and made him take them back and apologize to the owner, and pay for them. It may have been perfectly usual and normal behavior on her part. It had the effect she intended it to have: he remembered it, with mortification, for the rest of his life. By the time I knew her, her eyeglass case, her sewing, and her Bible were always in her lap or within reach of her rocker, and some of the psalms, as she quoted them, referred to a startling distance, but by then the world around her had grown dubious and evanescent. She was still contemptuous—as were her daughters—of those who maintained that we were descended from monkeys, and there were usually several tracts tucked into her Bible announcing, with apposite chapter and verse, what could be expected in the life to come. She was never altogether reconciled to my father's slipping away into Presbyterianism, even though the Presbyterian Church led him to college and to his ordination as a minister. She hoped it would be alright—meaning that she hoped it would be overlooked.

Her politics were as inflexible as her religion. Indeed there was probably no clear division between them. Both were aspects of the same
viewpoint and temperament, both had been formed by the same circumstances and at the same time. She would no more have voted for
a Democrat than she would have stolen a wallet or gone to Mass.
Somewhere in her heedless loyalty there remained an impression from
her youth of the Republican party as the party of Lincoln. It was also,
in the poverty of the river settlements, the party of respectability and
therefore both of social aspiration and conservatism. Her scorn of
"Dixie" (pronounced "Dixeh") had its origin in her childhood not so
many miles north of the Mason-Dixon Line, and the talk of the Civil
War and of friends who had helped runaway slaves escape to Canada,
but it was certainly emphasized in later years by the solidly Democratic allegiance of the South. But since her Republicanism was not
hampered by reason, she did not hesitate to make stern comments
on the Carnegies and Mellons, the rich who avoided paying the poor
an honest wage; and she spoke, or my father did, of early meetings
held by labor organizers—John L. Lewis among them—in her cellar.
I am not sure whether that would have been the cellar in Rimerton,
or the one later, in Kittanning, but I imagine it was the former; and
I suspect, if only on grounds of likelihood, that my grandfather, whose
politics may have been less impacted and more pragmatic than hers,
may have had something to do with any such gatherings.

And the children—Harry is the first of them for whom we have
a certain date. He was born in 1884. But there was one daughter, Ber-
tha, about whom there was always some unresolved mystery. The other
daughters spoke of her as being different, and called her a gypsy because she wore flashy jewelry and was said to have a good time. They
never had much to do with her. She may have been born before Harry.
In any event, from 1884 until the end of the century the babies continued to arrive every two or three years until there were seven all
told. After Harry came Alma, then Vince, Edna, Samuel, William (my
father) and Dewey. Dewey (pronounced "Dyeweh"), born the year of
the Admiral's "Damn The Torpedoes, Full Speed Ahead" attack on
Manila Bay, lived only a few years and died of some childhood disease
such as scarlet fever, leaving behind him a tiny rocking chair that remained in the family for five decades and more. It was always referred
to as Dewey's chair, and any mention of it had the faculty—at least

in my own experience—of making a whole room of the Rimerton house appear around its image: an upstairs back bedroom full of afternoon sunlight, with a plank floor, rag rugs, a bed covered with patchwork, a picture of Jesus, a few tan faded photographs in heavy frames, a smell of dry wood, a single window propped open looking out in late summer over the dusty vegetable patch going to seed, the parched outbuildings, and the glare of the river on which the green shadow grows from the far bank.

In large families there are bound to be marked differences in age among some of the children. Harry was at least twelve years older than Dewey. And after Dewey was born the household stayed on at Rimerton for another decade and more, while the marriage pulled apart and the family ties loosened—some of them.

Nobody has spoken of those years except by way of headshaking and sighs and reprobation of my grandfather's drinking. Perhaps none of the family could have described clearly much of the progress of that dissolution. My grandfather's absences while he worked on the river, or for whatever reason, grew more frequent and longer until he was away much of the time, and often no one at home knew where he was. When he showed up, my father said, he was usually drunk, and frightened them. Sometimes he had no money and his clothes were a disgrace. Sometimes he brought what seemed like a lot of money, acquired heaven knew how, and the household stocked up on food despite Grandma's misgivings, or he brought the staples himself: hams and flour and corn meal and dried beans. Sometimes he took to outlandish behavior: once he swept up all the homemade bread and hid it. Another time he flourished a pistol and shot the bucket at the pump full of holes, laughing, and then sent Edna or Alma to pump the bucket full of water, shouting "Fill it up! Fill it up!" Everyone thought he was serious, with that pistol, and later when they may have doubted that, they insisted on it; the story was beyond changing. On the other side, my grandmother's militant respectability stiffened. She took in more millinery work to feed the family, and she read the psalms, with her thimble on her finger.

TOMMY

JOHN WIDEMAN

John Wideman, winner of the 1984 PEN/Faulkner Award for his novel, Sent For You Yesterday, *spent most of his first thirty-one years in Pennsylvania, where his books and stories take place. "Certain locales," says Wideman, "Homewood in Pittsburgh [where he grew up], the areas of West Philly surrounding the Penn campus [where he went to college], have been threshed through my imagination so often I'm not always sure whether I'm seeing actual streets or the streets I need for my fiction to be true."*

This story, "Tommy," which originally appeared in TriQuarterly Review *under the title "Bobby," is based upon the experiences of his younger brother, Robert, now serving a life sentence in prison for murder. Wideman's most recent book, and his first nonfiction book, the highly praised* Brothers and Keepers, *focuses on his relationship with Robert. "We go home again all the time," Wideman says, "in a million different ways."*

Today Wideman teaches writing at the University of Wyoming, but coincidentally, one of his students at the University of Pennsylvania, where he taught more than a decade ago, is also collected in this anthology: David Bradley.

HE CHECKS OUT the Velvet Slipper. Can't see shit for a minute in the darkness. Just the jukebox and beer smell and the stink from the men's room door always hanging open. Carl ain't there yet. Must be his methadone day. Carl with his bad feet like he's in slow motion wants to lay them dogs down easy as he can on the hot sidewalk. Little sissy walking on eggs steps pussy-footing up Frankstown to the clinic. Uncle Carl ain't treating to no beer to start the day so he backs out into the brightness of the Avenue, to the early afternoon street quiet after the blast of nigger music and nigger talk.

Ain't nothing to it. Nothing. If he goes left under the trestle and up the stone steps or ducks up the bare path worn through the weeds on the hillside he can walk along the tracks to the park. Early for the park. The sun everywhere now giving the grass a yellow sheen. If he goes right it's down the Avenue to where the supermarkets and the 5 & 10 used to be. Man, they sure did fuck with this place. What he thinks each time he stares at what was once the heart of Homewood. Nothing. A parking lot and empty parking stalls with busted meters. Only a fool leave his car next to one of the bent meter poles. Places to park so you can shop in stores that ain't there no more. Remembers his little Saturday morning wagon hustle when him and all the other kids would lay outside the A & P to haul groceries. Still some white ladies in those days come down from Thomas Boulevard to shop and if you're lucky get one of them and get tipped a quarter. Some of them fat black bitches be in church every Sunday have you pulling ten tons of rice and beans all the way to West Hell and be smiling and yakking all the way and saying what a nice boy you are and I knowed your mama when she was little and please sonny just set them inside on the table and still be smiling at you with some warm glass of water and a dime after you done hauled their shit halfway round the world.

Hot in the street but nobody didn't like you just coming in and sitting in their air conditioning unless you gonna buy a drink and set it in front of you. The poolroom hot. And too early to be messing with those fools on the corner. Always somebody trying to hustle. Man, when you gonna give me my money, Man, I been waiting too long for my money, Man, lemme hold this quarter till tonight, Man. I'm getting over tonight, Man. And the buses climbing the hill and turning the corner by the state store and fools parked in the middle of the street and niggers getting hot honking to get by and niggers paying them no mind like they got important business and just gonna sit there blocking traffic as long as they please and the buses growling and farting those fumes when they struggle around the corner.

Look to the right and to the left but ain't nothing to it, nothing saying move one way or the other. Homewood Avenue a darker gray stripe between the gray sidewalks. Tar patches in the asphalt. Looks like somebody's bad head with the ringworm. Along the curb ground glass sparkles below the broken neck of a Tokay bottle. Just the long neck and shoulders of the bottle intact and a piece of label hanging. Somebody should make a deep ditch out of Homewood Avenue and just go on and push the row houses and boarded storefronts into the hole. Bury it all, like in a movie he had seen a dam burst and the flood waters ripping through the dry bed of a river till the roaring water overflowed the banks and swept away trees and houses, uprooting everything in its path like a cleansing wind.

He sees Homewood Avenue dipping and twisting at Hamilton. Where Homewood crests at Frankstown the heat is a shimmering curtain above the trolley tracks. No trolleys anymore. But the slippery tracks still embedded in the asphalt streets. Somebody forgot to tear out the tracks and pull down the cables. So when it rains or snows some fool always gets caught and the slick tracks flip a car into a telephone pole or upside a hydrant and the cars just lay there with crumpled fenders and windshields shattered, laying there for no reason just like the tracks and wires are there for no reason now that buses run where the 88 and the 82 Lincoln trolleys used to go.

He remembers running down Lemington Hill because trolleys come only once an hour after midnight and he had heard the clatter of the 82 starting its long glide down Lincoln Avenue. The Dells still working out on *Why Do You Have to Go* and the tip of his dick wet and his balls aching and his finger sticky but he had forgotten all that and forgot the half hour in Sylvia's hallway because he was flying, all long strides and pumping arms and his fists opening and closing on the night air as he grappled for balance in a headlong rush down the steep hill. He had heard the trolley coming and wished he was a bird soaring through the black night, a bird with shiny chrome fenders and fishtails and a Continental kit. He tried to watch his feet, avoid the cracks and gulleys in the sidewalk. He heard the trolley's bell and crash of its steel wheels against the tracks. He had been all in Sylvia's drawers and she was wet as a dishrag and moaning her hot breath into his ear and the record player inside the door hiccuping for the thousandth time caught in the groove of gray noise at the end of the disc.

He remembers that night and curses again the empty trolley scream-

ing past him as he had pulled up short half a block from the corner.
Honky driver half sleep in his yellow bubble. As the trolley careened
away red sparks had popped above its gimpy antenna. Chick had his
nose open and his dick hard but he should have cooled it and split,
been out her drawers and down the hill on time. He had fooled around
too long. He had missed the trolley and mize well walk. He had to
walk and in the darkness over his head the cables had swayed and
sung long after the trolley disappeared.

He had to walk cause that's all there was to it. And still no ride
of his own so he's still walking. Nothing to it. Either right or left, either
up Homewood or down Homewood, walking his hip walk, making
something out of the way he is walking since there is nothing else to
do, no place to go so he makes something of the going, lets them see
him moving in his own down way, his stylized walk which nobody
could walk better even if they had some place to go.

Thinking of a chump shot on the nine ball which he blew and
cost him a quarter for the game and his last dollar on a side bet. Of
pulling on his checkered bells that morning and the black tank top.
How the creases were dead and cherry pop or something on the front
and a million wrinkles behind the knees and where his thighs came
together. Junkie, wino-looking pants he would have rather died than
wear just a few years before when he was one of the cleanest cats in
Westinghouse High School. Sharp and leading the Commodores. Doo
Wah Diddy, Wah Diddy Bop. Thirty-five-dollar pants when most the
cats in the House couldn't spend that much for a suit. It was a bitch
in the world. Stone bitch. Feeling like Mister Tooth Decay crawling
all sweaty out of the gray sheets. Mom could wash them every day,
they still be gray. Like his underclothes. Like every motherfucking thing
they had and would ever have. Doo Wah Diddy. The rake jerked three
or four times through his bush. Left there as decoration and weapon.
You could fuck up a cat with those steel teeth. You could get the points
sharp as needles. And draw it swift as Billy the Kid.

Thinking it be a bitch out here. Niggers write all over everything
don't even know how to spell. Drawing power fists that look like a
loaf of bread.

Thinking this whole Avenue is like somebody's mouth they let some
jive dentist fuck with. All these old houses nothing but rotten teeth
and these raggedy pits is where some been dug out or knocked out

and ain't nothing left but stumps and snaggleteeth just waiting to go. Thinking, that's right. That's just what it is. Why it stinks around here and why ain't nothing but filth and germs and rot. And what that make me? What it make all these niggers? Thinking yes, yes, that's all it is.

Mr. Strayhorn where he always is down from the corner of Hamilton and Homewood sitting on a folding chair beside his iceball cart. A sweating canvas draped over the front of the cart to keep off the sun. Somebody said the old man a hundred years old, somebody said he was a bad dude in his day. A gambler like his own Granddaddy John French had been. They say Strayhorn whipped three cats half to death try to cheat him in the alley behind Dumferline. Took a knife off one and whipped all three with his bare hands. Just sits there all summer selling iceballs. Old and can hardly see. But nobody don't bother him even though he got his pockets full of change every evening.

Shit. One of the young boys will off him one night. Those kids was stone crazy. Kill you for a dime and think nothing of it. Shit. Rep don't mean a thing. They come at you in packs, like wild dogs. Couldn't tell those young boys nothing. He thought he had come up mean. Thought his running buddies be some terrible dudes. Shit. These kids coming up been into more stuff before they twelve than most grown men do they whole lives.

Hard out here. He stares into the dead storefronts. Sometimes they get in one of them. Take it over till they get run out or set it on fire or it gets so filled with shit and nigger piss don't nobody want to use it no more except for winos and junkies come in at night and could be sleeping on a bed of nails wouldn't make no nevermind to those cats. He peeks without stopping between the wooden slats where the glass used to be. Like he is reading the posters, like there might be something he needed to know on these rain-soaked, sun-faded pieces of cardboard talking about stuff that happened a long time ago.

Self-defense demonstration . . . Ahmed Jamal. Rummage Sale. Omega Boat Ride. The Dells. Madame Walker's Beauty Products.

A dead bird crushed dry and paper-thin in the alley between Albion and Tioga. Like somebody had smeared it with tar and mashed it between the pages of a giant book. If you hadn't seen it in the first place, still plump and bird colored, you'd never recognize it now. Looked now like the lost sole of somebody's shoe. He had watched it happen.

Four or five days was all it took. On the third day he thought a cat had dragged it off. But when he passed the corner next afternoon he found the dark shape in the grass at the edge of the cobblestones. The head was gone and the yellow smear of beak but he recognized the rest. By then already looking like the raggedy sole somebody had walked off their shoe.

He was afraid of anything dead. He could look at something dead but no way was he going to touch it. Didn't matter, big or small, he wasn't about to put his hands near nothing dead. His daddy had whipped him when his mother said he sassed her and wouldn't take the dead rat out of the trap. He could whip him again but no way he was gon touch that thing. The dudes come back from Nam talking about puddles of guts and scraping parts of people into plastic bags. They talk about carrying their own bags so they could get stuffed in if they got wasted. Have to court-martial his ass. No way he be carrying no body bag. Felt funny now carrying out the big green bags you put your garbage in. Any kind of plastic sack and he's thinking of machine guns and dudes screaming and grabbing their bellies and rolling around like they do when they're hit on Iwo Jima and Tarawa or the Dirty Dozen or the Magnificent Seven or the High Plains Drifter, but the screaming is not in the darkness on a screen it is bright, green afternoon and Willie Thompson and them are on patrol. It is a street like Homewood. Quiet like Homewood this time of day and bombed out like Homewood is. Just pieces of buildings standing here and there and fire scars and places ripped and kicked down and cars stripped and dead at the curb. They are moving along in single file and their uniforms are hip and their walks are hip and they are kind of smiling and rubbing their weapons and cats passing a joint fat as a cigar down the line. You can almost hear music from where Porgy's Record Shop used to be, like the music so fine it's still there clinging to the boards, the broken glass on the floor, the shelves covered with roach shit and rat shit, a ghost of the music rifting sweet and mellow like the smell of home cooking as the patrol slips on past where Porgy's used to be. Then . . .

Rat Tat Tat . . . Rat Tat Tat . . . Ra Ta Ta Ta Ta Ta Ta . . .

Sudden but almost on the beat. Close enough to the beat so it seems the point man can't take it any longer, can't play this soldier game no longer and he gets happy and the smoke is gone clear to his head so he jumps out almost on the beat, wiggling his hips and throwing up his arms so he can get it all, go on and get down. Like he is exploding to the music. To the beat which pushes him out there all alone, doing it, and it is Rat Tat Tat and we all want to fingerpop behind his twitching hips and his arms flung out but he is screaming and down in the dirty street and the street is exploding all round him in little volcanoes of dust. And some of the others in the front of the patrol go down with him. No semblance of rhythm now, just stumbling, or airborne like their feet jerked out from under them. The whole hip procession buckling, shattered as lines of deadly force stitch up and down the Avenue.

Hey man, what's to it? Ain't nothing to it man you got it baby hey now where's it at you got it you got it ain't nothing to it something to it I wouldn't be out here in all this sun you looking good you into something go on man you got it all you know you the Man hey now that was a stone fox you know what I'm talking about you don't be creeping past me yeah nice going you got it all save some for me Mister Clean you seen Ruchell and them yeah you know how that shit is the cat walked right on by like he ain't seen nobody but you know how he is get a little something don't know nobody shit like I tried to tell the cat get straight nigger be yourself before you be by yourself you got a hard head man hard as stone but he ain't gon listen to me shit no can't nobody do nothing for the cat less he's ready to do for hisself Ruchell yeah man Ruchell and them come by here little while ago yeah baby you got it yeah lemme hold this little something I know you got it you the Man you got to have it lemme hold a little something till this evening I'll put you straight tonight man you know your man do you right I unnerstand yeah that's all that's to it nothing to it I'ma see you straight man yeah you fall on by the crib yeah we be into something tonight you fall on by.

Back to the left now. Up Hamilton, past the old man who seems to sleep beside his cart until you get close and then his yellow eyes under the straw hat brim follow you. Cut through the alley past the old grade school. Halfway up the hill the game has already started. You have been hearing the basketball patted against the concrete, the hollow thump of the ball glancing off the metal backboards. The ball players half naked out there under that hot sun, working harder than niggers ever did picking cotton. They shine. They glide and leap and fly at each other like their dark bodies are at the ends of invisible strings. This time of day the court is hot as fire. Burn through your shoes. Maybe that's why the niggers play like they do, running and jumping so much cause the ground's too hot to stand on. His brother used to play here all day. Up and down all day in the hot sun with the rest of the crazy ball players. Old dudes and young dudes and when people on the side waiting for winners they'd get to arguing and you could hear them badmouthing all the way up the hill and cross the tracks in the park. Wolfing like they ready to kill each other.

His oldest brother John came back here to play when he brought his family through in the summer. Here and Mellon and the courts beside the Projects in East Liberty. His brother one of the old dudes now. Still crazy about the game. He sees a dude lose his man and fire a jumper from the side. A double pump, a lean, and the ball arched so it kisses the board and drops through the iron. He could have played the game. Tall and loose. Hands bigger than his brother's. Could palm a ball when he was eleven. Looks at his long fingers. His long feet in raggedy ass sneakers that show the crusty knuckle of his little toe. The sidewalk sloped and split. Little plots of gravel and weeds where whole paving blocks torn away. Past the dry swimming pool. Just a big concrete hole now where people piss and throw bottles like you got two points for shooting them in. Dropping like a rusty spiderweb from tall metal poles, what's left of a backstop, and beyond the flaking mesh of the screen the dusty field and beyond that a jungle of sooty trees below the railroad tracks. They called it the Bums' Forest when they were kids and bombed the winos sleeping down there in the shade of the trees. If they walked alongside the track all the way to the park they'd have to cross the bridge over Homewood Avenue. Hardly room for trains on the bridge so they always ran and some fool always yelling, *Train's coming* and everybody else yelling and then it's your chest all full and your heart pumping to keep up with the rest. Because the train couldn't kill everybody. It might get the last one, the slow one but it wouldn't run down all the crazy niggers screaming and hauling ass over Homewood Avenue. From the tracks you could look down on the winos curled up under a tree or sitting in a circle sipping from bottles wrapped in brown paper bags. At night they would have fires, hot as it was some summer nights you'd still see their fires from the bleachers while you watched the Legion baseball team kick butt.

From high up on the tracks you could bomb the forest. Stone hissed through the thick leaves. Once in a while a lucky shot shattered a bottle. Some gray, sorry-assed wino mother-fucker waking up and shaking his fist and cussing at you and some fool shouts *He's coming, he's coming.* And not taking the low path for a week because you think he was looking dead in your eyes, spitting blood and pointing at you and you will never go alone the low way along the path because he is behind every bush, gray and bloody-mouthed. The raggedy, gray clothes flapping like a bird and a bird's feathery, smothering funk covering you as he drags you into the bushes.

He had heard stories about the old days when the men used to hang out in the woods below the tracks. Gambling and drinking wine and telling lies and singing those old time, down home songs. Hang out there in the summer and when it got cold they'd loaf in the Bucket of Blood on the corner of Frankstown and Tioga. His granddaddy was in the stories. Old John French one of the baddest dudes ever walked these Homewood streets. Old, big-hat John French. They said his granddaddy could sing up a storm and now his jitterbug father up in the choir of Homewood A.M.E. Zion next to Mrs. Washington who hits those high notes. He was his father's son, people said. Singing all the time and running the streets like his daddy did till his daddy got too old and got saved. Tenor lead of the Commodores. Everybody saying the Commodores was the baddest group. If that cat hadn't fucked us over with the record we might have made the big time. Achmet backing us on the conga. Tito on the bongos. Tear up the park. Stone tear it up. Little kids and old folks all gone home and ain't nobody in the park but who supposed to be and you got your old lady on the side listening or maybe you singing pretty to pull some new fly bitch catch your eye in the crowd. It all comes down, comes together mellow and fine sometimes. The drums, the smoke, the sun going down and you out there flying and the Commodores steady taking care of business behind your lead.

"You got to go to church. I'm not asking I'm telling. Now you get those shoes shined and I don't want to hear another word out of you, young man." She is ironing his Sunday shirt hot and stiff. She hums along with the gospel songs on the radio. "Don't make me send you to your father." Who is in the bathroom for the half hour he takes doing whatever to get hisself together. Making everybody else late. Singing in there while he shaves. You don't want to be the next one after him. "You got five minutes, boy. Five minutes and your teeth better be clean and your hands and face shining." Gagging in the funky bathroom, not wanting to take a breath. How you supposed to brush your teeth, the cat just shit in there? "You're going to church this week and every week. This is my time and don't you try to spoil it, boy. Don't you get no attitude and try to spoil church for me." He is in the park now, sweating in the heat, a man now, but he can hear his mother's voice plain as day, filling up all the empty space around him just as it did in the house on Finance Street. She'd talk them all to church every Sunday. Use her voice like a club to beat everybody out the house.

His last time in church was a Thursday. They had up the scaffolding to clean the ceiling and Deacon Barclay's truck was parked outside. Barclay's Hauling, Cleaning and General Repairing. Young People's Gospel Chorus had practice on Thursday and he knew Adelaide would be there. That chick looked good even in them baggy choir robes. He had seen her on Sunday because his Mom cried and asked him to go to church. Because she knew he stole the money out her purse but he had lied and said he didn't and she knew he was lying and feeling guilty and knew he'd go to church to make up to her. Adelaide up there with the Young People's Gospel Chorus rocking church. Rocking church and he'd go right on up there, the lead of the Commodores, and sing gospel with them if he could get next to that fine Adelaide. So Thursday he left the poolroom, *Where you tipping off to, Man? None of your motherfucking business, motherfucker,* about seven when she had choir practice and look here, Adelaide, I been digging you for a long time. Longer and deeper than you'll ever know. Let me tell you something. I know what you're thinking, but don't say it, don't break my heart by saying you heard I was a jive cat and nothing to me and stay away from him he ain't no good and stuff like that I know I got a rep that way but you grown enough now to know how people talk and how you got to find things out for yourself. Don't be putting me down till you let me have a little chance to speak for myself. I ain't gon lie now. I been out here in the world and into some jive tips. Yeah, I did my time diddy bopping and trying my wheels out here in the street. I was a devil. Got into everything I was big and bad enough

to try. Look here. I could write the book. Pimptime and partytime
and jive to stay alive, but I been through all that and that ain't what
I want. I want something special, something solid. A woman, not no
fingerpopping young girl got her nose open and her behind wagging
all the time. That's right. That's right, I ain't talking nasty, I'm talking
what I know. I'm talking truth tonight and listen here I been digging you all these years and waiting for you because all that Doo Wah
Diddy ain't nothing, you hear, nothing to it. You grown now and I
need just what you got. . . .

Thursday rapping in the vestibule with Adelaide was the last time
in Homewood A.M.E. Zion Church. Had to be swift and clean. Swoop
down like a hawk and get to her mind. Tuesday she still crying and
gripping the elastic of her drawers and saying *No*. Next Thursday the
only singing she doing is behind some bushes in the park. *Oh, Baby.
Oh, Baby, it's so good.* Tore that pussy up.

Don't make no difference. No big thing. She's giving it to somebody else now. All that good stuff still shaking under her robe every
second Sunday when the Young People's Gospel Chorus in the loft
beside the pulpit. Old man Barclay like he guarding the church door
asking me did I come around to help clean. "Mr. Barclay, I wish I could
help but I'm working nights. Matter of fact I'm a little late now. I'm
gon be here on my night off, though."

He knew I was lying. Old bald head dude standing there in his
coveralls and holding a bucket of Lysol and a scrub brush. Worked
all his life and got a piece of truck and a piece of house and still running around yes sirring and no mamming the white folks and cleaning
their toilets. And he's doing better than most of these chumps. Knew
I was lying but smiled his little smile cause he knows my mama and
knows she's a good woman and knows Adelaide's grandmother and
knows if I ain't here to clean he better guard the door with his soap
and rags till I go on about my business.

Ruchell and them over on a bench. Niggers high already. They
ain't hardly out there in the sun barbecuing their brains less they been
into something already. Niggers be hugging the shade till evening less
they been into something.

"Hey now."

"What's to it, Tom?"

"You cats been into something."

"You ain't just talking."

"Ruchell man, we got that business to take care of."

"Stone business, Bruh. I'm ready to T.C.B., my man."

"You ain't ready for nothing, nigger."

"Hey man, we're gon get it together. I'm ready, man. Ain't never been so ready. We gon score big, Brother Man . . ."

They have been walking an hour. The night is cooling. A strong wind has risen and a few pale stars are visible above the yellow pall of the city's lights. Ruchell is talking:

"The reason it's gon work is the white boy is greedy. He's so greedy he can't stand for the nigger to have something. Did you see Indovina's eyes when we told him we had copped a truckload of color tee vees. Shit man. I could hear his mind working. Calculating like. These niggers is dumb. I can rob these niggers. Click. Click. Clickedy. Rob the shit out of these dumb spooks. They been robbing us so long they think that's the way things supposed to be. They're so greedy their hands get sweaty they see a nigger with something worth stealing."

"So he said he'd meet us at the car lot?"

"That's the deal. I told him we had two vans full."

"And Ricky said he'd let you use his van?"

"I already got the keys, man. I told you we were straight with Ricky. He ain't even in town till the weekend."

"I drive up then and you hide in the back?"

"Yeah dude. Just like we done said a hundred times. You go in the office to make the deal and you know how Indovina is. He gon send out his nigger Chubby to check the goods."

"And you jump Chubby?"

"Be on him like white on rice. Freeze that nigger till you get the money from Indovina."

"You sure Indovina ain't gon try and follow us?"

"Shit, man. He be happy to see us split. . . ."

"With his money?"

"Indovina do whatever you say. Just wave your piece in his face a couple times. That fat ofay motherfucker ain't got no heart. Chubby his heart and Ruchell stone take care of Chubby."

"I still think Indovina might go to the cops."

"And say what? Say he trying to buy some hot tee vees and got ripped off? He ain't hardly saying that. He might just say he got robbed and try to collect insurance. He's slick like that. But if he goes to the cops you can believe he won't be describing us. Naw. The pigs know that greasy dago is a crook. Everybody knows it and won't be no problems. Just score and blow. Leave this motherfucking sorry ass town. Score and blow."

"When you ain't got nothing you get desperate. You don't care. I mean what you got to be worried about? Your life ain't shit. All you got is a high. Getting high and spending all your time hustling some money so you can get high again. You do anything. Nothing don't matter. You just take, take, take whatever you can get your hands on. Pretty soon nothing don't matter, John. You just got to get that high. And everybody around you the same way. Don't make no difference. You steal a little something. If you get away with it, you try it again. Then something bigger. You get holt to a piece. Other dudes carry a piece. Lots of dudes out there holding something. So you get it and start to carrying it. What's it matter? You ain't nowhere anyway. Ain't got nothing. Nothing to look forward to but a high. A man needs something. A little money in his pocket. I mean you see people around you and on TV and shit. Man, they got everything. Cars and clothes. They can do something for a woman. They got something. And you look at yourself in the mirror you're going nowhere. Not a penny in your pocket. Your own people disgusted with you. Begging around your family like a little kid or something. And jail and stealing money from your own mama. You get desperate. You do what you have to do."

The wind is up again that night. At the stoplight Tommy stares at the big sign on the Boulevard. A smiling Duquesne Pilsner Duke with his glass of beer. The time and temperature flash beneath the nobleman's uniformed chest. Ricky had installed a tape deck into the dash. A tangle of wires drooped from its guts, but the sound was good. One speaker for the cab, another for the back where Ruchell was sitting on the rolls of carpet Ricky had stacked there. Al Green singing *Call Me*. Ricky could do things. Made his own tapes; customizing the delivery van. Next summer Ricky driving to California. Fixing up the van so he could live in it. The dude was good with his hands. A me-

chanic in the war. Government paid for the wasted knee. Ricky said,
Got me a new knee now. Got a four-wheeled knee that's gonna ride
me away from all this mess. The disability money paid for the van
and the customizing and the stereo tape deck. Ricky always have that
limp but the cat getting hisself together.

Flags were strung across the entrance to the used car lot. The wind
made them pop and dance. Rows and rows of cars looking clean and
new under the lights. Tommy parked on the street, in the deep shadow
at the far end of Indovina's glowing corner. He sees them through the
office window. Indovina and his nigger.

"Hey, Chubby."

"What's happening now?" Chubby's shoulders wide as the door.
Indovina's nigger all the way. Had his head laid back so far on his
neck it's like he's looking at you through his noseholes instead of
his eyes.

"You got the merchandise?" Indovina's fingers drum the desk.

"You got the money?"

"Ain't your money yet. I thought you said two vans full."

"Can't drive but one at a time. My partner's at a phone booth right
now. Got the number here. You show me the bread and he'll bring
the rest."

"I want to see them all before I give you a penny."

"Look, Mr. Indovina. This ain't no bullshit tip. We got the stuff,
alright. Good stuff like I said. Sony portables. All the same . . . still
in the boxes."

"Let's go look."

"I want to see some bread first."

"Give Chubby your keys. Chubby, check it out. Count em. Make
sure the cartons ain't broke open."

"I want to see some bread."

"Bread, Bread. My cousin DeLuca runs a bakery. I don't deal with
bread. I got money. See. That's money in my hand. Got plenty money
buy your television sets buy your van buy you."

"Just trying to do square business, Mr. Indovina."

"Don't forget to check the cartons. Make sure they're sealed."

Somebody must be down. Ruchell or Chubby down. Tommy
had heard two shots. He sees himself in the plate glass window. In

a fishbowl and patches of light gliding past. Except where the flood-lights are trained, the darkness outside is impenetrable. He cannot see past his image in the glass, past the rushes of light slicing through his body.

"Turn out the goddamn light."

"You kill me you be sorry . . . kill me you be real sorry . . . if one of them dead out there it's just one nigger kill another nigger . . . you kill me you be sorry . . . you killing a white man . . ."

Tommy's knee skids on the desk and he slams the gun across the man's fat, sweating face with all the force of his lunge. He is scrambling over the desk, scattering paper and junk, looking down on Indovina's white shirt, his hairy arms folded over his head. He is thinking of the shots. Thinking that everything is wrong. The shots, the white man cringing on the floor behind the steel desk. Him atop the desk, his back exposed to anybody coming through the glass door.

Then he is running. Flying into the darkness. He is crouching so low he loses his balance and trips onto all fours. The gun leaps from his hand and skitters toward a wall of tires. He hears the pennants crackling. Hears a motor starting and Ruchell calling his name.

"What you mean you didn't get the money? I done wasted Chubby and you ain't got the money? Aw shit. Shit. Shit."

He had nearly tripped again over the man's body. Without knowing how he knew, he knew Chubby was dead. Dead as the sole of his shoe. He should stop; he should try to help. But the body was lifeless. He couldn't touch . . .

Ruchell is shuddering and crying. Tears glazing his eyes and he wonders if Ruchell can see where he's going, if Ruchell knows he is driving like a wild man on both sides of the street and weaving in and out the lines of traffic. Horns blare after them. Then it's Al Green up again. He didn't know how, when or who pushed the button but it was Al Green blasting in the cab. *Help me Help me Help me. . . .*

Jesus is waiting . . . He snatches at the tape deck with both hands to turn it down or off or rip the goddamn cassette from the machine.

"Slow down, man. Slow down. You gonna get us stopped." Rolling down his window. The night air sharp in this face. The whir of tape dying then a hum of silence. The traffic sounds and city sounds pressing again into the cab.

"Nothing. Not a goddamn penny. Wasted the dude and we still ain't got nothing."

"They traced the car to Ricky. Ricky said he was out of town. Told them his van stolen when he was out of town. Claimed he didn't even know it gone till they came to his house. Ricky's cool. I know the cat's mad, but he's cool. Indovina trying to hang us. He saying it was a stickup. Saying Chubby tried to run for help and Ruchell shot him down. His story don't make no sense when you get down to it, but ain't nobody gon to listen to us."

"Then you're going to keep running?"

"Ain't no other way. Try to get to the coast. Ruchell knows a guy there can get us IDs. We was going there anyway. With our stake. We was gon get jobs and try to get it together. Make a real try. We just needed a little bread to get us started. I don't know why it had to happen the way it did. Ruchell said Chubby tried to go for bad. Said Chubby had a piece down in his pants and Ruchell told him to cool it told the cat don't be no hero and had his gun on him and everything but Chubby had to be a hard head, had to be John Wayne or some goddamned body. Just called Ruchell a punk and said no punk had the heart to pull the trigger on him. And Ruchell, Ruchell don't play, brother John. Ruchell blew him away when Chubby reached for his piece."

"You don't think you can prove your story?"

"I don't know, man. What Indovina is saying don't make no sense, but I heard the cops ain't found Chubby's gun. If they could just find that gun. But Indovina, he a slick old honky. That gun's at the bottom of the Allegheny River if he found it. They found mine. With my prints all over it. Naw. Can't take the chance. It's Murder One even though I didn't shoot nobody. That's long, hard time if they believe Indovina. I can't take the chance. . . ."

"Be careful, Tommy. You're a fugitive. Cops out here think they're Wyatt Earp and Marshall Dillon. They shoot first and maybe ask questions later. They still play wild, wild West out here."

"I hear you. But I'd rather take my chance that way. Rather they carry me back in a box than go back to prison. It's hard out there, Brother. Real hard. I'm happy you got out. One of us got out anyway."

"Think about it. Take your time. You can stay here as long as you need to. There's plenty of room."

"We gotta go. See Ruchell's cousin in Denver. Get us a little stake then make our run."

"I'll give you what I can if that's what you have to do. But sleep on it. Let's talk again in the morning."

"It's good to see you, man. And the kids and your old lady. At least we had this one evening. Being on the run can drive you crazy."

"Everybody was happy to see you. I knew you'd come. You've been heavy on my mind since yesterday. I wrote a kind of letter to you then. I knew you'd come. But get some sleep now . . . we'll talk in the morning."

"Listen, man. I'm sorry, man. I'm really sorry I had to come here like this. You sure Judy ain't mad?"

"I'm telling you it's OK. She's as glad to see you as I am. . . . And you can stay . . . both of us want you to stay."

"Running can drive you crazy. From the time I wake in the morning till I go to bed at night, all I can think about is getting away. My head ain't been right since it happened."

"When's the last time you talked to anybody at home?"

"It's been a couple weeks. They probably watching people back there. Might even be watching you. That's why I can't stay. Got to keep moving till we get to the coast. I'm sorry, man. I mean nobody was supposed to die. It was easy. We thought we had a perfect plan. Thieves robbing thieves. Just score and blow like Ruchell said. It was our chance and we had to take it. But nobody was supposed to get hurt. I'd be dead now if it was me Chubby pulled on. I couldna just looked in his face and blown him away. But Ruchell don't play. And everybody at home. I know how they must feel. It was all over TV and the papers. Had our names and where we lived and everything. Goddamn mug shots in the Post Gazette. Looking like two gorillas. I know it's hurting people. In a way I wish it had been me. Maybe it would have been better. I don't really care what happens to me now. Just wish there be some way to get the burden off Mama and everybody. Be easier if I was dead."

"Nobody wants you dead. . . . That's what Mom's most afraid of. Afraid of you coming home in a box."

"I ain't going back to prison. They have to kill me before I go back in prison. Hey, man. Ain't nothing to my crazy talk. You don't want to hear this jive. I'm tired, man. I ain't never been so tired. . . . I'ma sleep . . . talk in the morning, Big Brother."

He feels his brother squeeze then relax the grip on his shoulder. He has seen his brother cry once before. Doesn't want to see it again. Too many faces in his brother's face. Starting with their mother and going back and going sideways and all of Homewood there if he looked long enough. Not just faces but streets and stories and rooms and songs.

Tommy listens to the steps. He can hear faintly the squeak of a bed upstairs. Then nothing. Ruchell asleep in another part of the house. Ruchell spent the evening with the kids, playing with their toys. The cat won't ever grow up. Still into the Durango Kid, and Whip Wilson and Audie Murphy wasting Japs and shit. Still Saturday afternoon at the Bellmawr Show and he is lining up the plastic cowboys against the plastic Indians and boom-booming them down with the kids on the playroom floor. And dressing up the Lone Ranger doll with the mask and guns and cinching the saddle on Silver. Toys like they didn't make when we were coming up. And Christmas morning and so much stuff piled up they'd be crying with exhaustion and bad nerves before half the stuff unwrapped. Christmas morning and they never really went to sleep. Looking out the black windows all night for reindeer and shit. Cheating. Worried that all the gifts will turn to ashes if they get caught cheating, but needing to know, to see if reindeer really can fly.

Pam Rhodes

As time
goes by

A LION BOOK

Copyright © 2004 Pam Rhodes
This edition copyright © 2004 Lion Hudson

The author asserts the moral right
to be identified as the author of this work

A Lion Book
an imprint of
Lion Hudson plc
Mayfield House, 256 Banbury Road,
Oxford OX2 7DH, England
www.lionhudson.com
ISBN 0 7459 5169 4

First edition 2004
10 9 8 7 6 5 4 3 2 1 0

All rights reserved

A catalogue record for this book is available
from the British Library

Typeset in 12/14 DeVinne
Printed and bound in China

Acknowledgments
Every effort has been made to trace
relevant copyright holders. If there are
any inadvertent omissions in these
acknowledgments we apologize to those
concerned.

All images copyright © Brand X Pictures.

p. 16: 'As years come in' copyright ©
Dorothy L. Sayers. Used with permission.

pp. 29, 65: extracts by Dorothy Parker,
copyright © The National Association for
the Advancement of Colored People
(NAACP) and the Estate of Dorothy Parker.
Lion Hudson thanks the NAACP for
authorizing this use of Dorothy Parker's
works.

pp. 30–31: extract from 'May Every Day'
copyright © 1981 Frank Topping. Published
in *Working at Prayer* by Lutterworth Press.
Used with permission.

pp. 32, 68, 80: 'Lines on Facing Forty'
(1942), 'A Word to Husbands' (1957) and
'Crossing the Border' (1955), by Ogden
Nash. All copyright © Linell Nash Smith
and Isabel Nash Eberstadt. Published in the
UK by Andre Deutsch Ltd.

p. 57: 'Take this Moment' by John Bell and
Graham Maule. Copyright © 1998 Wild
Goose Resource Group, Iona Community,
Glasgow G51 3UU, Scotland. Used with
permission.

Contents

Introduction

It happens to us all. Time moves on, and yet our view of ourselves remains quaintly unchanged. In spite of the thickening waistline, bald spot on top, hot flushes – and the perplexing increase in policemen, doctors and vicars who are surely far too youthful to do their jobs properly – we are as young as we feel, rather than as old as we probably look!

And our surprise at how quickly the years pass is not confined to those of us who find small print getting irritatingly smaller. Twenty-somethings can feel over the hill as their 'born to be wild' days become a distant memory. The big Four-O birthday can strike fear into the heart of someone who has apparently reached middle age when inside they feel they're still struggling to get through puberty. Retirement can come all too soon when your head is still buzzing with things to do, places to go and bills to pay. Whoever we are, time marches on relentlessly while we gallop along trying to catch up with it.

Of all the things that help us cope with the 'getting older' syndrome, such as good health, bone structure, friends, genes and bank balance, the best quality must surely be a down-to-earth sense of humour, closely followed by a genuine wish to count our blessings rather than either our birthdays or other people's faults.

And for us all, who are unique and extraordinary as each and every one of us is, there's an instinctive longing for more, something beyond this mortal life, which can give purpose and meaning to our time and existence here. We want to matter. We want to love and be loved. We want this world to be a better place for ever because of our presence here now.

So this book is for everyone who appreciates life, love and laughter, no matter how many candles they've blown out over the years. Live today. Live every day. Treasure every precious moment!

As Others See Us

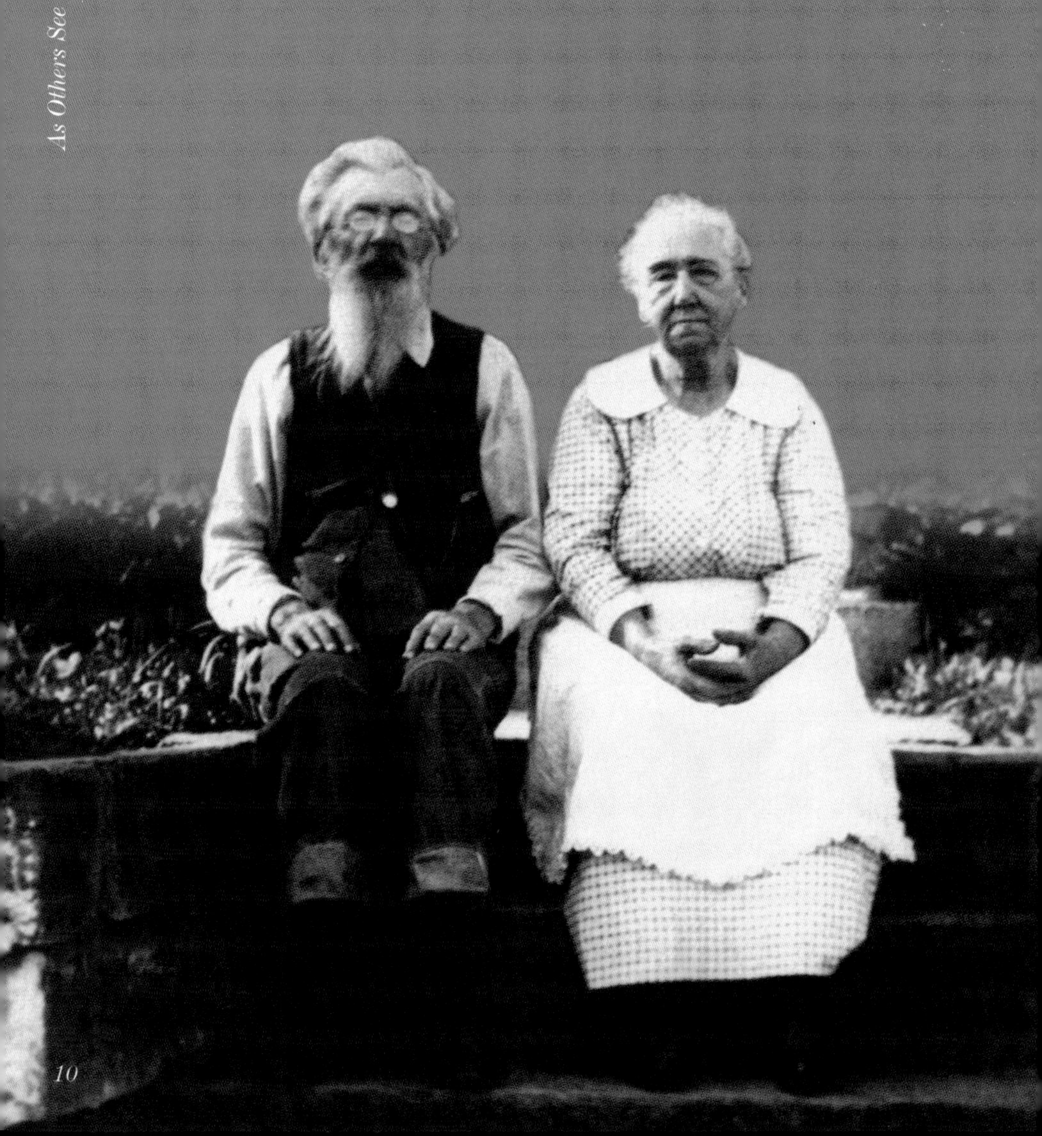

As Others See Us

… even if they do think you look your age

It ain't what you do,
it's the way that you do it!

... *even if they do think you look your age*

At my age, when a girl flirts with me in the movies, she's after my popcorn.

Milton Berle

You know you're getting old when the candles cost more than the cake.

Bob Hope

Middle age is when your wife tells you to pull in your stomach, and you already have.

Jack Barry

Middle age is when your old classmates are so grey and wrinkled and bald, they don't recognize you.

Bennet Cerf

It is a terrible thing for an old woman to outlive her dogs.

Tennessee Williams

A woman is as old as she looks
before breakfast.
Edgar Watson Howe

She was once 'cool' –
but Mr Gravity's been very
unkind to that woman.
Edina, from Absolutely Fabulous

If God had to give a woman
wrinkles, he might at least
have put them on the soles
of her feet.
Ninon de Lenclos

No woman should ever be quite accurate
about her age. It looks so calculating.
Oscar Wilde

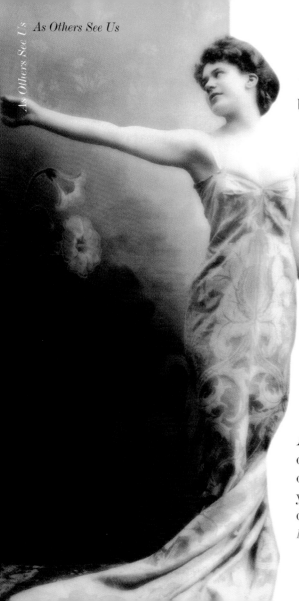

Women are most fascinating between the age of thirty-five and forty after they have won a few races and know how to pace themselves. Since few ever pass forty, maximum fascination can continue indefinitely.

Christian Dior

Sex appeal is fifty per cent what you've got – and fifty per cent what people think you've got.

Sophia Loren

After forty, a woman has to choose between losing her figure or her face. My advice is to keep your face, and stay sitting down.

Barbara Cartland

You grew old first not in your own eyes, but in other people's eyes; then, slowly, you agreed with their opinion of you.

Julian Barnes

To what do I attribute my longevity?
Bad luck.

Quentin Crisp

Better a bald head than no head at all.

Maurice Chevalier

I don't know what the big deal is about old age. Old people who shine from inside look ten to twenty years younger.

Dolly Parton

When you've reached a certain age and think that a facelift or a trendy way of dressing will make you feel twenty years younger, remember – nothing can fool a flight of stairs.

Denis Norden

It ain't what you do, it's the way that you do it!

To succeed with the opposite sex, tell her you're impotent. She can't wait to disprove it.

Cary Grant, attributed

If you want to be a dear old lady at seventy, you should start early, say about seventeen.

Maud Royden

They don't tell;
They don't yell;
They don't swell;
And they're grateful
as hell.

*Anon,
'Ode to
Women
Over Fifty'*

I'll tell you how to stay young. Hang around with older people.

Bob Hope

As you get old, you're grateful for it.
Nigella Lawson, on wolf-whistling

Man comes of age at sixty,
woman at fifteen.
James Stephens

'You are old, Father William,'
the young man said,
'And your hair has become very white.
And yet you incessantly
stand on your head,
Do you think at your age it is right?'
Lewis Carroll

As years come in and years go out
I totter towards the tomb,
Still caring less and less about
Who goes to bed with whom.
Dorothy L. Sayers

Know yourself.
Don't accept your dog's
admiration as conclusive
evidence that you are
wonderful.
Ann Landers

BEWARE
OF
THE DOG

When my time has come to go,
I pray to God I'll not say so –
If only I had…
What if I…
I wish…
I'll simply say –
I did.

Derek Dobson

How did I git to be a hundred
years old? Well, when I moves,
I moves slow. When I sits,
I sits loose. And when I
worries, I goes to sleep.

Appalachian mountain woman

Wrinkles should merely
indicate where smiles
have been.

Mark Twain

To enjoy your work and accept
your lot in life – that is a gift
from God. People who do this
rarely look with sorrow on the
past, for God has given them
reasons for joy.

From Ecclesiastes 5:19–20

You're never too old
to become young.

Mae West

Life is uncertain.
Eat dessert first.

Ernestine Ulmer

It ain't what you do,
it's the way that you do it.

'Fats' Waller

As We See Ourselves

How we feel…
… and how we feel about it
We have good days and bad days…
… and learn a thing or two along the way

How we feel...

The average, healthy, well-adjusted adult gets up at 7.30
in the morning feeling just plain awful.

Jean Kerr

I don't feel old. In fact, I don't feel anything till noon.
Then it's time for my nap.

Bob Hope

You stoop to tie your shoelaces and ask yourself,
'What else can I do while I'm down here?'

George Burns

I'm at an age where my back goes out more than I do.

Phyllis Diller

You know you're getting old when
   everything hurts and what doesn't
   hurt doesn't work.
Hy Gardner, attributed

I have everything I had
twenty years ago, only
it's all a little bit lower.
Gypsy Rose Lee

I can tolerate without
   discomfort being waited on
hand and foot.
Osbert Lancaster

How old would you be if you
   didn't know how old you are?
Satchel Paige

23

Old age is a shipwreck.

Charles de Gaulle

As for me, except for an occasional heart attack,
I feel as young as I ever did.

Robert Benchley

At my age, I don't even buy green bananas.

Anon

I smoke cigars because at my age, if I don't have
something to hang on to, I might fall down.

George Burns

A man is only as old as the woman he feels.

Groucho Marx

People don't come in my size until they're old… I used to think people were born with big bones and large frames, but apparently these grow when you're about sixty-eight.

Maeve Binchy

A man is as old as his arteries.

Tomas Sydenham

A woman is as young as her knees.

Mary Quant

All would live long, but none would be old.

Benjamin Franklin

... and how we feel about it

I love living. I have some problems with my life,
but living is the best thing they've come up with so far.
Neil Simon

I'm over the hill – but the climb was terrific!
Graffiti

The only difference between a man of
forty and one of seventy is thirty years
of experience.
Maurice Chevalier

Retirement at sixty-five is
ridiculous. When I was sixty-
five, I still had pimples.
George Burns

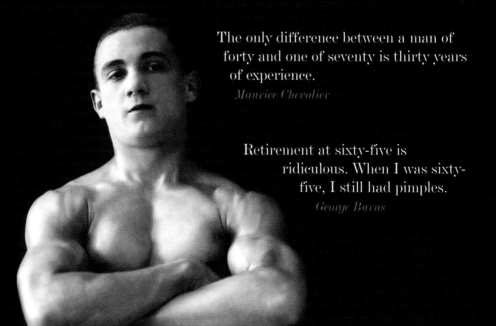

I refuse to admit that I am more than fifty-two,
even if that does make my sons illegitimate.

Nancy Astor

You must ask someone else.
I am only sixty.

*Princess Metternich, asked when a woman
ceases to be capable of sexual love*

The fountain of youth
is dull as paint,
Methuselah is my
favourite saint.
I've never been so
comfortable before,
Oh, I'm so glad I'm not
young any more.

Alan Jay Lerner

Mr Salteena was an elderly man of forty-two.

Daisy Ashford

I wish I loved the human race;
I wish I loved its silly face;
I wish I loved the way it walks;
I wish I loved the way it talks;
And when I'm introduced to one,
I wish I thought What Jolly Fun!

Walter Alexander Raleigh

Boys will be boys, and so will a lot
of middle-aged men.

Albert Hubbard

To me, old age is always fifteen
years older than I am.

Bernard Baruch

The greatest thing about
getting older is that you
don't lose all the other ages you've been.

Madeleine L'Engle

In youth, it was a way I had
To do my best to please.
And change, with every passing lad,
To suit his theories.

But now I know the things I know,
And do the things I do;
And if you do not like me so,
To hell, my love, with you!
Dorothy Parker

No wise man ever wished
to be younger.
Jonathan Swift

Age is not important
unless you're a cheese.
Helen Hayes

You're only old once!
Dr Seuss

If only I could live
A life that was good
If only, if only,
If only I could.

I wish that I could
For everyone's sake
Discover some way
To undo each mistake.

If only I could
When my mind sees red
Allow that I should
Be laughing instead.

If only I knew
When I should be meek
Or when to be bold
Or stand up and speak.

If only I could
Say my prayers
as I should.
If only, if only,
If only I could.

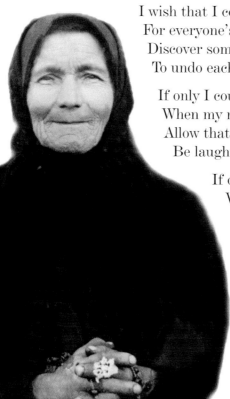

May every day
Begin with space
Enough to see
My saviour's face.

May every hour
Possess within it
The space to live
A prayerful minute.

And may I find
From night's alarms
The space between
My saviour's arms.
Frank Topping

Old age comes from God. Old age leads
on to God. Old age will not touch me,
only so far as he wills.
Pierre Teilhard de Chardin

When it comes to staying young,
a mindlift beats a facelift any day.
Marty Bucella

We have good days and bad days...

I have a bone to pick with Fate,
Come here and tell me, girlie,
Do you think my mind is maturing late,
Or simply rotted early?

Ogden Nash

It's being so miserable keeps me happy.

Anon

They tell you that you'll lose your mind when you grow older. What they don't tell you is that you won't miss it very much.

Malcolm Cowley

You know you're getting older when you try to straighten out the wrinkles in your socks and discover that you're not wearing any.

Leonard L. Knott

I did feel like smiling yesterday
And I may again tomorrow
But not today
Not today.
'Give us a smile,' they say.
So for them, I try.
But thank you, God, for letting me be glum.
Thank you for letting me be me.
Thank you for staying with me when the smile is far away.

Paul Bettison

All the things I really like to do are either illegal,
immoral or fattening.

Alexander Woollcott

I get up every morning and dust off my wits,
Go pick up the paper and read the 'o-bits'.
If my name isn't there I know I'm not dead,
So I get a good breakfast and go back to bed.

Anon

It's not perfect, but to me on balance
Right Now is a lot better than the
Good Old Days.

Maeve Binchy

I merely took the
energy it takes to
pout and wrote some
blues.

Duke Ellington

God has not promised skies always blue,
Flower-strewn pathways all our lives through;
God has not promised sun without rain,
Joy without sorrow, peace without pain.

God has not promised smooth roads and wide,
Swift easy travel needing no guide;
God has not promised that we shall not bear
Many a burden, many a care.

But God has promised strength for the day,
Rest for the labour, light for the way,
Grace for the trials, help from above,
Unfailing sympathy, undying love.

Annie Johnson Flint

... and learn a thing or two along the way

When you're about thirty-five years old, something terrible always happens to music.
Steve Race

Now I'm over fifty, my doctor says I should go out and get more fresh air and exercise. I said, 'All right, I'll drive with the car window open.'
Angus Walker

The really frightening thing about middle age is that you know you'll grow out of it.

Doris Day

If I'd known I was gonna live this long, I'd have taken better care of myself.

Eubie Blake, on reaching the age of one hundred

You can take no credit for beauty at sixteen. But if you are beautiful at sixty, it will be your own soul's doing.

Marie Stopes

Let us take care that age does not make more wrinkles on our spirit than on our face.

Michel de Montaigne

My grace is enough for you, for my power is made perfect in weakness.

From 2 Corinthians 12:9

Lord, thou knowest better than I know myself that I am growing older and will some day be old. Keep me from the fatal habit of thinking I must say something on every subject and on every occasion. Release me from craving to straighten out everybody's affairs. Make me thoughtful but not moody; helpful but not bossy. With my vast store of wisdom, it seems a pity not to use it all, but thou knowest, Lord, that I want a few friends at the end.

Keep my mind free from the recital of endless details; give me wings to get to the point. Seal my lips on my aches and pains. They are increasing, and love of rehearsing them is becoming sweeter as the years go by. I dare not ask for grace enough to enjoy the tales of others' pains, but help me to endure them with patience. I dare not ask for improved memory, but for a growing humility and a lessening cocksureness when my memory seems to clash with the memories of others. Teach me the glorious lesson that occasionally I may be mistaken.

Keep me reasonably sweet. I do not want to be a saint – some of them are so hard to live with – but a sour old person is one of the crowning works of the devil. Give me the ability to see good things in unexpected places, and talents in unexpected people. And give me, O Lord, the grace to tell them so. Amen.

Seventeenth-century nun's prayer

As you grow older you will discover that you have two hands – one for helping yourself, the other for helping others.

Audrey Hepburn

Accept me, O Lord, just as I am,
In my frailty, my inadequacy, my
    contradictions and my confusions.
Accept me, with all those discordant currents
    that pull me in so many directions.
Accept all of this, and help me to live with what I am,
That what I am may become my way to you.

Based on the Suscipe me, a prayer made by novices on entering a Benedictine community

I look forward to being older, when what you look like becomes less and less an issue – and what you are is the point.

Susan Sarandon

As Things Really Are

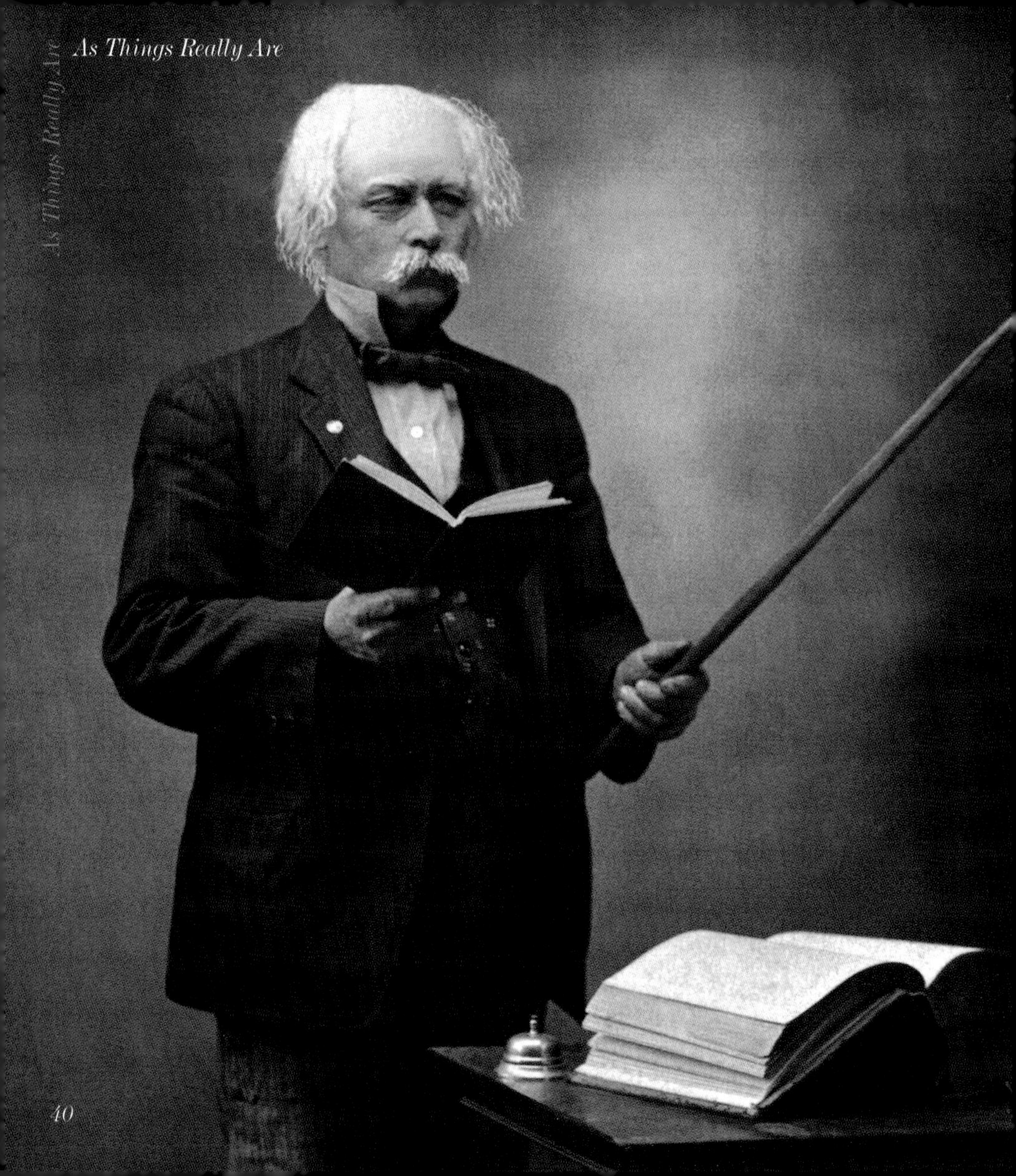

As Things Really Are

A word of warning…

… to the wise

The trick is growing up…

… without growing old

A word of warning…

Don't eat health foods! You
need all the preservatives you
can get!
Anon

Kissing don't last.
Cooking do.
George Meredith

God gave burdens, also shoulders.

Jewish saying

Never lend your car to anyone to whom you have given birth.

Erma Bombeck

As you get older, don't slow down. Speed up. There's less time left!

Malcolm Forbes

Never eat more than you can lift.

Miss Piggy

Sex with older men? I say grab it. But if your man has had a heart attack, don't try to jump-start his pacemaker. Whisper, 'This could be your last one. Let's make it good.'

Phyllis Diller

Early to rise and early to bed,
Makes a man healthy and wealthy and dead.
James Thurber

The older one grows, the more one
likes indecency.
Virginia Wood

You were born an original.
Don't die a copy.
John Mason

Avenge yourself –
live long enough to be
a problem to your kids.

Be kind to your children.
They may choose your rest home.
Notices seen in a café in Palm Springs

No matter how big or soft or warm your bed is, you still have to get out of it.

Grace Slick

You're ageing when your actions creak louder than your words.

Milton Berle

If you're gonna be a failure, at least be one at something you enjoy.

Sylvester Stallone

Time is a dressmaker specializing in alteration.

Faith Baldwin

If you rest, you rust.

Helen Hayes

... to the wise

I'm not young enough to know everything.
J.M. Barrie

I base most of my fashion taste
on what doesn't itch.
Gilda Radner

There must be quite a few
things a hot bath won't
cure, but I don't know
many of them.
Sylvia Plath

Cancer,
schmancer –
as long as
you're healthy.
Yiddish proverb

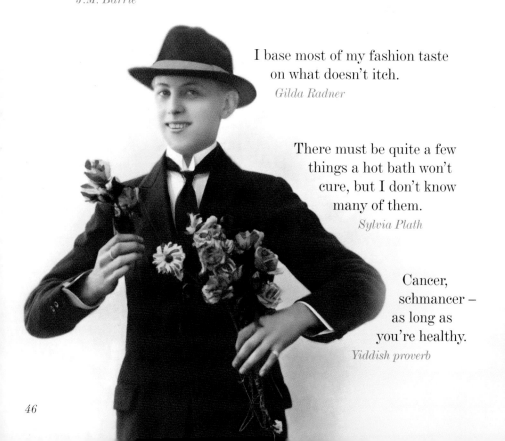

The most popular labour-saving device is still money.
Phyllis George

I've been rich and I've been poor. Rich is better.
Sophie Tucker

A new broom sweeps clean, but an old one knows the corners.
Traditional proverb

I've buried a lot of ironing in the backyard.
Phyllis Diller

The old law about 'an eye for an eye' leaves everybody blind.
Martin Luther King

Life does not have to be perfect to be wonderful.
Annette Funicello

Always forgive your enemies –
nothing annoys them so much.
Oscar Wilde

When a man has compassion for others, God
has compassion for him.
The Talmud

Within your heart keep one
still, secret spot where dreams
may go.
Louise Driscoll

Angels whisper to a man when
he goes for a walk.
Raymond Inman

There is something sadder
than growing old – remaining
a child.
Cesare Pavese

No one cares how much you
know until they know how
much you care.

Don Swartz

Of all the things that wisdom provides
to help one live one's entire life in happiness,
the greatest by far is friendship.

Epicurus

Variety's the very spice of life
That gives it all its flavour.

William Cowper

We are the choices we make.

Meryl Streep, as said in The Bridges of Madison
County, *by Robert James Waller*

A ship in harbour is safe – but that is not what ships are for.

John A. Shedd

You can't control the past, but you can ruin a perfectly good present by worrying about the future.

Anon

There is a way to look at the past. Don't hide from it. It will not catch you if you don't repeat it.

Pearl Bailey

This is the day that the Lord has made. Let's rejoice and be glad in it.

From Psalm 118:24

Do what you can, with what you have, where you are.

Theodore Roosevelt

Expect a miracle!

Anon

The one important thing I've learned over the years is the difference between taking one's work seriously and oneself seriously. The first is imperative; the second is disastrous.

Margot Fonteyn

We're all only fragile threads, but what a tapestry we make.

Jerry Ellis

Use it or lose it!

Anon

A little praise
Goes a great ways.

Ralph Waldo Emerson

After all, tomorrow is another day.

Scarlett, in Gone With the Wind, *by Margaret Mitchell*

The trick is growing up…

The family with an old person in it possesses a jewel.

Chinese saying

One's prime is elusive. You little girls, when you grow up, must be on the alert to recognize your prime at whatever time of your life it may occur. You must then live it to the full.

Muriel Spark

Either you are interesting at any age or you are not. There is nothing particularly interesting about being old – or being young, for that matter.

Katharine Hepburn

The young have aspirations that never come to pass, the old have reminiscences of what never happened. It's only the middle-aged who are really conscious of their limitations.

Saki

It's never too late to have a happy childhood.

Anon

If you want to be adored by your peers and have standing ovations wherever you go, live to be over ninety.

From the obituary of George Abbott in The Times

From birth to age eighteen,
a girl needs good parents.
From eighteen to thirty-five,
she needs good looks.
From thirty-five to fifty-five,
she needs a good personality.
From fifty-five on,
she needs good cash.

Sophie Tucker

When I grow up, I want
to be a little boy.

Joseph Heller

People who are lonely are
those who do not know what
to do with the time when
they are alone.

Quentin Crisp

To be seventy years young is
sometimes far more cheerful
and hopeful than to be forty
years old.

Oliver Wendell Holmes

Just remember,
once you're over the hill,
you begin to pick up speed.

Charles M. Schulz, attributed

Middle age, by which I mean
anything over twenty and
under ninety…

A.A. Milne

Middle age is when the best
exercise is discretion.

Laurence J. Peter

The truth of the matter
is that you always know
the right thing to do.
The hard part is doing it.

H. Norman Schwarzkopf

Shall we make a new rule of
life from tonight: always to
try to be a little kinder than
is necessary?

J.M. Barrie

Forgetting is the cost of
living cheerfully.
Zoe Atkins

As long as I have food and
remote control, I'm happy.
Margie Klein

Yesterday is ashes; tomorrow
wood. Only today does the
fire burn brightly.
Eskimo saying

Things don't change.
You change your way of
looking, that's all.
Carlos Castaneda

Age is other things too. It is wisdom, if one has lived
one's life properly. It is experience and knowledge.
And it is getting to know all the ways the world turns,
so that if you cannot turn the world the way you want,
you can at least get out of the way so you won't get
run over.
Miriam Makeba

Anyone who keeps the ability to see
beauty never grows old.
Franz Kafka

Take this moment, sign and space;
Take my friends around;
Here among us make a place
Where your love is found.

Take the time to call my name;
Take the time to mend
Who I am and what I've been,
All I've failed to tend.

Take the tiredness of my days;
Take my past regrets,
Letting your forgiveness touch
All I can't forget.

Take the little child in me,
Scared of growing old.
Help me here to find my worth,
Made in Christ's own mould.

Take my talents, take my skills,
Take what's yet to be.
Let my life be yours, and yet,
Let it still be me.

John Bell and Graham Maule

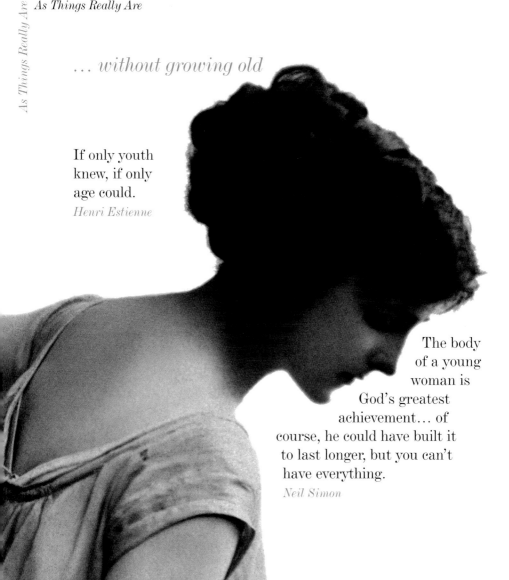

... *without growing old*

If only youth
knew, if only
age could.
Henri Estienne

The body
of a young
woman is
God's greatest
achievement... of
course, he could have built it
to last longer, but you can't
have everything.
Neil Simon

The secret of staying young is to live honestly, eat slowly – and lie about your age.

Lucille Ball

Old age? That's the period of life when you buy a see-through nightgown and then remember you don't know anybody who can still see through one.

Bette Davis

You can't help getting older, but you don't have to get old.

George Burns

To carry a grudge is like being stung to death by one bee.

William H. Walton

Old men and comets have been reverenced for the same reason – their long beards, and pretences to foretell events.

Jonathan Swift

I never heard of an old man forgetting where he had buried his money! Old people remember what interests them – the dates fixed for their lawsuits, and the names of their debtors and creditors.

Marcus Tullius Cicero

God gave us our memories so that we might have roses in December.

J.M. Barrie

A man ninety years old was asked to what he attributed his longevity. 'I reckon,' he said with a twinkle in his eye, 'it's because most nights I went to bed and slept when I should have sat up and worried.'

Dorothea Kent

Sometimes it is more important to discover what one cannot do than what one can do.

Lin Yutang

There are three signs of old age.
Loss of memory… I forget the other two.

Red Skelton

With the ancient is wisdom, and in length of days is understanding.

From Job 12:12

Your prayers and thoughts go out further than you think, and as you wait in patience and in communion with God, you may be made ministers of peace and healing and be kept young in soul.

The Religious Society of Friends

Age is a question of mind over matter. If you don't mind, it doesn't matter.

Dan Ingman

Love, Sweet Love

Love to remember…

… and love that lasts

Love to remember…

Lovers remember everything.

Ovid

When our organs have been transplanted
And the new ones made happy to lodge in us,
Let us pray one wish be granted –
We retain our zones erogenous.

E.Y. Harburg

Quite a few women told me, one way or
another, that they thought it was sex, not
youth, that's wasted on the young…

Janet Harris

It's so long since I've had sex
I've forgotten who gets tied up.

Joan Rivers

He'd have given me rolling lands,
House of marble,
    and billowing farms,
Pearls, to trickle
    between my hands,
Smouldering rubies,
    to circle my arms.
You – you'd only a lilting song,
Only a melody, happy and high,
You were sudden and swift
    and strong –
Never a thought for another had I.

He'd have given me laces rare,
Dresses that glimmered with frosty sheen,
Shining ribbons to wrap my hair,
Horses to draw me, as fine as a queen.
You – you'd only to whistle low,
Gaily I followed wherever you led.
I took you, and let him go –
Someone ought to examine
    my head!

Dorothy Parker

When I am dead, you'll find it hard,
  says he,
To ever find another like me.

What makes you think,
  as I suppose you do,
I'll ever want another man like you?

Eugene Fitch Ware

Grow old along with me,
The best is yet to be!

Robert Browning

When I was cuter,
Each night meant another suitor,
I sleep easier now.

Cole Porter

'Tis better to have loved and lost than
never to have loved at all.

Alfred, Lord Tennyson

Mender of toys, leader of boys,
Changer of fuses, kisser of bruises,
Bless him, dear Lord.

Mover of couches, soother of ouches,
Pounder of nails, teller of tales,
Reward him, O Lord.

Hanger of screens,
counsellor of teens,
Fixer of bikes,
chastiser of tykes,
Help him, O Lord.

Raker of leaves,
cleaner of eaves,
Dryer of dishes,
fulfiller of wishes...
Bless him, O Lord.

Jo Ann Heidbreder

If ever two were one, then surely we,
If ever man were loved by wife,
    then thee…
    Thy love is such I can no way repay,
    The heavens reward thee manifold
    I pray.

Anne Bradstreet

Habit causes love… love
    depends on habit quite as much
    as the wild ways of passion.

Lucretius

Young love is a flame, often
    very hot and fierce, but still
    only light and flickering.
    The love of the older and
    disciplined heart is as
    coals deep-burning,
    unquenchable.

Henry Ward Beecher

Sexiness wears thin after a while and beauty fades, but to be
married to a man who makes you laugh every day, ah, now
that's a treat.

Joanne Woodward

I love you no matter what
you do – but do you have to
do so much of it?

Jean Illsley Clarke

He lay beside me all those years
while I turned and twisted
myself to fit beside him.

Elaine Kraf

You love me so much, you want to put me in your pocket.
And I should die there smothered.

D.H. Lawrence

To keep your marriage brimming,
With love in the loving cup,
Whenever you're wrong, admit it;
Whenever you're right, shut up.

Ogden Nash

You can bear your own fault, and
why not a fault in your wife?

Benjamin Franklin

A thing of beauty is a joy for ever.

John Keats

I've grown accustomed to the trace
   of something in the air,
Accustomed to her face.

Alan Jay Lerner

I love thee, I love but thee,
With a love that shall not die.
Till the sun grows old,
And the stars are cold,
And the leaves of the
Judgement Book unfold.

Bayard Taylor

With thee conversing I forget all time,
All seasons, and their change,
   all please alike.
Sir John Lubbock

Love itself is what is left when being
in love has burned away.
Louis de Bernières

How life catches up with us and
teaches us to love and forgive each
other!
Judy Collins

Life has taught us that love does not
consist in gazing at each other but in
looking outward together in the same
direction.
Antoine de Saint-Exupéry

A sound marriage is
not based on complete
frankness; it is based
on sensible reticence.
Morris L. Ernst

And I will love thee still,
   my dear,
Till a' the seas gang dry.
Robert Burns

... and love that lasts

Dawn love is silver
Wait for the west:
Old love is gold love
Old love is best.
Katherine Lee Bates

Love is what you have been through
with somebody.
James Thurber

Remember, no matter how many candles you blow out
this year, there is one gal who will always think of you
as young, strong and handsome – your mother.
Susan D. Anderson

Age does not protect you from love. But love, to some
extent, protects you from age.
Jeanne Moreau

None of us are as young as we were.
So what? Friendship never ages.
W.H. Auden

Two people, yes,
two lasting friends,
The giving comes,
the taking ends.
Elizabeth Jennings

Long friendships
are like jewels,
polished over time
to become beautiful
and enduring.
Celia Brayfield

The good thing about
friends is not having to
finish sentences.
Brian Jones

Friendship is far more tragic than love. It lasts longer.

Oscar Wilde

The only way to have a friend is to be one.

Ralph Waldo Emerson

A friend is someone who knows all about you and loves you just the same.

Anon

Immature love says, 'I love you because I need you.' Mature love says, 'I need you because I love you.'

Erich Fromm

No one is too heavy or too old to need and receive God's love.

Barbara Johnson

Time engraves our faces with all the tears we have not shed.

Natalie Clifford Barney

Your absence has not taught me how to be alone. It merely has shown that when together we cast a single shadow on this wall.

Doug Fetherling

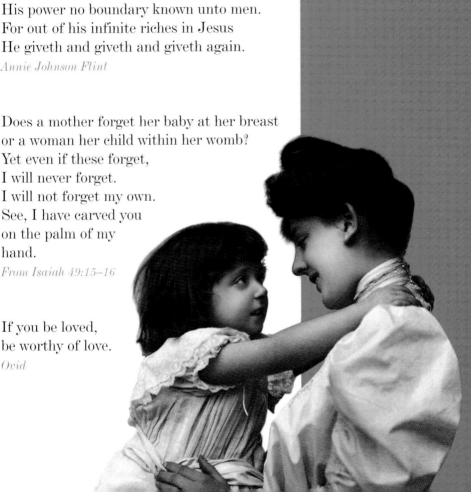

His love has no limit, his grace
  has no measure,
His power no boundary known unto men.
For out of his infinite riches in Jesus
He giveth and giveth and giveth again.

Annie Johnson Flint

Does a mother forget her baby at her breast
or a woman her child within her womb?
Yet even if these forget,
I will never forget.
I will not forget my own.
See, I have carved you
on the palm of my
hand.

From Isaiah 49:15–16

If you be loved,
be worthy of love.

Ovid

I will be your God throughout your lifetime –
until your hair is white with age. I have
made you, and I will care for you. I will
carry you along and save you.

From Isaiah 46:4

We love because he first loved us.

From 1 John 4:19

How long does
youth last?
So long as we
are loved.

*The Golden Book of
Countess Diana*

O God of love, we pray you
   to give us love:
Love in our thinking,
   love in our speaking,
Love in our doing,
And love in the hidden places
   of our souls;
Love of our neighbours near and far;
Love of our friends old and new;
Love of those with whom we find it
   hard to bear,
And love of those who find it hard
   to bear with us;
Love of those with whom we work,
And love of those with whom we
   take our ease;
Love in joy, love in sorrow;
Love in life and love in death;
That so at length we may be worthy
   to dwell with you
Who are eternal love.

William Temple

Now, Then and For Ever

Time to take stock…

… and count your blessings

Time to take stock…

If God came in and said, 'I want you to be happy for the rest of your life,' what would you do?
Bernie Siegel

Man arrives as a novice at each age of his life.
Nicolas Chamfort

The young fool has first to grow up to be an old fool to realize what a damn fool he was when he was a young fool.
Harold Macmillan

Everyone is the age of their heart.
Guatemalan saying

Each generation imagines itself to be more intelligent than the one that went before it, and wiser than the one that comes after it.

George Orwell

Senescence begins
And middle age ends
The day your descendants
Outnumber your friends.

Ogden Nash

Anyone can get old. All you
have to do is to live long
enough.

Groucho Marx

I'll never make the mistake
of bein' seventy again!

Casey Stengel

Life would be infinitely happier if we could only be born at the age of eighty and gradually approach eighteen.

Mark Twain

No man is ever old enough to know better.

Holbrook Jackson

'Tis very certain the desire of life prolongs it.

Lord Byron

Hot water is my native element. I was in it as a baby, and I have never seemed to get out of it ever since.

Edith Sitwell

The most powerful thing you can do to change the world is to change your own beliefs about the nature of life, people, reality, to something more positive.

Shakti Gawain

God, give me the serenity to accept
  things which cannot be changed;
Give me courage to change
  things which must be changed;
And the wisdom to distinguish the
  one from the other.

Dr Reinhold Niebuhr

What makes old age hard to bear is not the failing of one's faculties, mental and physical, but the burden of one's memories.

Somerset Maugham

When all else fails, pray.

Tim and Beverley La Haye

When as a child I laughed and wept, time crept.
When as a youth I dreamed and talked, time walked.
When I became a full-grown man, time ran.
When older still I daily grew, time flew.
Soon I shall find, while travelling on, time gone.
O Christ! Wilt Thou have saved me then?
Amen.

Henry Twells

But a lifetime of happiness!
No man alive could bear it.
It would be hell on earth.

George Bernard Shaw

Life is my college.
May I graduate well,
and earn some honours.

Louisa May Alcott

When things go wrong,
  as they sometimes will,
When the road you're
  trudging seems all uphill,
When care is pressing you
  down a bit,
Rest, if you must –
  but don't you quit!

Anon

The gardener's rule applied
to youth and age: when
young, 'sow wild oats',
but when old, grow sage.

H.J. Byron

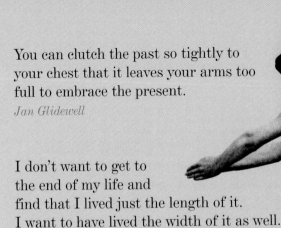

You can clutch the past so tightly to
your chest that it leaves your arms too
full to embrace the present.
Jan Glidewell

I don't want to get to
the end of my life and
find that I lived just the length of it.
I want to have lived the width of it as well.
Diane Ackerman

You have not done enough, you have never
done enough, so long as it is still possible that
you have something to contribute.
Dag Hammarskjöld

Nothing can bring you peace but yourself.
Ralph Waldo Emerson

I adore life, but I don't fear death. I just prefer to die as late as possible.

Georges Simenon

If I die, I forgive you. If I recover, we shall see…

Spanish proverb

I look back on my life like a good day's work. It was done and I am satisfied with it.

Grandma Moses

I don't believe in dying. It's been done. I'm working on a new exit. Besides, I can't die now – I'm booked.

George Burns

Lord bless the folk that somehow never get there,
The people who intended something fine;
The folk who might have lived a little nobler,
The men who always seemed to fail to shine;
The people who have tried to keep their temper,
And yet who seemed to lose it all the more;
The ones who haven't made their name in business,
Who should be rich, yet always would be poor;
The folk who aren't as clever as they might be,
Who aren't as good and feel their efforts vain:
Lord bless all these, and Lord, bless me among them,
And give us all the heart to try again.

Anon

If every day is an awakening,
you will never grow old. You will just
keep growing.

Gail Sheehy

It's not the years in your life but
the life in your years that counts.

Adlai Stevenson

When my life is finally
    measured in
Months, weeks, days, hours,
I want to live free of pain,
Free of indignity,
    free of loneliness.
Give me your hand,
Give me your understanding,
Give me your love –
Then let me go peacefully
And help my family to understand.

From a Belarus Hospice publication

... *and count your blessings*

Cherish all your happy moments.
They make a fine cushion for old age.
Booth Tarkington

There is no such thing in anyone's life
as an unimportant day.
Alexander Woollcott

If I had to live my life again, I'd
make all the same mistakes –
only sooner.
Tallulah Bankhead

If you have good children, why
do you need wealth? And if you
have bad children, again why do
you need wealth?
Turkish proverb

For age is opportunity no less than youth itself,
     though in another dress.
And as the evening twilight fades away,
The sky is filled with stars, invisible by day.

Henry Wadsworth Longfellow

The past is history,
The future mystery,
But today's a gift.
That's why it's called the present.

Anon

As the dew to the blossom,
     the bed to the bee,
As the scent to the rose,
     are those memories to me.

Amelia C. Welby

The past with its pleasures, its
rewards, its foolishness, its
punishments, is there for each
of us for ever – and it should be.

Lilian Hellman

I don't like to look back in
anger or even mild regret. It
has all been most enjoyable.

Noel Coward

Count your blessings,
     not your crosses,
Count your gains,
     not your losses.
Count your joys
     instead of your woes,
Count your friends
     instead of your foes.
Count your health,
     not your wealth.

Proverb

Drop your still dews of quietness
Till all our strivings cease,
Take from our lives the strain and stress,
And let our ordered lives confess
The beauty of your peace.

John Greenleaf Whittier

Colours fade,
temples crumble,
empires fall –
but wise words endure.

Edward Thorndike

Old age has a great sense of
calm and freedom. When
the passions have relaxed
their hold, you have escaped
not from one master
but from many.

Plato

The world is full
of wonders and
miracles, but
man takes his
little hand and
covers his eyes
and sees
nothing.

Israel Baal Shem

May you live
all the days
of your life.

Jonathan Swift

I live alone, dear Lord,
Stay by my side.
In all my daily needs
Be thou my guide.
Grant me good health,
For that indeed, I pray,
To carry on my work
From day to day.
Keep pure my mind,
My thoughts, my every deed,
Let me be kind, unselfish
In my neighbour's need,
If sickness or an
    accident befall,
Then humbly, Lord, I pray,

Hear thou my call,
And when I'm feeling low
Or in despair,
Lift up my heart
And help me in my
    prayer.
I live alone,
    dear Lord,
Yet have no fear
Because I feel
    your presence
Ever near.

Anon

91

The older I get, the greater power I seem to
have to help the world. I am like a snowball
– the further I am rolled, the more I gain.

Susan B. Anthony

The miracle is this – the more we share,
the more we have.

Leonard Nimoy

Then Jesus said, 'Come to me, all of you
who are weary and have heavy burdens,
and I will give you rest.'

From Matthew 11:28

Only the young die good.

Oliver Herford

I don't regret a damn thing. I came,
I went, and I did it all.

Kim Basinger

I want the mornings to last longer
and the twilight to linger,
I want to clutch the present to my bosom
and never let it go.
I resent the tyranny of the clock in the hall
nagging me to get on with the day,
I am a time traveller but a traveller
who would rather walk than fly.
And yet – there is a lot to be said for growing old.
The major battles in life are over
though minor skirmishes may still occur.
There is an armistice of the heart,
a truce with passion,
Compromise becomes preferable to conflict
And old animosities blur with time.
There is still one last hurdle to cross
and the joy of your life measures
your reluctance to approach it.
But if you have lived your life with love
there will be nothing to fear,
Because a warm welcome will await you
on the other side.

Sir Harry Secombe, written after a stroke

I wanted a perfect ending. Now I've learned,
the hard way, that some poems
don't rhyme, and some stories
don't have a clear beginning,
middle and end. Life is about
not knowing, having to change,
taking the moment and making
the best of it without knowing
what's going to happen next.
Gilda Radner

My favourite word is YES.
Lenore Kandell

Last Will and Testament:
Being of sound mind,
I spent all my money.
Anon

The song has ended,
but the melody lingers on...
Irving Berlin